# THE NAME'S STILL CHARLIE
A Biography of Lieutenant-Colonel Charles Green DSO

# THE AUSTRALIAN ARMY HISTORY COLLECTION
A joint venture between the Australian Army History Unit and Australian Military History Publications

| | |
|---|---|
| *A Most Unusual Regiment* | M.J. Ryan |
| *Australian Army Unit Colour Patches* | Phil Blackwell |
| *Battle of Anzac Ridge* | Peter D. Williams |
| *Battlefield Korea* | Maurie Pears |
| *Between Victor and Vanquished* | Arthur Page |
| *Bowler of Gallipoli* | Frank Glen |
| *Chemical Warfare in Australia* | Geoff Plunkett |
| *Chiefs of the Australian Army* | James Wood |
| *Country Victoria's Own* | Neil Leckie |
| *Defenders of Australia* | Albert Palazzo |
| *Doves Over the Pacific* | Reuben R.E. Bowd |
| *Duntroon* | Darren Moore |
| *Fight Leaders* | Butler, Argent & Shelton |
| *Fragile Forts* | Peter Oppenheim |
| *History of the RACT 1973–2000* | Albert Palazzo |
| *Hassett* | John Essex-Clark |
| *Lionheart* | David Coombes |
| *Little by Little* | Michael Tyquin |
| *Madness and the Military* | Michael Tyquin |
| *Never Late* | Gordon Dickens |
| *Operation Orders* | Pat Beale |
| *Only One River to Cross* | A.M. Harris |
| *Persian Expedition* | Alan Stewart |
| *Red Coats to Cams* | Ian Kuring |
| *Surgeon and General* | Ian Howie-Willis |
| *To Pierce the Tyrant's Heart* | Greg Blake |
| *Vets at War* | Ian M. Parsonson |
| *Warrior Poets* | Robert Morrison |
| *Warrior of Kokoda* | Bill Edgar |
| *Winning with Intelligence* | Judy Thomas |

# THE NAME'S STILL CHARLIE
A Biography of Lieutenant-Colonel Charles Green DSO

OLWYN GREEN

*A remarkable story of courage and love*

2010

First published – 1993
This edition published in Australia – 2010

by
AUSTRALIAN MILITARY HISTORY PUBLICATIONS
13 Veronica Place, Loftus 2232 Australia.
Phone: 02- 954 2-6771 Fax: 02-954 2-6787
Website: www.warbooks.com.au

Written by Olwyn Green.
This work is copyright. Apart from any fair dealing for the purpose of study, research, criticism or review no part may be reproduced by any process without written permission.
Enquiries should be directed to the publisher.

Additional typesetting: Margaret McNally, Canberra, ACT
Cover: Typesmith Pty. Ltd. Ellis Lane, NSW
Printed by: Trojan Press, Thomastown, VIC
ISBN: 978-0-9805674-3-4

*This book is produced in co-operation
with Australian Army History Unit*

Army History Unit strives to maintain the highest quality in the books it supports for publication but occasionally that standard can not be achieved.

This book is a facsimile of the original 1993 edition but unfortunately the scanning process has not been able to provide our usual high standard.

It has been decided to proceed with publication in this form to enable Charles Green's life story to be reprinted.

Roger Lee

# Contents

| | | |
|---|---|---|
| Illustrations | | vi |
| Acknowledgments | | viii |
| Preface | | xi |
| 1 | Youth | 7 |
| 2 | From man to soldier | 19 |
| 3 | A sea change | 39 |
| 4 | Palestine—Waiting | 45 |
| 5 | The Desert—Consternation | 60 |
| 6 | Bardia—"Ripeness is all" | 70 |
| 7 | Tobruk—The motley soldiers | 78 |
| 8 | Greece—"A terrible beauty" | 83 |
| 9 | Greece—Escape | 107 |
| 10 | After Greece—"A home thought" | 130 |
| 11 | Syria to Ceylon—"A strange interlude' | 138 |
| 12 | Home—Marriage vows | 152 |
| 13 | Anticipation | 162 |
| 14 | 2/11 Bn—The Battalion remembers | 170 |
| 15 | 2/11 Bn—Aitape to Wewak | 182 |
| 16 | 2/11 Bn, Wewak—"To shine in use" | 202 |
| 17 | What happened to the dreams? | 213 |
| 18 | Cloudless days | 226 |
| 19 | The cow | 237 |
| 20 | Korea—Getting the feel of the Battalion | 240 |
| 21 | Korea—"This cold and lonely feeling" | 256 |
| 22 | The last hours | 285 |
| Epilogue | | 292 |
| Epilogue: second edition | | 295 |
| Contributors | | 311 |
| Copyright acknowledgements | | 313 |
| Reference works consulted | | 316 |
| Index | | 319 |

# Illustrations

| | |
|---|---:|
| Charles Green in Japan | xiv |
| Officers, NCOs and men of 41 Battalion, 1936 | 18 |
| Enlisted men of Ulmarra district, 1939 | 19 |
| Officers of 2/2 Battalion, 1940 | 50 |
| Charlie Green and Lieutenant Travers, Egypt, 1940 | 51 |
| Lieutenant Charlie Green and Arab horse | 64 |
| Charlie Green packed and ready to move, 1940 | 65 |
| Bardia township. | 65 |
| Chilton, Wootten, Edgar and Dougherty | 80 |
| Middle East map and 'Bobby' Tobruk | 81 |
| Adrian Buckley and men at Aliakmon River | 90 |
| Lieutenant Bruce Brock and in 'Effendi' garb | 91 |
| Greek terrain and donkey transport | 120 |
| Escape party including Chilton, Green and Brock | 121 |
| Olwyn Warner – a photograph sent to Charlie | 158 |
| Wedding day for the Greens, 1943 | 159 |
| Charlie Green: new commander of 2/11 Battalion | 172 |
| Men of 2/11 Battalion in the Wewak area | 173 |
| Charlie Green and Olwyn, Grafton , 1946 | 218 |
| Charlie Green and his daughter Anthea, 1949 | 218 |
| Smiths saying goodbye to the Greens, 1949 | 219 |
| Charlie and Anthea, 1950 | 219 |
| Charlie in Japan and with 3 RAR officers, 1950 | 244 |
| Welcome party, Pusan, Korea | 245 |
| Green with Lieutenant Argent | 245 |
| Green with Harding and Bouchier, Korea, 1959 | 254 |
| Charlie Green with Brigadier Coad, 1950 | 255 |
| Brigadier Coad visits 3 RAR. | 266 |
| Coad and Green conferring | 267 |
| Coad and Green map reading | 280 |
| Painting of Charlie Green | 281 |
| Coad and Green with tank | 284 |
| The burial of Charlie Green | 284 |

## *Illustrations*

| | |
|---|---|
| Re-burial of Charlie Green and his grave | 285 |
| Men of 3 RAR riding on a tank | 300 |
| The Broken Bridge | 301 |
| Olwyn and Bruce Ferguson, 1950s | 304 |

# Acknowledgements: First Edition

This is a true story so far as memory permits. It took many years to research and to collect from soldiers, their willingly-given oral and written accounts of what they could so vividly remember, without which 1 could not have pieced it all together.

The idea came in 1980 in Lismore during the unveiling of the memorial cairn to my husband who died in 1950. Lieutenant-Colonel Peter Brooks ED, and Warrant Officers R.W. Chamberlain and R.J. Armstrong (41 Battalion CMF) are credited with initiating the memorial to ensure that Charles Green should not he forgotten.

I am indebted to all the people mentioned in this book who helped me rediscover Charlie and understand soldiering. Their names are recorded, according to their unit, in the appendices – sadly, many of them have since died. Special mention must be made of two significant contributions: Bruce Brock's long account of the escape from Greece, written shortly before he died and the tribute by Claude Boshammer which came after I thought the task was finished.

2/2 Battalion Association and 2/11 Battalion Association generously gave permission to use their histories, documents and journals. 2/11 Battalion has since published a book, described not as a history but as a collection of contributions from members of the unit.

The staff at the Australian War Memorial in Canberra were most helpful and, upon request, had all the relevant war diaries ready for me. Prior to its publication they also gave me access to the manuscript of the Australian official history of the Korean War by R.J. O'Neill.

My story would not have been published but for two 3 RAR veterans, Mick Servos and Jack Gallaway. Jack thought it worth introducing to the University of Queensland Press.

At a more personal level I am indebted to Margaret Barter, recently awarded a PhD for her fine study of the 2/2 Battalion. Margaret freely gave me help and information.

I also appreciate help given with early drafts by my friends, Chris Campbell and Beth Ingram. I am especially grateful to Ardyce Harris and Alan Haagensen for so willingly undertaking the difficult task of proof-reading. For the original publication of my book, I thank the staff at University of Queensland Press for their support and Barbara Ker Wilson provided sensitive editing.

## Acknowledgements: Second Edition

As I related in the 1993 edition of my book, it was not until 1980 at the unveiling of the Charlie Green Memorial Cairn, at the 41 Battalion RNSWR HQ Lismore, that I became aware of Charlie Green's remarkable service to the Australian Army. Then I decided to write his story.

Since the book's publication in 1993, realising that the Korean War has had little recognition, I have widely researched others who served in the RAR in Korea, and formed the material into a collection that is deposited in the Australian War Memorial. To indicate what I have since learned about Charlie and the Korean War, I have written an epilogue for this edition of the book.

Today, I am more aware of the origin of the Anzac legend and its formative influence on all branches of the army. The creation of the Green Memorial in Lismore illustrates the digger ethos – soldiers giving freely of time and spirit to honour a man like Charlie, who is regarded as "a soldier's soldier." Since 1980, I have kept contact with 41 Battalion, and have viewed its records.

Not until then, did I fully realise the considerable voluntary team-work that went into the production of the memorial in Lismore in 1980.

I want to record, in this edition, those who contributed to the 1980 Green Memorial. If that event had not occurred, I would never have discovered the story of Charlie Green for myself and for history. In 1980 it was 41 Battalion's Adjutant, Captain Gerard Nelson of the Regular Army, who noted Charlie Green's exceptional military record (Charlie had commanded a battalion in each branch of the Australian Army).

The Commanding Officer in 1980, Lieutenant Colonel Peter Brooks, was inspired to build and manage the project of creating the memorial to Charlie (who began his career in 41 Battalion and who in 1948, as a lieutenant-colonel, was appointed to re-raise 41 Battalion). In 1980, assisting the CO was his 2 I/C Major Tony Streeter. Research of Charlie Green's military record was done by Captain Bennett, WOII R.W. Chamberlain and WOII R.J. Armstrong. The Commander of 2 Division, Major General K. Murray, gave his support; whilst the Commandant of RNSWR, Major General R.J. Sharp, organised the creation of the cairn itself. It was Brigadier N.R. Charlesworth, a veteran of 3 RAR, who gave the address at the unveiling ceremony in 1980.

I am grateful to my friend, Ardyce Harris, for her assistance in producing this revised edition. To this task she brought her considerable editing skills, persuading me not to range too widely in subject matter, but to write what is, in effect, a conclusion to the Charlie story.

I thank my family and friends for the support and assistance they have given me over the years. Lastly I thank the Army History Unit for its decision to assist with the reprinting of the book.

# Preface

In this revised edition the original text is kept intact and in a new Epilogue I provide subsequently acquired material that is, in effect, a conclusion to the book.

It was 30 years after Charlie's death that a significant thing happened that led to the writing of the book and the changing of my life. When Charlie died in 1950, I had no qualifications, having left school at thirteen. I achieved the seemingly unattainable goal of attending university and gaining meaningful employment to support my daughter, Anthea, and myself.

This would not have been possible without support I received from the Department of Veterans' Affairs Rehabilitation Scheme. In 1958, I graduated from Sydney University with a BA and soon after was employed as an English teacher in the Department of Technical Education, NSW. In 1979, due to the terms of my employment, I retired.

Between Charlie's death and my retirement I had little contact with things military. In response to the trauma of his death, I tried to shut out the past and make a new life. The interval between 1950 and 1979, remains a sort of 'separate life'.

The recognition of Charlie Green's war service, at the 41st Battalion's 1980 memorial ceremony, was the stimulus for writing this book.

By the time it was first published in 1983, I had begun to understand more fully, the significance of his service; he was the youngest AIF battalion commander in World War II; he had the distinction of having commanded a battalion in each branch of the Australian army (AIF, CMF and RAR); he commanded the Royal Australian Regiment's first unit (3RAR) in its first action in the Korean War.

To this date, he is the only battalion commander of the Royal Australian Regiment to be killed in action.

Realising how little I knew about the Korean War, let alone Charlie's service, I felt compelled to learn and record more. To become more professionally informed, I enrolled in a Post Graduate Research Degree Course at Macquarie University in 1997. However, in 2000 I was diagnosed as having bowel cancer and withdrew from the course.

Realising that the oral history research I had completed was of importance, I converted it into a collection of papers and, in 2003, deposited them in the Private Records Section of the Australian War Memorial (Ref PR00466.) I have also used my research material to write articles and stories for various military journals, newsletters and a website: http://www.kmike.com/oz/album.htm.

In the Epilogue I provide comment on matters I believe I now better understand: the importance of the continuing influence of the Anzac Story on our nation; reasons the Korean War has not received recognition; and how I responded to the loss of my husband in war. In conclusion, I review how the picture of Charlie the soldier has developed over many years, and the supposition that by idealising him I had prolonged my grieving.

*Preface*

> *Or was there too little said*
> *For ease or resolution –*
> *Summer scarcely begun*
> *And violets,*
> *A few picked, the rest dead?*
>
> *Pastorale.* Hart Crane

> *The art of war calls for a vaster amount of knowledge and more inborne talents than any of the other arts . . .*
>
> George von Behrenhurst
> 1733-1814

Charlie: *"You'll call me Sir."*
Soldier: *"What about when we are on leave?"*
Charlie: *"The name's still Charlie.*

# 1
# Youth

> And I was green and carefree, famous among the barns
> About the happy yard and singing as the farm was home,
> In the sun that is young once only,
> Time let me play and be
> Golden in the mercy of his means,
> And green and golden I was huntsman and herdsman, the calves
> Sang to my horn, the foxes on the hills barked clear and cold,
> And the Sabbath rang slowly
> In the pebbles of the holy streams.
>
> from *Fern Hill* by Dylan Thomas

Charlie Green grew up in the years between the great wars on a farm at Swan Creek, about four miles from Grafton, New South Wales.

He was born on 26th December, 1919, and christened Charles Hercules. His parents were Bertha de Ville, originally from Yugilbar, and Hercules ("Herc") John Green, who came from Windsor, NSW. There were two other children: Doris, the eldest and Alvan, the youngest, who died recently.

To begin unravelling the past, I went back one winter day to Swan Creek, still only a settlement. A few buildings nestle around the bridge that crosses the creek just north of South Grafton, on the Pacific Highway. It is only a few houses larger than it was when Charlie was a youth. I can remember because I grew up in Ulmarra, a village a few miles farther north. I was born four years after Charlie.

I remember the Greens' wooden house with its verandas as it was in 1942, when he took me home to meet his parents. The house stood on a hill, out of flood reach, at the cutting near the bridge, alongside the tiny wooden Anglican Church, that Bertha Green would quietly tend. She laundered the white communion cloths and put flowers from her garden on the altar for the Sunday service. But for the church, the Greens' place would have been another typical North Coast farm, with its galvanised iron tanks, a few shade trees, a paling fence to keep out the animals and a front door that was never used.

What had happened to Swan Creek, and the surrounding district in the thirty years since I had last seen it shocked me. Charlie held, or acquired during the war, a sustaining dream of a secure future on an ideal farm. It's as well he never knew the changes brought by time. I, on the other hand, regarded a dairy farm as a prison. We never saw eye to eye on that. And it was on that issue, I always thought, that our lives turned.

What I found at Swan Creek, the source of Charlie's dream, was a decaying dairy industry. There were no more carts or trucks clanking to the butter factory with brimming cans of cream. Fertile river flats lay idle below paddocks that were no longer filled with languid, munching cows, emerald lucerne patches, potatoes or head-high corn. Instead, empty dairies were tumbling down and flaking wooden farm houses stood forlornly, as though wondering where everyone had gone. A few of the frost and drought-scorched paddocks were scattered with skeletons of gum trees.

One gum tree has become a legend.

It stands alone where the new road was deliberately curved to avoid it. People wanted the big tree preserved because when Charlie Green was a boy, he and a friend, Val Turner, climbed high up into it and carved their initials. The tree is dead now and so are Charlie and Val. Nature has sculpted its own memorial to a boy who, like the tree, was once fine, strong and tall.

I looked for people who knew Charlie. There were few left but their memories, once stirred, gave up sharp and racy vignettes.

Mrs Want "lived up the road a bit, at the two fig trees on the side of the hill". She was ninety, and had been in the same house all her married life, nearly seventy years. We sat on the veranda, drinking tea, and the old lady pointed to the hill behind her house: "He used to play cricket up there with my boys." I looked beyond the paling fence to the hill. For a moment I thought I heard the happy cries of young boys in the crisp winter breeze. Then she pointed down the road to Swan Creek. "When he left school, he worked on that cutting with his horses. He was always such a hard worker. And he loved his horses."

Many of the memories of Charlie focused on Swan Creek itself, which was not big enough to be marked on a map. It was a little world that produced a large soul.

I remember Swan Creek merely as a wooden bridge, a place that frightened me as a small child when my father used to drive over it. The bridge used to rattle and I always hated the creek, choked with purple hyacinth, imagining that if one fell in, there could be no escape. I wasn't to know my fate was contained there at Swan Creek.

Living in a small community means, inevitably, that everyone knows you. The Greens were known as a sturdy, thriving family, their roots going deep into the soil: generations of farmers, back to Australia's first settlers, and further back, to England.

Herc, Charlie's father, was an uncompromising man. He set himself the task of being the best: the best farmer, owning the biggest and best property in the district. He proudly related how he got married to Bertha with only two pounds in his pocket, a terrible mortgage over his head and a bullet in his chest. A rifle had accidentally gone off as he was getting through a fence, and the bullet had never been removed. Herc had only one year of formal education, yet he could read, though scarcely write. Even so, he was, through his skill, the unofficial "vet" and agricultural guru of the district. That he was a genius with animals, no one questioned. He kept cattle dogs that were so well-trained that he could work them from the veranda of his house by a series of whistles. Such was his control over his dogs that one blue cattle dog became savagely protective of everything Herc owned. Herc's solution for keeping the dog, yet preventing it from doing terrible damage with its bite, was to pull out its fangs. At a very early age Charlie assisted his father with the animals. Someone who remembered the Greens well commented: "Herc was a remarkable horse doctor, but he was a hard man; in fact he was a rotten old bastard."

Bertha, Charlie's mother, was one of life's uncelebrated angels. Her patience and virtue were immeasurable. I never knew a cross, mean or petty word to pass her lips. She had big, brown eyes, a broad forehead, a fine straight nose, and olive skin, all of which her beloved Charles inherited. She also passed on to him her inner strength, equanimity and diligence. In all her married life Bertha missed only a handful of days serving in the dairy. Though she moved in Herc's shadow, she preserved her independence of mind and unfailing sense of humour. Her worth did not go unnoticed. The old lady of the fig trees said, "She worked terribly hard but she never let it lean on her."

Bertha's father had a significant influence on the family. They were all very much in awe of him, yet amused by his eccentricities. "Old Harry" de Ville, as he was known, was a church elder who drove a buggy, wore black clothes and had a long white beard. His wife, who rode submissively beside him would be enjoined never to look back: "Don't look round, woman, or you'll be turned to salt!" His grandchildren loved to hear his story of how he helped to arrest the bushranger Tommy Ryan at Yugilbar, one of the most interesting places in the district with a castle where one of the colony's most appealing romances was enacted. The castle was the abandoned dream of a man called Ogilvie, who built it for his bride-to-be — who never arrived from England: a reminder of the fragility of dreams.

Bertha's influence, though significant, was not so obvious in Charlie, but his grandfather's and his father's were. The Green children were all clever and, not surprisingly, imbued with a drive to excel in whatever they did. Someone else said: "Herc's desire for a touch of glory was screwed into all of them."

But Charlie was no mere offshoot of his ancestors. Charlie was different; he had a touch of greatness in him. His wasn't the impulse to glory so much as the satisfaction he enjoyed from his own ability. And there was more to him. Despite his frugal soil, he inclined towards the softer, more imaginative things in life. He had a vein of poetry and a fineness of spirit that neither menial work nor war could erase.

Even as a little boy, his sister Dot recalled, Charlie was always a bit special. "As a little fellow he was all eyes: wonder, excitement, fear." What was very noticeable, she said, was the way he always managed to mastermind everything that was going on when the kids were playing. He was, too, a leader in mischief, getting his playmates into dangerous situations. Though there were few toys, Charlie, his young brother Alvan and the neighbours' children made toboggans out of pieces of tin; canoes out of galvanised iron; billy carts out of scraps of timber; and their imaginations turned the landscape into the backdrop of grand adventures. "None of us ever thought to question what he asked us to do," reminisced one of his playmates.

Dot tells the vivid story of Charlie's canoe:

> Mr A., the schoolteacher, who lived across the way, was a figure of fun who could not control his little swarm. The boys fought, smoked, ran the tanks dry and goaded him into wasting half the day lecturing them or wielding the cane. He had a son who, by contrast, was indulged. He owned a magnificent canoe that he paddled around the creek. Somebody, probably Dad, christened him Hiawatha.
> 
> Charlie, envious of Hiawatha's canoe, begged Dad to get him one. Dad said "No". Charlie brooded for a day or two, then went back to Dad. "Can we build one, then?" — "Yes, on one condition. I want to see it before you take it out."
> 
> Charlie masterminded the building. He and Alvan got sheets of corrugated iron and bent them into the desired shape. To make it waterproof, they plugged up the cracks with clay. Then they made a double-ended paddle, real Hiawatha-style.
> 
> Ready for the launching, Charlie went to Dad: "Dad, the canoe is finished."
> 
> Dad took a good look at it and croaked, "Take the bloody thing down to the lagoon and put it in."

While the boys headed for the lagoon, Dad, anticipating a quick sinking, called to Mum: "Come and watch this."

They put their precious creation in the water. Charlie got in and Alvan pushed him out. The canoe wobbled and dipped. For breathtaking minutes, he wobbled and dipped, then all of a sudden he got his balance and away he paddled, around and around.

Another schoolmaster, Bill Turner, replaced Hiawatha's inept father. His children were very friendly with the Greens. Shirley Turner, younger than Alvan, remembered with love and nostalgia her youth at Swan Creek. "I lived at the Greens', following the boys around. Most of the time they wouldn't let me play with them. I was too young." Wistfully she recalled that some of the happiest moments of her life was over at Greens' place, talking to them in the cow bails, while they milked, or in the kitchen. At afternoon teatime, just before milking, they would all be there: Here lying on his couch smoking his pipe, Mrs Green making tea. "I don't remember where Dot was, but the boys would be skylarking and teasing me."

When I asked about Charlie, she hesitated and her mouth quivered as she was visited by his image. "I remember him as he looked: tall, muscly, brown and very handsome. He was the epitome of the best of youth — full of energy and innocence."

As Charlie grew older, there was less time for play. The farm came first. When they are old enough, children on farms have to work. It is an endless round. At sunrise and sunset, the cows are milked, the cream separated and the washing-up done in the dairy. In between, there are the other jobs: the crops, the calves, the pigs and the fowls. Then there is school to fit in.

Charlie's schooling was very brief. I have a collection of books that he won as prizes at the Swan Creek one-teacher school, a testimony to his potential. In 1932, he cycled to high school in Grafton. Not many of the local youth in those days got to high school. Charlie remained there for only one year. Academic pursuits had no value in an ethic that placed the supreme value on possessing the Clarence River's best farm.

Nor was there any impulse in Charlie towards learning, intelligent though he was. His bent was for action.

By the time I passed Swan Creek on my own way to high school, Charlie, four years older than me, would have been a busy young farmer. I got on the school bus, a square red contraption called the "Butter Box", in Ulmarra. The memory of those bus rides is still a nightmare. The boys — Horsey, Little Horsey, Puss, Dog and Nosepecker, to mention a few, were large, steaming, screaming, bad-mouthed lads always ready to stop the bus for a fight, or to fire catapults at us girls in the front. On that bus I nearly lost forever any romantic impulses I might have had.

Charlie Green had his first skirmish with death in about 1930. One misty, drizzly morning when horses tend to get frisky, eleven-year-old Charlie was trying to harness one of the draught horses for the day's work. The horse kicked him in the face, the blow catching a corner of one eye and smashing his nose and teeth. Many people in the district remember this incident. Herc told how he had to put his hand into the boy's smashed face to keep the air passages free until they got him to hospital in Grafton.

He was absent from school for nearly a year. Apart from nearly losing his life, he had lost most of his teeth. As was the practice in those times, the rest of his teeth were extracted and he was given dentures. When he returned to school his appearance was changed. His nose was thicker and he bore a scar across his mouth. As the years went on his face became more shrunken. One had only to look at his face to realise that had he not lost his teeth so young he would have been not just handsome, but exceedingly handsome.

In spite of this accident Charlie held a lasting love of horses and had considerable skill with them. After he left school at thirteen, he set himself up in a contracting business — in addition to his farm work. Somehow, he acquired two draught horses to do such jobs as ploughing and to get some work on the new highway that was being built. As the old lady recalled, he worked with his horses on the cutting at Swan

Creek. At an early age he was showing initiative and willingness to take responsiblity beyond his years.

While it became legendary that Charlie worked hard, it was also legendary that he ate like a horse. In the Crown Hotel at Grafton, I heard this memory:

> Charlie Green was a big growthy lad that could work like one of his draught horses. When he went to help on one of his neighbour's farms with potato planting or corn picking, they reckon they could never fill him up. He'd eat everything in sight.

To delve into people's memories after fifty years, and to find consistency reassured me of the validity of my task. Tom Mawhinney from the Ulmarra district and a soldier-comrade of Charlie's remembered him thus: "At fifteen years of age, we had a young man who was in no way unusual, not keen on study, a good eater, with a wonderful capacity to handle horses." I never ceased to be fascinated, during my search for Charlie, at the things people remembered and the turns of phrase they used.

When he was sixteen, Charlie Green did something no one can really explain to me. It was the first fateful step that took him out of the little world of Swan Creek into the unknown. He joined the militia. His sister recalled that he was often busy polishing his buttons and boots and studying military manuals. Camps would take him away for the occasional weekend. Soon he was a sergeant and within a couple of years he was wearing the bright pip of a second lieutenant. At the time, nobody in the family realised this interest was to take him away from the farm, where he was expected to dedicate his life to realising Herc's dream.

Perhaps at this point C.H., as Charlie was often called, made one of his bids to be his own man. Maybe his first was when he acquired his horses and worked on the cutting at Swan Creek. What I cannot determine is whether Charlie ever worked out exactly what his dream was (though towards the end of the war he articulated it as a farm). I am sure he didn't want to follow Herc's dream or mine. If I were to mark the spot where the seeds of his life's conflict were sown, I'd do it here. After this, Charlie was to be continually facing crossroads, his impulse to achievement luring him on; limitations and loyalties counter-tugging.

As Charlie grew older the farm and the militia did not take up all his time. There was cricket, for one thing. As the lady at the fig trees remembered, the boys started playing when they were very young. Our next glimpse of Charlie the cricketer is when he was about sixteen or seventeen, tall brown and eager, donning his "creams" to play in a Saturday afternoon cricket match. Herc allowed Charlie the privilege of playing sport. Bertha and his sister could carry on in the dairy until he got home. "Charlie was the apple of Dad's eye," recalls his sister, quoting a conversation: when Charlie got in from cricket one afternoon, Herc said, "How many runs did you get, son?" Charlie replied, "I got four wickets." The Greens knew themselves. This, they would say, is the typical Charlie. You record the successes, not the failures. And so you are born a winner, not a loser.

Nobody had to leave Swan Creek to enjoy a social life or meet sweethearts. It all came to them. Over the road from Greens' place, also near the bridge, a great barn of a hall was built in 1934. Herc and Charlie, when he was older, played an active part in everything that went on in the hall. It wasn't long before both Charlie and Alvan realised that if they were to participate in the dances held there, they would have to learn to dance.

They didn't bother to remove the blucher boots they worked in to practise dance steps on the wooden front veranda — the only time the veranda was used, I think. Acquiring what is supposed to be a gracious skill in this burlesque manner appealed to their sense of fun. It might have avoided, too, any misgivings they had about such a suspect thing as dancing. This nonchalant way of taking the edge off embarrassment was characteristic of Charlie — it's probably a very Australian trait.

"Noop," said Alvan, speaking of Charlie, "had very big feet that weren't really suited to blucher boot training." Charlie's big feet are nearly as legendary as his big appetite. His batmen, after forty years, remember that: they were required to clean his boots.

The Swan Creek Hall became renowned for its dances — and all that went with them. On Saturday nights everyone would come from down the river, from Grafton, from other districts. They came in buses, on bikes, on horses. There were wonderful suppers, the kind that only country people can produce. Adults kept things under control inside. Small children lay rolled up like packages under the benches surrounding the walls, sleeping through the din. Outside in the paddocks some of the local larrikins had their bottles hidden. And if I know them, there would have been the occasional fist flying. The boys always stood at the front of the hall, looking over the girls before they made the plunge. One witty lad I once knew told me: "You pick them by their ankles. That's how you tell their breeding." The local band shone in noise, if not in excellence. It was the age of Glen Miller and *Midnight Serenade* or *In the Mood*. The Swan Creek versions burst out of that barn of a building into black frosty nights or balmy, tropical evenings.

Charlie's sister gave me another glimpse of Charlie's first romantic impulses. He was seen some evenings, spruced up, setting out on his bicycle to visit a girl in Ulmarra. With typical Green humour she told me about one occasion fixed in the family memory. The night Charlie came to grief. "Charlie set out one evening, but returned after an amazingly short interval. "He had," Dot chuckled, " had an unfortunate accident that hurt him in an unfortunate place — and broke the bicycle." For Charlie it was funny but it was also embarrassing. He didn't like to be caught on the wrong foot. His natural instinct to preserve his dignity was part of his "presence". (He had, men say, that presence born leaders possess.)

I do not know whether Charlie would have been interested, then, in any more sophisticated things. The only cultural activity would have been the local concert. There was always someone who could play Chopin, or recite a poem. Other than that, there was the wireless and the Municipal Library in

Ulmarra. That was all. I remember my own astonishment at discovering people who had read every book in the library.

The exciting events of the week were, predictably, tennis, cricket, football, a dance, or the travelling picture show. Mr Penn, "The Picture Show Man", used to bring his big red van to our district regularly. Chairs would be lined up in the local halls, then we would sit and wait, hoping the machines wouldn't break down, with kids sending the place into chaos as they ran around through many unplanned intermissions. The picture shows were one of the exciting events of my young life. In Ulmarra, my teenage years were similar to Charlie's. I left high school at thirteen to work in my father's newsagency. Every morning at six I would sort newspapers for the cream runs. I did not finish work until seven or eight at night as the shop remained open until the people of the village all went home, after picking up a paper, some tobacco or simply popping in for a chat. I disliked the long hours, but I did enjoy the people I met. On Sunday afternoon I played tennis. Tennis was my passion, the most exciting thing in my own country-town life.

Growing up in the thirties meant that we heard a lot about the Depression. Though times were hard for Charlie on the farm, and for my father's business, we had relative security. Nevertheless, the lessons of the Depression inhibited daring and initiative. The priority was security: the safe job and money in the bank. Few young people escaped the narrow regime of leaving school at fourteen and going to work if they could get it. When World War 2 broke out, opportunity came for an exit from the valley — by way of the army. Going into the army was a suspension of normal life — or an end. It was not escape.

If the war had not occurred, it is difficult to imagine what would have happened to Charlie Green. Given his subsequent life history, this is a tantalising thought. I cannot see him easily leaping the boundaries of that environment: he had little education and he had no encouragement to turn his eyes away from the farm towards those less honourable, less manly occupations of "townies" and "city slickers". But he had already shown a certain impulse to break out.

Charlie's adolescence, though not easy, was happy. And all that hard work, developing initiative, ingenuity and industry, were the resources he was to draw on throughout the rest of his life, to compensate for his lack of education. Then, suddenly, the mould that was intended for him was cracked. He found himself thousands of miles away, in the company of sophisticated, university trained men. There he had to adjust to the daunting role of a commander of men — in battle.

The seeds of the man are in the youth. Harry Bell, who went to school with Charlie and soldiered with him in the 2/2 Battalion, AIF, discerned one overriding trait, in the adolescent Charlie: coolness. Already he had a quality for leadership, one to which Napoleon gave primacy. Napoleon said, "the first quality of a commander is a cool head". That quality of Charlie's was to be set down in several war books and in Dr O'Neil's history of the Korean War. Harry said: "I admired and envied him. He was clean and unspoilt, if you know what I mean. He never let his youthful impulses govern him — with girls and sex. Yes, and he was a bit detached. It was his coolness that got me. While I was always in a turmoil in those days, he was unaffected by the things that cursed me. He seemed to have no complexes."

And so it was that while Charlie Green was innocently managing his horses, having an occasional game of cricket, going to dances and polishing the buttons on his new subaltern's uniform, momentous things were happening in Europe to hurtle him, and many, many others into a different life.

Two caricatures strutted on the European stage in the thirties. One moustached figure with stiff swinging arms screeched glory to embittered thousands; another, square-faced, booted, and ornamented, promised an empire and the transforming of the Mediterranean into a large Latin lake. Little, hopeless people succumbed to those grand promises. The scene was set for a great drama, a tragedy — and there were few who escaped a part.

Officers, NCOs and men of 41 Militia Battalion, Grafton Drill Hall, 1936. Sergeant Charles Green – second row sixth from left.

## The name's still Charlie

Men of Ulmarra District who enlisted in the AIF, October, 1939. L-R (front): Vic Davis, Bill Grant, Charlie Green, Bill Ulrick, George Finlayson. (rear): George Roberts, Bill Sullivan, Lester McArtney, Bill Wright, Ron Pattemore, Max Finlayson, Errol Pattemore, Tom Mawhinney.

# 2
# From man to soldier

> In all men's heart it is.
> Some spirit old
> Hath turned with maligned kiss
> Our lives to mould.
>
> *On Receiving News of the War*
> by Isaac Rosenberg

In 1939, in the little town of Ulmarra, we waited by our wireless sets, with our minds no longer on the cricket ground in England but switched back to the hell of the "not so great, Great War" which people were still talking about. We feared a replay of the horror that men had endured only twenty years earlier. Of going to the western front to live like rats in muddy trenches. Of going over the top under barrages of shells. Of being mown down in scores. Of struggling towards the terrible wire. Of the shattered limbs, the gas-congested lungs and the troubled minds. Could men endure all that futile destruction again?

On September 1, the news reached us. Hitler had attacked Poland, without warning. A new kind of war had begun: the blitz. Before long we knew how war had changed. The new war was one of mobility and speed, of planes raining down bombs, of trucks and tanks sweeping across countries and U-boats lurking in the sea-lanes. The world's rhythm had changed. Life went into high gear. Most people would never again be close to the patient cycle of nature. We were hurrying into the age of big bombs, press buttons and flimsy relationships.

That spring of 1939, we huddled around those wirelesses

as we were to do for the next six years, waiting for the distant BBC voice to spell out what "they" were doing with our men and our lives. On September 3, we heard Neville Chamberlain's despondent voice from Downing Street, uttering the words that sealed our fate: "This country is at war with Germany." A little over an hour later, Australia's Prime Minister, Robert Menzies, sonorously told us that, as a result, it was his "melancholy duty" to tell us: "Australia is also at war." We were at war, because Britain was.

I was nearly sixteen, old enough to be aware that the sacrifices for this war were to be made by my generation. I felt despair and fear. The men would go to the front again and would die. We women would be like my grandmother and all those others who had been robbed of their men: they dusted the pictures of the young soldiers in khaki; they kept mementoes in boxes on their dressing-tables and cried, often, for the rest of their lives.

Charlie Green and fourteen other boys from Ulmarra and district joined up in 1939 the day recruiting opened. There is a photo of thirteen of them. Those men who are left keep records of the fate of each man. They mark them off now, as they die. In 1981, Tom Mawhinney, a sergeant major in 2/2 Battalion, in which all but one of them served, told me their fates: "George Roberts, whereabouts unknown; Bill Sullivan, killed in action, Greece; Lester McArtney, Grafton; Bill Wright, Tucabia; Ron Pattemore, Ballina; Max Finlayson, deceased; Errol Pattemore, a missionary, whereabouts unknown; Tom Mawhinney, South Grafton; Vic Davis, Sydney; A.H.W. Grant, Sydney; seated in middle, C.H. Green, killed in action; Bill Ulrick, Grafton; George Finlayson, deceased." Tom said: "Two not included in the snapshot are Jack Ulrick, of Grafton, and Jim Newman, in Strathfield. The only one of those who did not get drafted into the 2/2 Battalion was Bill Grant, who went into 2/3 Battalion." Today the only survivors are Ron Pattemore, Errol Pattemore and Jack Ulrick.

None of those who volunteered immediately — the "thirty-niners" — could have had the innocence, the sense of excitement for "the big adventure" that their fathers, the Anzacs, had. But they had a reputation to live up to (especially if they had fathers who were diggers), a job to do. And a man "couldn't back off".

Herc Green was not an Anzac so Charlie did not have a father model compelling him. For Herc, the war was an interruption to his grand plans for his farm, his stud herd, and his boys, especially Charlie, "the apple of his eye". He suffered, torn between pride for his talented son and frustration of his own ambitions.

Everyone knew what Herc wanted. Nobody can tell me what prompted Charlie to join up immediately, obviously against his father's wishes. He would have felt it was the honourable thing to do, I am sure. It is possible though, as his enthusiasm for the militia shows, that he sensed he had a talent. The war would have provided him with an opportunity to explore it. Or he might simply have wanted to break out of his narrow existence, to be his own man.

There's no certainty about many of Charlie's motives; he tended to keep things to himself. His reticence was to be commented on, often. F.O. Chilton — Sir Fred — who became Charlie's CO, made a point when he said Charlie was a poor communicator in personal matters, but never in army matters. Sir Fred went right to the heart of the matter. Poor communication was our problem, Charlie's and mine, mainly because we avoided the disagreeable. Hindsight tells me my belief that we were always in perfect communion was an illusion. Love goes forward through the flak shoulder to shoulder — the way soldiers do. And what soldiers call mateship could, I believe, be called love.

For another observer, C.H. had depths not to be plumbed. Bruce Brock was tantalised by what he perceived as the "mystery" of C.H. He wrote in 1984:

> You are probably the only person who knew the real C.H.G. You saw most of his facets. I know there was another C.H. that few suspected existed but I never found out what it was. I realise it existed but it just didn't come to the surface with us."

Charlie would not have consciously put up a barrier or created a mystery. He was self-contained, not secretive or defensive. He was a courageous, clear thinker who didn't concern himself with the trivial. There are clear intimations that though he was realistic, he was also a big dreamer. Our tragedy wasn't our inability to communicate our dreams, but our inability to admit they weren't coming true. They couldn't come true because neither was giving what the other wanted. And that was too awful to admit. We weren't to know that silence doesn't erase. Instead, it would postpone an eruption that had to occur, in some unexpected place at some later time. This book is an eruption.

Most men, except the more perceptive, such as Bruce Brock, read Charlie as a simple man, a dedicated soldier, and a born leader who promised to develop into one of the country's outstanding commanders. And when Charlie was so strangely cut down in the flowering of his talent in 1950, men saw an archetypal mystery to seize upon. They would say, knowingly, proudly: "Charlie Green had a field marshal's baton in his haversack."

At no time in Charlie's life can one be absolutely certain how interested he was in making a career in the Army. Dedication to a miliary career can clash with personal desires, like family life. Before the outbreak of war in 1939, Charlie showed his obvious interest in the army by being prepared to study. He didn't like studying, yet he was observed riding his bike to Ulmarra one night a week, after milking, to have extra lessons on military manuals from Sergeant-Major Harry Preston of 41 Battalion. Who better to learn from than Harry, a Great War veteran. He was every inch a sergeant-major: erect, crisp, keen, brightly polished and with a voice he could throw for miles. He had gleaming, alert eyes in a freckled face. At the outbreak of war, it was Harry who suggested Charlie should go straight to Sydney to enlist "to get in on the ground floor". No doubt he had confidence in the potential of his pupil.

Charlie is remembered vividly the day he turned up at the 2/2 Battalion recruiting office to enlist. This is one of those instances of memory that flashes forth clear and bright. But as the memory belongs to Sir Ivan Dougherty, many would not be surprised. In 1939, Sir Ivan was second in command of the newly formed 2/2 Battalion of the second AIF. Sir Ivan did not put any interpretation on the following recollection; he merely related it — quizzically. It is not typical of Charlie. I think it was Herc's influence bursting out.

The scene is 2/2 Battalion HQ, Ingleburn, 1939. 2/2 Bn drew its recruits from northern NSW. Charlie arrives, in his militia uniform, with the single pip of a subaltern. He says he wants to apply for an appointment as an officer. He is told: "Sorry, sir, we can't take you. Today we are only enlisting other ranks." Charlie takes off his officer's tunic, flings it down and says, "Well, here I am."

Apparently there were second thoughts. He did get an appointment as a lieutenant and it was a very early one, as his AIF number indicates. Astoundingly, thirty years later, many men reminiscing about Charlie can recite that number: NX121. It's a number to be proud of. The "N" indicates NSW. Three digits indicate officer, whereas four indicate other ranks. Most important, though, is how low the number is. High-ranking officers, the first appointees, took the lowest numbers. 121 was a low number for a junior officer.

Getting an appointment to the 2/2 Battalion was by no means automatic. The CO, the famous Lieutenant Colonel George Wootten, hand-picked his officers, gathering around him one of the finest teams in the AIF. They performed brilliantly in war and later, in peace. Today many are knighted.

It is important to recognise the significance of the Battalion, the army unit that features in Charlie's life — in the life of any man who chooses to be an infanteer. A foot slogger, carrying a gun in the front line of battle, where the services of about twenty others are required to keep one man firing. An infantry battalion, probably the most important unit in any army, is a strangely beguiling phenomenon. Its concept is ancient and its psychology powerful. A battalion is where a soldier belongs: it's his family, his home. He fights for its colours and wears them with pride. The battalion gives him a clear identity — the first for some — and also immortality. That old soldiers don't die can be divined at any battalion reunion, especially in a quiet place, beyond the noisy surface show, where men remember sadly and sweetly.

In his military service, C.H. fought with three battalions. The fourth, the 41 Militia Battalion, is the one he served with before and after World War 2. Each battalion has its own character. Charlie learned the craft of leadership in his original fighting battalion, Nulli Secundus, the 2/2 of the second AIF. In 1945, aged twenty-five, he took command of another, the 2/11, nicknamed "Mud over the Water" or "Legs Eleven". Each of these AIF Battalions perceived Charlie a little differently; in each he had a different nickname. In 1950, he took command of a Regular Army Battalion, 3 RAR, which was given the task of representing Australia in the Korean War. 3 RAR earned itself the nickname "Old Faithful" and earned high praise from American generals.

It is fascinating to see unfold the human qualities that are quarried and explored in the making of the unique character of a battalion. A battalion is about 800 strong, as was its ancient counterpart, the Roman cohort. A modern battalion could amount to 1000 men, because of the inclusion of support sections with more sophisticated weaponry, such as rocket-launchers, or anti-tank guns. A battalion is autonomous. The Commanding Officer is in absolute control and bears concomitant responsibility. In action, the CO has his battalion's objective to achieve, but the way he chooses to do it is his weighty decision. The tactics. And there's far more to tactics than the application of some well-established principles of attack and defence. Though a battalion is autonomous and its CO in complete control, he is still answerable to his senior commanders: first, the brigadier who commands a brigade, and then further up the chain of command to the generals.

Within the Army's structure, a battalion is the main building block, as was the cohort to a legion in Caesar's time. The battalion is self-contained, a veritable army in miniature, except that it may draw on independently commanded artillery or tanks. (Or on the Air Force or, in some special circumstances, the Navy.) In operations, it may function independently or it may fight alongside other battalions, making a larger force with an overall commander. The fighting nucleus of a battalion is made up of its four rifle companies — "riflemen", "infanteers", "footsloggers" or "diggers" as they are variously called. The names picture their roles. They are the teeth and claws of the army, in the vanguard, closing with the enemy with rifle and bayonet; or else digging holes or trenches for protection — or, too often, to make their temporary home. They call themselves "the poor bloody infantry". For the reality is hard, and unglamorous.

A battalion does not come alive without good leadership to produce well-trained personnel with high morale. Morale is that magic ingredient a commander must forge in his battalion. Without it, men will not stand up and fight. Or be prepared to die: for his comrades, for his battalion. In that order. The character and destiny of a battalion rests, largely, on one man, the commanding officer, especially the first CO, the founding father.

Soldiers will tell you that a battalion that becomes an immortal entity with "a soul" of its own "is a goer". Thereafter, the initiated enjoy a bond beyond words. The strength of that indivisible bond derives from the nature of the stakes. Death and honour. A man is rewarded in the knowledge he has earned honour among his fellows and passed the big test, the personal test: "I measured up". The testimony to the warrior code is visible in history's armies. In uniforms, flags, medals and in the numbers of men, who, century after century, have been prepared to engage in trial by the sword.

But we may wonder, observing traditional concepts changing, who will want to be tomorrow's soldiers.

The 2/2 Battalion, Charlie's first, takes its character from its members and its history, which begins in 1914. When the Australian Government raised a second AIF for World War 2, it gave it the same nomenclature, certain in its belief that the Anzac tradition of Gallipoli would be continued by the Anzacs' sons. A heavy charge to lay on another generation. The 2/2's ancestor was 2 Battalion, AIF, blooded on Gallipoli and subsequently mauled and mutilated in France. Some of the names on its lists of battle honours chill the blood: Lone Pine, Somme, Pozières, Ypres, Passchendale, Amien, Hindenburg Line.

In World War 2, 2/2 Battalion was reborn on September 3, 1939. Its colours are purple over green — not the gold over green of World War I, because during World War 2 gold dye was unprocurable. To signify the second AIF, the colours sit on a rectangular grey patch, worn on the shoulder of the tunic. The rectangle denotes the sixth division, the first expeditionary force for World War 2. Its continuity with the five Divisions of World War 1 thus becomes apparent. The motto, Nulli Secundus — Second to None — is the motto of the British Coldstream Guards, raised in 1661 for King Charles II. Nulli Secundus had a lot to live up to. Which it did. The tangible signs are fifteen battle honours, 129 decorations won by individuals and a formidable list of casualties.

The 2/2 was one of the great Battalions — immortal, unique. You are assured of that when you hear men talking:

"We fought like tigers for it."
"It was home: mother, father, family."
"A Battalion is God's gift to men."

Another soldier, writing about his battalion, the 2/11th, expresses similar sentiments:

To arrive in the Battalion was to be keenly aware that you had got somewhere, like arrival in one of the world's great cities, after travel through many sleepy half-awake hamlets.

In 1916, Banjo Paterson put into verse the essence of war experience. In this extract (from *Australia 1916*) he expresses the special bond between a soldier and his battalion:

They battled, the old battalion,
  Through the toil of the training camps,
Sweated and strove at lectures,
  By the light of the stinking lamps.

Marching, shooting, and drilling;
  Steady and slow and stern;

Awkward and strange, but willing
All of their job to learn.
Learning to use the rifle;
Learning to use the spade;
Deeming fatigue a trifle
During each long parade.
Till at last they welded
Into a concrete whole,
And there grew in the old battalion
A kind of battalion's soul.

The 2/2, great enough and individual enough to take its place among "the world's great cities", was imprinted at its inception. When a battalion is born, its first CO, provided he has those hard to define qualities that his special role requires, puts his indelible stamp on a battalion, giving it its character and style. Those COs who follow him mar this at their peril. While the battalion is a stern master to its members, it is merciless to its custodian, the commander. Any soldier will tell you.

The 2/2 Battalion's first CO, Lieutenant Colonel George Wootten, was incomparable. He served in World War 1 and between the wars he was a militiaman. He was summed up as one who would stand no nonsense, yet was fair. He was, above all, very capable. With his unquestionable authority, he was able to command respect and confidence. One soldier described him, affectionately, as "an ungainly big thing, but he looked magnificent on a horse". He had the nickname "Blood and Guts" which over the years got reduced to just "Guts". To sum up the men's appraisal of him, he was big and tough.

Second Seconders, speaking of their original CO and his equally inspiring successors, Colonels Chilton and Edgar, will say: "That's why our Battaliion was always a goer." Soldiers know the genuine from the false; just as they know when it's time to stand and fight, or run and survive; when it's time to obey, or time to jack up. I think Charlie Green's talent as a commander of men was fed by the examples set in 2/2 Battalion by its leaders and by the understanding he got there of the inimitable digger.

Arriving at the Battalion is one day no soldier forgets. Charlie's arrival is recorded by Captain Bill Toohill, who drove Charlie to camp on November 3, 1939. They were joining Colonel Wootten's staff in preparation for the arrival of the troops the next day. It was a balmy day as they travelled through Ingleburn's rolling farmlands. In a few weeks, soft green fields were covered in huts and dirt roads were covered with marching soldiers throwing up clouds of dust.

Then the recruits arrived. They staggered off their troop trains, were assembled and began their first route march — into camp. Immediately they were in another world, under the rule of martial law — a shock to most Australians, who are not readily amenable to discipline. They came from all walks of life — from the bush, the farms, the forests, from offices, banks and schools. They carried their gear in anything from sugar bags to suitcases. They were dressed in suits and moleskins. They arrived in a range of moods and in varying degrees of sobriety. They quipped and sang. Within hours their sardonic humour began to jell. The latecomers were to hear, as would the poor unesteemed reinforcements in years to come: "You'll be sorry." The army tried to stop this call in the Middle East. It never succeeded.

Amongst this motley lot were wags, larrikins, and some really "bad lots" (these the Battalion got rid of) and the real heroes, the average stout-hearted "poor bloody infantryman". Somewhere amongst them were the men who survived to tell us their stories.

Colonel Wootten stood in his hut, looking out of the window at them arriving and exclaimed, "Good God. What have I done to deserve this?" Well might he ask. One man confessed that at first "We were fair buggers. We didn't want anyone telling us what to do." An Australian soldier might give over the control of his life to the Army. The Army, however, can never control the soldier's humour, his deadly weapon. His humour alleviates the hard-to-put-up-with, and attacks the unliked

— or it is playfully used to take just a little bit of the mickey out of officers in particular. The wags were soon at work. One of the officers who marched them in from the railway station on the first day was wearing his splendid Light Horse uniform: riding breeches, polished leggings, spurs, riding crop, Sam Browne belt, gleaming brass. A tipsy aside was heard along the ranks: "Gawd, look at the bloody pansy." Duncan Goslett, a fine officer, who later won an MC and command of his own battalion, never lost his nickname. Nor did it bother him. Forty-odd years on, his wife Tammy maintained that legend. She used to make "Pansy" dolls for the 2/2 Battalion Association to raffle for the funds that are used to assist old diggers and to keep the group together.

The changing of men into soldiers now began. At battalion level it happens with training and drilling. When 1000 uniformed men can move as one man, a lot has been achieved. They have learned to obey orders, to cooperate and to persevere. From this they obtain satisfying pride. They inspire it, too. As Padre Read of the 2/2 said, looking back on his army life: "What a thrill it was to see the Battalion on parade."

Training to be an infantryman, a footslogger, is unromantic, hard work. After long, arduous route marches in new army boots, dressed in the famous "giggle suit", they would attend weapon training. When they were ready, they were introduced to mock battles, probably still using World War 1 principles and models. As infanteers, they had to learn the importance of the ground, the place where they were safest. They had to dig-in for defence and learn the features that would protect them as they moved. The day was to come, when the real bullets were flying, when they would gratefully bury their face in mud or sand for protection. They soon learned that they ate, slept, marched and fought in or on the ground. What they remember most clearly of those early days, years after, is how they dug trenches and filled them in; dug and filled in . . .

To spur them along, there was always the awesome Sergeant-Major. All sergeant-majors seem to fashion themselves to the stereotype: barking, bawling, frightening. I was told about an early SM, one Sanderson, who did his job so well the soldier said: "When he spoke, you'd jump like a lion. And you could hear him at Bourke." He warned them when they first went into camp: "You blokes are going to hate me."

Trying to make soldiers toe the line is an officer's most difficult job, especially in the Australian army. At first it was a problem for Charlie. He made mistakes and he learned from them. His biggest mistake was to threaten. Apparently, so the story goes, he said one day to his platoon, in a fit of exasperation: "If you don't do what I tell you, I'll charge you." That was it. He had done it. Quick as a flash some wag nailed him. For that moment of hasty folly, he won himself the nickname "Charger". The name stuck until he transferred to another battalion. There he gained another nickname, "Chuckles". Today it depends on the unit, whether he is remembered as "Charger", "Chuckles" or "Greenie". How "Chuckles" came about is described later on. Each nickname marked a significant phase of his development. He had the problem, too, of handling the "caste system". Traditionally, officers and other ranks do not fraternise. It was difficult for Charlie to know how to treat the men who had enlisted with him, whom he had known all his life. One man, a schoolfriend, observed Charlie struggling with this problem: "I think he was taken aside and advised. He soon became the officer. He learned, quickly, to draw the line so that everybody knew where it was."

Another instance showed his early struggle with learning how to discipline men. "He was inclined to be bumptious and to bully us," said one of the self-confessed "buggers". "On one occasion, when he realised he'd gone too far, he apologised to us. He was respected for that." He showed he could be flexible and be ready to right a wrong, which was long remembered and appreciated. "We were picked on for smoking during a lecture. We were sent to Lieutenant Green. He knew what had happened, because he was at the lecture. When we went to the orderly room, he let us off. He said, 'Get to buggery out of here and don't come back.' "

A less hard-headed man, who saw the world through different coloured glasses, gave me his impression of his first days in the Army in C Company — the same company as Charlie Green. The storyteller was Jack Boorer, a countryman from Gloucester. He fought in the Bardia, Greek and New Guinea campaigns. In the Owen Stanleys, New Guinea, he was struck by a volley of machine-gun bullets. One shattered his spine; another lodged in the wallet he carried in his left-hand breast pocket. (I've seen the wallet and wondered at the chanciness of war.)

Jack was a man whose pride in the Battalion and its feats shone bright. In no way was his view of life soured by the ravages war made on his body. This is how Jack remembered 1939:

> Some of us blokes from C Company were watching at a distance as Major Ivan Dougherty, the second-in-command, briefed some officers on organising heavy equipment. They were standing under a tree. Among them were the CO, Wootten, Buckley, "Pansy" Goslett, the "Black Prince", Calwell and Charlie. I looked at them and thought to myself "What wonderful giants of men". They looked inspiring and it gave me a tremendous sense of pride. I was right, too, they were giants of men in every way. The pride we felt in them soon ran through the whole Battalion. We wanted to be the best and look the best.

I heard Jack argue with some of the boys at a Battalion reunion about the origin of Charlie's nickname "Charger". He declared his was the correct story. On his side of his argument Jack had the weight of an impeccable pedigree: his number was NX1507. Sitting in his wheelchair, Jack told me:

> When we arrived at Ingleburn there was nothing there, just a few carts, some tents and old huts. We had to build a rifle range in a hurry to begin training. Charlie Green was in command of the nucleus of C Company which had the job of preparing the rifle range. They had no vehicles for transport to and from the site of the rifle range, some distance away. Horses were provided as an alternative means of transport. Charlie chose a beautiful, big black animal. He had someone saddle it and bring it up to him. This took place in front of the company. He mounted it and it bolted, immediately it charged right through the ranks of the

onlookers, sending them in all directions. He stayed on. The boys, seeing the possibilities in this, yelled and shouted to make the horse bolt even more. Which it did. He still stayed on. That's how he got his name, "Charlie the Charger". That wasn't quite the end of the story. Charlie always rode that horse even though it was always bolting and the troops were always yelling at it to make it worse. But one day, another officer, not knowing about all this, got on the black horse. He was wearing a cape that flapped, frightening the horse. The horse, out of control, charged into traffic on the road. After that the horse disappeared. It was beautiful, but it was dangerous. It could have killed someone.

Charlie had those enviable countryman's skills, horsemanship and ingenuity. But he didn't have the advantage of a university education as most of his fellow officers had. Frederick Chilton, who was to be their next commanding officer, said: "He overcame his educational disadvantages fairly quickly because he was very intelligent and quiet. Indeed he soon displayed outstanding qualities; he learned to relate well to both officers and men; he was firm; he had a strong character; and there was one other important thing — he had presence."

If men were aware of Charlie's background, they didn't discuss it. Some knew he was "only a cow-cocky finding it hard to compete with university men". Others, when they learned of his youth and his background, were visibly astonished. One said: "I can't believe he was only nineteen then. He seemed to be about thirty, experienced and better educated than I was." Jack Boorer was surprised too. He said: "Now I understand why he didn't get a promotion immediately, as I thought he should have. He was brilliant and I could never understand why they didn't put him at the drawing board" [planning tactics]. As an afterthought, Jack added: "The important thing was he looked the part: he looked good and clean."

The troops had their own problems to contend with. Most of them were only nineteen too, full of spirits and mischief. They started furphies about how their tea was being laced with bromide; they made up bawdy songs to sing on route marches and many of them went on leave and got drunk. If they misbehaved they had their pay docked. And every Saturday, it seemed, they got inoculated or vaccinated.

After a hard day's training they would have enjoyed a few beers, but the canteens were dry. Their frustration level with canteens was low, and when one of the civilian contractors, out to make a quick buck, started fleecing them, they retaliated. One night the canteen disappeared in a mysterious blaze. "Mysterious happenings" in the army spell mischief — or worse, discontent. In battle zones, for example, officers' latrines, which have the privilege of being surrounded with hessian, are very prone to direct hits from the "enemy".

The church parades were not well attended until the men discovered that the alternative was fatigue duty. That meant clearing tree stumps out of the ground, digging ditches, or similar tasks. Suddenly they became religious to a man.

Leave was not without its hazards, as the Army was only too ready to remind them. One digger explains it all in a letter home:

> "We have to go and see a picture about women. You can imagine what it's about; so it will do us no harm. Anyway it's compulsory."

Ulmarra changed a lot when war broke out. I was in a position to observe. My father's newsagency was a kind of gathering place. The farmers and the cream carriers would do the rounds of the town each day. They'd go to the factory to deliver their cream, then to the post-office, the store — and the newsagent. In our newsagency, behind a partition at the back of the shop, was a barber's salon. Men liked to wait for a haircut or shave. It gave them an opportunity to yarn: to fix up the world. What wisdom and what a fund of yarns I heard through the thin partition! There was one old man called Tom, whose ringing voice and distinctive laugh always drew an audience. When old Tom came in the shop, I knew my day was made. He would tell stories of the old days on the Clarence and other tales ten feet high. There's one favourite I myself tell, about a farmer who bought a motor car that he tried to pull up like a horse, with a "whoa", because he forgot about the brake pedal.

In a small town where people live so closely, the departure of fifteen boys left a gap. I missed two of them in particular, Bill Sullivan and Jack Ulrick, because they were in my tennis team. The year war broke out we were playing competition tennis. That meant that each Saturday we played at a different centre. Sometimes we played on our home courts; sometimes we travelled around the district by car.

Those golden, carefree days. Motoring along gravel roads among the canefields, over the river by punt to Southgate, or out into the dry, scrub country to those district courts, sometimes privately owned or else near a corrugated iron hall, quaint buildings still to be seen occasionally on the Australian landscape. The courts were always freshly marked and the little shed filled with people waiting for a game. In the afternoon great teapots were filled and plate after plate came out: sponge cakes, scones, tarts, and lamingtons resting on crisp doilies.

Jack Ulrick and Bill Sullivan developed quickly as tennis players, especially as doubles partners. They'd move into the net and play with their opponents like a cat with a mouse. When they were ready they would smash the ball, usually over the wire fence. I was too short to reach many shots. Bill would hit me on the bottom with his racket to send me into the net, where impulsiveness and urgency would cause me, when I got the opportunity, to whack the ball — into the net or out. Then they would give me a playful lecture on the art of the game.

When I heard about them on a Bren carrier, still together in Greece in the thick of the battle, I could envisage them so clearly: brave, joking and daring. Bill did not survive.

Coming home from tennis, muscles tired, there'd be post mortems on the game, maybe a song or two. It would be late afternoon, that hushed, gentle time of the day. Long, soft shadows fell across the stony road. We had to go slowly along those shadow-dappled roads. Sometimes there was a deep pothole, or worse, we would strike a patch of corrugation so

## From man to soldier 35

bad we were forced to travel either very slowly or dangerously quickly. As you would expect, the driver of our tennis party, in one of those tourers of the 1930s, took the quick way. It added to the fun. "Hang on" he'd say, and put his foot on the accelerator.

When Jack and Bill, and all the other boys, went to the war life seemed to come to a halt. That was the end of long, leisurely afternoons among the scones and tea.

Europe had come to a halt too, but only a temporary one. After the fury of the September blitz on Poland, the quiet they call the "Sitzkrieg" was an eerie one. Everyone must have known that static trench warfare was a thing of the past and that the miles of fortifications on the Maginot line were redundant. Even so, few could have anticipated the dizzy pace or the fury of the great steel German war machine that would start rolling over Europe in May 1940.

Charlie's 2/2 Battalion, in training at Liverpool in 1939, were route marching and digging trenches in preparation for service in Europe in the style of World War 1, not dreaming of what lay in store: deserts, mountains and jungles.

Christmas 1939 was 6 Division's last in Australia for a long time. Before "Blamey's Mob", as 6 Division was called, was sent overseas in January 1940, they were given final leave.

Final leave. For the soldier, a delayed realisation. Maybe it would be final. He'd go home, to say goodbye. As most of the Second Seconders came from the country farms, they would have been feted in their district. But, more than likely, the young bravado would have wanted to see his mother. As their letters show, young soldiers think a lot about their mothers. That is the only tangible sign of their concern and their vulnerability.

On that ominous "Final Leave", the soldier becomes sharply conscious of all the familiar, suddenly precious things he might never see again. His eyes store greedily all that he wants to bank in his mind. Scenes to call up, consolingly, later, as he crouches in a foxhole, on some cratered battle ground on the other side of the world. Like the kitchen at tea-time. His dog waiting for him to come home. The wistful sweetheart. But there would be a lot of jolly talk to hide what he was feeling: pain, fear, excitement, uncertainty. The future had no landscape.

For anyone who once farewelled a soldier nothing could be more evocative than Vera Lynne singing "We'll meet again, don't know where, don't know when. But I know we'll meet again some sunny day . . ." That song went round the world during the war years, echoing the pain of all those who were saying goodbye. That is what war is — all goodbyes.

I saw Charlie Green when he was on his final leave. It turned out to be a fateful encounter. Though I was only 16, I had now been working for two and a half years in my father's newsagency. When Charlie came into the shop I knew who he was, by his tallness and his officer's uniform. I've never forgotten that incident. Immediately, I sensed some strange connection had been made. He suddenly appeared, and stood there looking down at me — straight tall, handsome, manly. I noticed his eyes, particularly, and his clear brown skin. His eyes were large, velvety brown and soft. His body might have indicated reserve, but his eyes were softly shining. He bought a fountain pen. I wished him luck. He thanked me and left. That was all.

No sooner had the men returned from leave, than the preparation for their departure was evident.

On January 4, 1940, 16 Brigade of 6 Division of the second AIF marched through the streets of Sydney prior to embarkation. They were eight abreast, fixed bayonets gleaming. They thrilled the hearts of Sydney, according to the *Sydney Morning Herald*:

> These men of Australia's brave new army, young, bronzed, clear-eyed, and so obviously conscious in their demeanour of their high responsibility and the confidence which a nation reposes on them,

were the answer to Berlin's wishful propaganda. They were worth, in terms of patriotic showmanship, ten times all the supply ships and the foodships which Australia has sent to the European war zone since the war began. One was reminded, as they strode forward with youthful step, heads erect, eyes shining with the glow of health and the pride of achievement, of John Masefield's first impression of the old Anzacs. "For physical beauty and nobility of bearing they surpassed any men I have ever seen. They walked and looked like kings in old poems."

Describing the march in a letter home, Ernie Osbourne drew attention to those spectators who didn't feel so thrilled. As the boys marched along, one stirrer in the crowd yelled out: "Five bob a day murderers!" But as Ernie wrote: "one of our mates who was there knocked him off his feet, and the crowd cheered."

"They walked and looked like kings in old poems." The journalist used the weight of Masefield's words to attempt to pinpoint the incredible fascination of soldiers in action — whether they are marching in unison, drilling on the parade ground or charging with fixed bayonets through a sand dune or up a razorback. I try to deny my own fascination, knowing that the price of all that discipline, courage, comradeship and — yes — nobility, is *death*. High stakes.

Only the soldiers understand the price. As Sassoon, the deglorifyer, reminds us in his poem *Suicide in the Trenches:*

"You smug faced crowds with kindling eye
Who cheer when soldiers march by,
Sneak home and pray you'll never know
The hell where youth and laughter go."

Five days after the march, the Brigade was secreted to Darling Harbour, for security reasons, to embark for an unknown destination — somewhere overseas. For all the secrecy, a crowd was there to farewell the new generation of Anzacs. There were the last hugs, the false smiles, the women's tears, the often repeated plea "don't forget to write".

When the men at 2/2 Battalion got aboard their ship, the *Otranto,* they crowded the rails or climbed high on the rigging to shout farewells and cooees. As the ship pulled out the streamers stretched and the shouts were deafening. The harbour was filled with ships and small craft that saluted the boys going off to war with sirens blowing and ferries crowing. Noise and bravado.

It was goodbye to Australia, to home, to the sweetheart for these men for a long time. One soldier said of their first night at sea: "I had a lot of trouble sleeping. I couldn't help thinking about it all and what I'd left behind."

What Charlie Green felt, uprooted from everything he had known, can only be conjecture.

# 3
# A sea change

> — though we break with swords
> A great oppression and a greater wrong,
> Stumbling along uncertain paths towards
> A time when laws are just and peace is strong —
> Though we give freedom to the race of men,
> Yet who shall give us back Ourselves again?
>
> *The Soldiers* by Alexander Turner

At sea in the Indian Ocean, Charlie Green was in a first-class cabin on the hastily converted *Otranto,* which a coat of black paint had transformed into a troop ship. There was a steward to clean the cabin and a batman to look after him personally. At home, in Swan Creek, he would have been the servant of the sun and the cows, milking at sunup and sundown. Despite the contrast, he smoothly took on the caste of officer, among men born to that station.

Officer and gentleman. The ideal; the expectation. Charlie in some ways didn't measure up; he did not come from the gentleman class and he did not have a formal education. His fellow officers no doubt noticed his occasional lapse in grammar and other telltale signs. But the soldiers, it seems, didn't notice. If you drew their attention to it, they seemed surprised because they hadn't noticed, nor considered that it would be an issue. To them, Charlie was a born leader. He had authority, presence, and they could trust his judgment. He commanded respect for he was a natural gentleman who, through his strength of character and wholeness of self, had a refinement that education doesn't necessarily produce. It leaves you wondering what a formal education might have done for C.H. I don't think it would have robbed him of that simplicity that was admired. It might have equipped him to realise his full potential after the war, when all his talent lay fallow.

Men looking back on C.H., the young officer, saw that he was "talented", "quiet and reserved". One man said, "He had armour hard to crack". If he meant that Charlie put up defences, I disagree. More likely he was treading cautiously, finding his way in his own time. More to the point, "He didn't let anything lean on him". Not surprisingly, he eventually became noted for his "sure touch" and his "coolness", which emanated from his wholeness.

Jack Boorer repeatedly commented on the importance of officers "looking the part", especially the field commanders, on whom their lives and their honour (no less valued) depended. Jack said wonderingly, "It's the way they look that sticks. It does something to you." Of Charlie in particular, he went on: "You'd look at him and say: "How lucky we are to have a man with his ability and to be able to get there at his age!" It was Jack who made that interesting comment: "He looked good and clean."

That something emanating from C.H.'s inner self was noticed by officers as well. It was described as "presence" by F.O. Chilton (Sir Fred). Another fellow officer, the late Sir John Dunlop, of 2/2 Battalion, wrote this about the young Charlie Green of 1940:

> Some people possess a basic ethos which allows them to stand tall. It is probably most evident in men on the land. They know by experience that they can deal with elemental things; they are unfazed by responsibility and they widen their horizons from the sound base of their early training.

World War 1 historian Dr Charles Bean has drawn attention to the qualities of Australian countrymen that made them the best soldiers, the real Anzac, the mythical Australian image. Is it because Charlie Green fitted the myth that men who were more educated and often much older were ready to defer to him as a leader? That is why I wonder if a polished Charlie with a private school accent could have achieved what he did when he was a commander in battle.

He was one of them, yet he had ability, too. So he gained their grateful confidence.

For all the troops, whether officer or other ranks, the voyage over was "a bit of a holiday". It was the start of "the big adventure" that was opening up the world, an experience only the Army could provide. For a while they could forget what lay in store. Though there was training, there were, too, the beer ration, their mates to yarn with, play cards with, and gamble with.

The convoy arrived at Colombo, a landfall which gave the troops the first hint of their still secret destination. They had "a heck of a day" in Colombo. The highlight was the now legendary rickshaw racing. The soldiers confiscated rickshaws from the natives, popped the owners into them and then held races. The wide-eyed, startled owners hung on for grim life while the soldier audience cheered and barracked — and had a few bets, of course.

Charlie Green was seen visiting the cricket ground, "that small gem of a place", scene of some famous matches. And I daresay Charlie was one of the junior officers who had the difficult task of marching red-faced, boisterous troops back to the ship.

Summing up the day in Ceylon, in one digger's words, "It was a beautiful day but it had a bad ending." Almost to a man the troops had dysentery so badly "they thought they were dying". Drinking the native brew from the exotic palm made it worse for some. Back at sea, the heat was so bad and men so ill that their mates, at least those who were able, carried the really ill men up on to the deck to get some air.

In Ceylon the troops did what was to become a practice. They bought souvenirs. One of the special purchases was moonstones, for their mothers and girl friends. I received a memento from Ceylon. My first present from a man: a beautiful moonstone pendant. Jack, my idol of the tennis courts, sent it to me. My joy was clouded when someone looked at the chain and said ruefully: "Moonstones are very unlucky." After the casualties in Greece, when Bill, the other boy of the tennis courts, was killed and Jack was captured, I never wore those milky, mysterious looking stones again.

News of the arrival of AIF mail got around in Ulmarra. We would gather near the post-office or at my father's shop with letters, photos and souvenirs in our hands, eager to exchange news and check up on all the boys of the district.

Back at sea, after their wild day in Colombo, the soldiers were too sick to care that their destination was still officially unknown. Obviously, like their fathers, they must be heading for the Suez Canal, then England, and then into trenches in Europe.

They bubbled over with excitement when they first saw the Canal. Near the entrance, Sir Anthony Eden, Secretary of State for War, double-breasted and very English, used a pilot boat to visit each ship to welcome Australia's fighting men to the war zone, with a tribute to their readiness to offer their services.

At midnight on February 12, 1940, the troops arrived at their disembarkation point: El Kantara, on the east side of the Canal, at the junction of the Cairo-Palestine line. "It looked like an oasis." The British engineers, on duty looking after the canal, turned on a memorable breakfast of sausages — camel sausages, they told the troops — and lashings of wonderful tea. "It was the best we had since we left home." It's interesting how soldiers remember where they enjoyed a cuppa. The closer to the front line, the better the tea tastes and the more frequently they'll try to brew it.

At Kantara, the Australians were about twenty miles from a 1916 battlefield, made famous by the Australian cavalry. At Romani, the great leader, Chauvel, routed the Turks with his daring young Lighthorsemen. True to Dr Bean's remarks about countrymen making the best soldiers, Chauvel was reared on a property on the Upper Clarence, beginning his army career in the Upper Clarence Light Horse. Had C.H. lived he might have been the second Clarence River man to become a general.

The men boarded an antique train, still not knowing where they were headed, but assuming it was Egypt, where the

Anzacs had trained. It wasn't long before they realised that the chill desert they were crossing was the Sinai. And that their destination was not Egypt after all. It was Palestine.

They were sent to Palestine because the British Government was intent upon keeping control of the Middle East. In Palestine, the Australians were in reserve, to be trained to a pitch of readiness for quick deployment. At the same time they had the job of maintaining a garrison. Keeping the peace between Arabs and Jews, they discovered, required constant vigilance and active patrolling.

In Australia there was a lot of controversy about the use of the 6 Division and its senior appointments. The Labor Party wanted the Australians kept at home, arguing that Japan was a menace to Australia's safety. Regular Army staff were indignant that part-time soldiers were being given high commands. In February, 1940, as 6 Division was arriving in Palestine, the Government began to raise another division, the 7th. General Sir Thomas Blamey was given the top appointment: Commander-in-Chief — a militia man with World War 1 experience. Preference throughout the AIF went to militia officers many of whom also had World War 1 service. The rather bitter feeling that resulted was still alive in 1950 when Charlie Green, an AIF man, was given command of the Australian contingent to the Korean War.

Blamey's promotion to Commander-in-Chief left a vacancy in the command of 6 Division. Major General Iven Mackay filled that position and in the re-shuffle "Tubby Allen" became 2/2 Battalion's new brigadier. "Nulli Secundus" retained "Guts" Wootten as their CO and the gentle "lovable" Ivan Dougherty as second-in-command. Often, when Wootten was seconded to other duties, Dougherty acted in command, and before 2/2 Battalion went into battle he had his own battalion. F.O. Chilton, who acted as Dougherty's second-in-command and became his lifelong friend, was then appointed CO of 2/2, and it was under him that the Battalion was blooded. All remarkable men. "That's why we were always a goer," 2/2 men always say.

Ideally, wartime appointments are based on one consideration only: the man who can best serve the interests of his country and his men so that they may acquit themselves with honour, whether in victory or defeat. He is the one who puts his men first. It was that ideal of unity that Colonel Brooks and his part-time soldiers of the 41 Byron Scottish Regiment had in mind when they built the memorial to Charlie Green.

Charlie's transition from simple farmer to officer with an impressive potential could have gone unnoticed. But what happened after the war couldn't go unnoticed. War took Charlie out of his lifestream. When it ended there was for him no going on, and no going back. One would expect a man like C.H. to make the return easily. That he didn't begs for an explanation, especially as his attempt to break out of his impasse led to his end. If I could understand, I might be able to wake up in the mornings without the lump of lead in my chest. Consequently, all that Charlie experienced is relevant. Even the next part of the story, the long wait in Palestine, before the second generation of Anzacs were blooded.

# 4
# Palestine — Waiting

> I walk the ancient hills of God —
> The hills and plains of Israel's land —
> So tread I where my Saviour trod,
> But with a rifle in my hand.
>
> *An Infantryman in Palestine* by Val Anderson

On February 13, the troops arrived at Julis Camp. Julis, some twelve miles from Gaza and about fifty miles from Jerusalem, was the site of a regiment of British soldiers, the Black Watch, most of whom were being hurried back to Britain. The Australians were to take over their job of keeping a garrison — a kind of occupation force — and continue intensive training for an unknown future. "All that the Tommies left us were latrines, showers and a canteen hut" the Australians record. With British-type issue tents, the diggers began to build their tent city. No sooner had they got their tents up than it rained . . . and rained. When the rain stopped and the land greened before their eyes, they believed it truly was the land of milk and honey, as the Bible told them.

Julis camp was on the west side of a hill adjoining an orange grove. From the top of the hill you could look down a wide valley dotted mainly with Arab villages and more orange groves. In the north-west part of the valley a series of white dots were the cottages of the Jewish village of Gan Yavne. Set in carpets of brilliant green pastures or crops were the chocolate patches of ploughed ground. To the east reared up the gaunt Judaean mountains in whose foothills they were to spend much time on "doovers" (military exercises). Away to the west was the sparkling blue Mediterranean.

Charlie would have enjoyed the view from the hill. Looking along that valley, alive with rural activity, he would have thought of the farm back home, and, as soldiers will, mused: "I wonder what they are doing now." He always felt the pull of the earth. No matter where he went he would cast his eyes over the ground and pick up soil, running it through his fingers and smelling it. Once, somewhere near Mudgee, when we had gone for a tour around New South Wales looking at properties, he stopped the car beside a ploughed paddock. It looked like finely grated chocolate; it was the richest darkest soil I have ever seen. He leaned through the fence, picked up a handful of soil, rubbed it through his fingers, sniffed it and exclaimed: "It's so good you could eat it!" And he emptied his matchbox and stuffed it full of chocolate soil to carry home.

For many, not for all, a year in Palestine wasn't long enough. "There was never enough time to see it all," Jack Boorer told me. First, there was homage to pay, to wander through the cemetery at Gaza looking at the Australian Light Horse graves, easily identified by their Rising Suns. The gum trees stirred feelings of nostalgia and then they would fossick through the old grassed-over trenches to see if they could find a bullet or some shrapnel to souvenir.

Their photos indicate what impressed most. The Biblical places took precedence. And in Charlie's album there was a series of photos of Tiberias that still bore the marks of Roman genius in walls, moats, villas and gardens. What an eye-opener it all was to boys from the Australian outback or from the city dole queues.

One place the Australians could go that did not seem so alien to them was the modern, relatively clean Tel Aviv. Tel Aviv was a Jewish city, so the women were not concealed and untouchable. Diggers could go to street cafes, and along the beach front. There were cabarets, crowds of pleasure seekers, blaring music, garish modern stucco buildings in a harsh blaze of sun. It reminded them of Bondi, they said. Except that everyone spoke Hebrew, or Yiddish.

Charlie was invited by Frederick Chilton, the man who became their CO and his friend, to accompany him, with his party, on a trip through the Sinai desert to Akaba and then to Jordan. A photo Charlie took of the Sea of Gallilee might date from that trip; the fishing boats could have belonged to the Disciples. Already, Charlie Green's experience was sufficient for Sir Fred to make a pertinent observation: "The army widened his horizons. I couldn't imagine him settling down again to the narrow regime of a dairy farm." There's no doubt Charlie was stimulated by all he saw. Often he would say to me, "I'll take you back there one day. I'd love you to see it."

There are a lot of funny stories about how the Australians "duped the Arabs" who swarmed around the camp like flies, scavenging, especially ready to make lightning swoops on weapons for their own war. One that Charlie told me is typical. The scene is a railway station in Palestine. An Arab is peddling oranges through the window to soldiers on a troop train. He takes money from one soldier, then, seeing that the train is about to depart, dawdles and stalls to avoid handing over the oranges. The train begins to jerk into motion . . . the Australian, quick as a flash, leaps into action. He seizes his rifle, points it at the Arab, slips the safety catch and lets out a bloodcurdling yell. Immediately he is showered with oranges that the terrified Arab flings through the window before streaking off in terror. When the Australian troops first arrived, oranges were a penny each. By the time they left they were ten for a penny. They learned to deal with the Arabs.

The Australians' role as peacekeepers brought the immediate realisation of the terrible tension brooding over everything because of the struggle between the Arabs and Jews for possession of the Holy Land, to which each claimed an inalienable right. The struggle kept erupting. There were sneak raids, terrorist raids, riots, as well as the Arabs' own tribal conflicts and blood feuds. If a village were under suspicion for any kind of disruptive activity, an army patrol would be sent to watch it. First there would be the show of strength, riding around the village in a truck bristling with soldiers and guns. Then the patrol would camp nearby. That's how soldiers got to see village life at close quarters and got invited to village feasts by the local Mukhtar.

Adrian Buckley told me about those social occasions. "Buck" was Charlie's closest friend in the Army. He was also in C Company and engaged in good-natured rivalry with C.H. as a platoon commander. Like Charlie, he was a farmer, from the wheat-sheep belt at Tamworth. He had those same country qualities of resourcefulness, ingenuity, industriousness. He was very intelligent and possessed an impish sense of humour. Altogether, he seemed less serious. Whereas Charlie was tall, big-boned and dark, Buck was tall, fair, sharper featured and slighter of stature. These days, though still remarkably fit and still farming, Buck says he cannot remember much about the war. But he can remember very clearly how he and Charlie suffered Arab hospitality.

Etiquette, Buck pointed out, was a complicated matter. The Arabs press incredible amounts of food on to their guests, who are obliged to eat all the host decides to offer. Not to do so is a deadly offence. And the guest has to eat in the same manner as the host. Adrian said he didn't mind eating with his fingers but "when the mukhtar began eating the bloody bones as well . . ." This is what a man could be expected to consume: first there were two roasted pigeons, a small fowl, bread and salad. Then, when the guests thought they were finished, around came a platter with a leg of lamb on it. And after that a plate piled high with melon and grapes . . .

Both the Arab and the Jewish newspapers in Palestine hailed the soldiers of the AIF as the true sons of their fathers, the Anzacs, "The best troops in the British Empire". The Germans announced it to the world as well — sarcastically. Lord Haw Haw, the Irishman who broadcast Goebbel's propaganda, told the world in his very British accent that it was no secret that Churchill's "cowboys" had arrived.

Chauvel's Desert Mounted Corps had blazed Australia's way into the history of Palestine in World War 1. Joined by some infanteers who had survived Gallipoli, his cavalry, distinctive in their emu-plumed slouch hats, attacked the Turks at Beersheba. They thundered across the Turkish trenches, leapt off their horses and bayonet charged with such daring the routed Turks declared: "They are madmen."

The second generation of Anzacs had their heads filled with the Anzac legend. "We are the best", they thought. They felt the flush of pride and the urge to live up to the reputation, especially when Polish or Free French soldiers would see the slouch hat and salute. Or when a local, an Arab or a Jew, would approach them, hand held out, saying: "Proud to meet you, Aussie."

But they were not prepared for another reputation the Anzacs of World War 1 had earned. They learned it in a way that might have been damaging to their morale. But instead, it enflamed them, for it was too late to change the Australian character. General Wavell (Field Marshal Lord Wavell), Commander of all the British troops in the east, went to Gaza in April 1940 to inspect the AIF and to address the troops. All the Australians remember of Wavell's address is his denunciation of the men who had come to fight for the Empire. Lord Wavell said the Australians had gained a most unfortunate reputation in 1915 in Egypt. He didn't want it to happen again. He wanted the Australians to show the Egyptians that "their notion of the Australians as rough, wild, undisciplined people, given to strong drink" was incorrect. Chastised like schoolboys, they were all indignant, even the officers. A more constructive approach would have been to balance those remarks with recognition of the first AIF's contribution. The Australians smarted for the honour of the sixty thousand men who had died. The Australians, the ones always pushed into the vanguard by the British because they were such wonderful "shock troops", who earned the title "Lords of Death"! A consequence of their vanguard role was their casualty rate — the highest in the British forces for men and officers alike.

In spite of Wavell's complaints about the Australians, including some recent minor incidents, he nevertheless sent the second AIF in first to attack the Italian-held fort, Bardia — Australia's first campaign in World War 2.

Other British officers followed Wavell's lead and continued the criticism of the Australians. As did British writers such as Vera Brittain. In 1941, the not-so-effective British commander in Greece, General Maitland Wilson, again pre-judged the colonials. Even in 1950 in Korea, the prejudice was still alive. Possibly British officers perpetuated the label "undisciplined" fearing that British troops would get out of hand under Australian influence.

The following incident couldn't have happened in the British Army — nor in the German. Where else but in the Australian Army? This story not only involves Charlie, it epitomises the Australian soldier, very impatient with pomp, ceremony and "doovers" where you fight only imaginary enemies, not fair dinkum ones.

One day in Palestine when Charlie was acting OC of C Company, he had a few problems. There had been a very strenuous and taxing doover. After, there was a ten-mile march back to camp where the troops were obliged to wait on the parade ground, tired, dirty, hungry and very thirsty. They had to wait for an appreciation. This day it was from the CO himself, "Guts" Wootten. Furthermore, they knew they were in for one of Wootten's blastings (he didn't mince words) as they had blown it.

Bluey had had enough. In front of all, he walked off the parade ground, with his rifle at the slope, took off his gear, threw down his slouch hat — his most significant act — and declared: "I've had it. I'm going home. You can stick the AIF . . ."

It is not surprising that the British Army, steeped in discipline and tradition, found the Australians apparently unsoldierly.

The Ned Kelly myth suggests that our trait of lawlessness is ingrained, hammered in at our rough beginnings. Because the Ned Kelly theme keeps recurring in music, literature and art, it strikes a chord we recognise and even admire. But it is not solely Ned's lawlessness that Sydney Nolan conveys in his haunting images of the bushranger's stand in his ingenious ploughshare armour.

One Anzac legend which originated in Egypt in 1915 is more about mischief than lawlessness. A brawl broke out between Australians and Egyptian police at a brothel. This became known as the "Battle of Wazzir". Accounts of it

Officers of 2/2 Battalion AIF, 1940.

L-R (front): Captains B.S. Black, D.E. Michelson, J.C. Rishworth, Major F.O. Chilton, Lieutenant-Colonel I.N. Dougherty, Lieutenant-Colonel G.F. Wootten DSO, Captain G.A. Bertram, Major C.R.V Edgar, Captains P.A. Cohen, W.B. Caldwell, L.Y Armati (MO).
(centre): Padre Read, Lieutenants A.S. Wilson, A.A. McLellan, Captain G.H. Godbold, Lieutenants E.E. Taylor, A.H. Baird, J.W. Dunlop, G.S. Cox, K.H. Loftus, D.N. Fairbrother, E.H. King.
(rear): Lieutenants C.N. Swinton, W.J. Crosby, C.E. Green, B. Brock, D.B.L. Goslett, B.H. Travers, A.H. Champion, A.A. Buckley and J.G. Hendry.

Visiting the Great Pyramid, Egypt, December 1940.
Charlie Green (L) and B. H. Travers (R).

abound, varying from comic to scathing. Here is C.J. Dennis' version, accurate in detail, yet inimitably racy in the telling:

*From the winders come piannees an' some giddy
 duchess pairs;
An' they piled 'em on the roadway in the mire,
An' 'eaped them 'igh wiv fal-derals an'
 pretty parlor chairs
Which they started in to purify wiv fire.
Then the redcaps come to argue, but they jist
 amused the mob;
For the scavengers wus warmin' to their job.*

In 1940, the 2/2 Battalion (2nd AIF) on leave in Cairo sought the Wazzir site, readily identifiable by an emu-plumed slouch hat hanging from the ceiling. Then there was some kind of re-enactment. It is recorded that another piano flew out of a window.

A scathing version of this appears in British novelist Olivia Manning's *The Levant Trilogy*. Manning embellished the story by having the Australians throw not only a piano out the window but also a British airman, enjoining him: "Now FLY, you bastard." She added that for this the Australians "were confined to barracks for public safety".

The characters given legendary status in 2/2 Battalion's history, *Purple over Green,* directly relate to the national/battalion psyche. There's a hero, a dog, a fabrication, and a tall story. (We'll catch up with them again later.) The hero is an inspiring Sergeant Major, Harry Honeywell, who escaped from Greece with Charlie and died a hero's death on the Kokoda Track. The dog, Bobby Tobruk, illustrates the soldiers' unsuspected sentimental streak. Herb Hazarus is no surprise for he was invented to plague officers. And there is the larger-than-life character, Lofty Stafford, whom I see as being in the line of both Ned Kelly and Shakespeare's fools — a comic outlaw.

Lofty Stafford could not have existed in the British Army — nor the German. Charlie, who did not talk much about war (and I didn't think to ask), told me fascinating stories about that big clown. At the time I thought they sounded a bit "tall".

There's some nostalgia about how I learned more about Lofty. I had gone to see Adrian Buckley, a close friend of Charlie's in 2/2 Battalion, at Tamworth, wanting to fill in gaps in Charlie's story. After the initial surprise of the frosty hair, there was the same Buck of twenty-odd years ago: his steady quizzical gaze, quick wit, ready smile, his warm hospitality. As Charlie was, as they all are, he was reluctant to talk. He did loosen up to tell some jokes and funny stories. With a shock, I realised I had heard them before — from Charlie. So when we walked through the green fields of his farm under a high blue sky to a far paddock to see his "inventions"— pieces of labour-saving machinery — Charlie seemed close.

"He would have loved all of this," I ventured.

"Yes, he would," Buck replied in a measured voice, the words falling heavily on the light blue day.

This is how Buck remembered Lofty:

"Lofty Stafford towered over everyone. He was about six foot four, and wore size twelve shoes. He was always in a giggle suit and if you spoke to him about it, he always claimed he couldn't get a uniform to fit. He was a swarthy man with black hair and a big, droopy moustache. In civilian life he worked for Wirth's circus, sometimes as a clown.

"We could never get him to do anything right on the parade ground. He spoilt everything. For that reason he kept getting moved from company to company.

"He had the disconcerting habit of addressing everyone, irrespective of rank, as 'Brother'. He became the king of two-up. He would sneak his profits into my tent to hide them under my mattress. I told him I wanted him to count it. He would say, 'Take what you want, Brother'."

Lofty's nonconformism on the battlefield comes later. The best known Lofty incident occurred when he was wheeled up before the CO on yet another minor charge. Lieutenant Colonel Wootten said testily: "Well, Stafford, you're here again. You're not a criminal type — yet you're always up before me for something or other. I don't know what to do with you."

Private Stafford: "Well, Brother, I'm willing to forget it if you will."

That's only half the picture, as you'll see. If Lofty had been a mere comic, he would not have become a legend. He won a place in men's hearts because he was a comic with a lion's heart. His daring and courage were different, too. Lofty is, I think, the Australian character writ large.

Buck's reticence to talk about the darker side of war is typical. It is a soldier trait worthy of as much attention as the more visible high-jinks. Soldiers are renowned for unwillingness to talk, especially about front-line experience. (I've noticed this changes somewhat when soldiers realise their history could be lost.) At first I believed it was some kind of pact to protect their loved ones from the horror. But possibly there is another important explanation. Unfortunately for the soldier himself, he is not prepared, or able, to express his deepest emotions, such as fear or grief. He can throw pianos out of windows but he cannot cry. The following revelations indicate the pain behind the silence:

One soldier said, "When I start talking about war, I get nervous and shake. I can't stop it. In any case you couldn't explain. Even if you could, nobody would believe you."

A British veteran of World War 2 explained the gap of silence between soldier and civilian as a result of the effect of war combined with lack of understanding. He said, "War experience cut us off. It cut us off from our elders and it cut us off from our children. They could not or did not want to envisage what happened in war."

In more recent times, the gap was never greater than for the Vietnam veteran.


It was General Wavell's remarks which began this exploration of the Australian character in relation to discipline, a required "virtue" in a soldier. An undisciplined army would be a rabble; they would not be the choice for shock troops, as the Anzacs were. The test of discipline and morale in soldiers is that they'll stand up and fight. A bit of horseplay or some rugged individualism doesn't make a slack army.

A Battalion officer, Sir John Dunlop, comments on the state of morale in the 2/2 Battalion:

> How then did we achieve the good morale, and I agree that it was good, very good, that was in evidence before the first Lybian campaign, the attacks on Bardia and Tobruk? Well, there is one trivial little story which I remember and which I think has some value. There was for a time a continuation of what was known as the "Smith's Weekly" syndrome, all about Australian soldiers being undisciplined, sloppy in dress and in drill and so on. There was a story that an English sentry somewhere in Palestine complained to his Guard Commander that an Australian armed party had marched past him and that he had paid the proper compliment (which meant he had presented arms) and as he said to his officer, "the Australians took no notice of me whatever" (which meant, did not give him an "eyes right"). The officer is supposed to have replied: "You were lucky, Tompson, Australians usually throw stones."
>
> Well, it happened that one of our most ocker NCO's — his name was Tanner — was sent to the British NCO school at Sarafend where he witnessed and was struck by the quite magnificent standard of parade ground drill of the English. He came back to the unit enthusiastic about this, demonstrated this to the CO and the CO made him demonstrate it to the battalion on parade one morning. The battalion thought if the English can do this, so we can do it just as well, and by golly, they did. It is a curiosity but it is a fact that drill is a morale builder on its own. One does somehow get a sense of unity by performing fairly intricate parade ground exercises as one man.

At Julis Camp the Australians got to work, drilling and training — the ninety per cent element of boredom that is part of a soldier's life and prepares him for the ten per cent element of fear that is battle.

At first, during the quiet of the phoney war, and despite the quick attack of steel on Poland, the Australians' early training was still for trench warfare in Europe. "We dug trenches and filled them in; we dug trenches and filled them in . . ." bewailed the troops. They did gas mask training; jabbed a swinging sandbag with a bayonet, went through the naming of the parts of their weapons, fired them on the Jaffa rifle range, and slogged over the land of the Bible for long hard thirty-mile route marches — with Arabs following to sell oranges and drinks. They were always thirsty. The Army provided the playing fields: tournaments in boxing, running, rugby. There was a padre of every denomination to conduct church parades. Before long, the AIF had its own newspaper and a picture theatre. It was nearly like home.

It was in Palestine that C.H.'s ability was noticed by Colonel Wootten, in particular. Very early he said: "That boy will go a long way." Brock Effendi could remember that the CO "sensed Charlie's ability". Bruce told of a particular incident. "After a special exercise in platoon attacks there came the usual post mortem and I well remember George saying, 'Excellent. Almost perfect, Green, but remember always maintain your objective'. From George, that was praise indeed."

One of the boys, I am not sure now whether it was Jack or Woop Waters, told me he thought it was Charlie who coined the word "doover" for a training exercise.

Out in the rough Hebron hills one day, Charlie had again taken C Company for the OC who was away, probably at a school. They were on a "doover". Even out in the hills, an Arab would turn up with a laden camel. This day he had melons. He hooshed down his camel ready to start his trading. Some of the boys, with the intention of having some fun, had brought some "sendem", a well-known outback potion that stung. Someone squirted some under the camel's tail. The camel bellowed, staggered up and loped off over the hills with the yelling Arab streaking after it. The gleeful lads watched them disappear over the horizon: "the camel going, the Arab going, and the melons flying." Charlie lined the company up. "Some of you bastards hit him with something. I know."

While most training exercises were irksome, there was one place in Palestine a soldier would willingly go. Most photo albums have a snap of Askalon, a camp on the shores of the Mediterranean, not far from Julis. It was a site selected for training and recreation. There they could swim, run on the beach and bivouac overnight. Sometimes there was a bit of pontoon training. It's not surprising that C.H. was often sighted at Askalon, enjoying the sand, the sun and water that he loved. Also, he used to ride horses that he borrowed from the British. Harry Bell, his old school friend, saw him racing along the beach one day. Harry said, almost grudgingly, "He was no dolt on a horse." As the old lady at the fig trees in Swan Creek remembered, Charlie loved horses, and at every opportunity in Palestine, he would be on a beautiful Arab horse.

When men are at the front, in action, mail is their main concern. The Army realises that mail is essential to a soldier's morale. It was no less important to the soldiers waiting and training in Palestine. The period in Palestine was described by the boys as "lifeless". Lifeless, because normal life was suspended. In Palestine, "mail day was the day we lived for" they said, and the boys would watch the mail plane fly over, wondering what the news from home would be.

> ". . . then, like a bird
> With silvered wings, we saw the plane
> Heading, with mail, to Galilee.
> Above the sandhills, out to sea,
> And in the clouds we saw again
> Our homes; the noonday shimmering sun
> On farm, and beach, and station run;
> The shearers nodding as we pass
> Each stand; the silos crammed with wheat,
> The sheepdogs panting in the heat;
> The breakers' curl, the lash of foam,
> The aching, taunting thoughts of home."

*Air Mail — Palestine* by David McNicoll

A hush fell on the camp as they clasped their letters, photos and parcels and went off to read, alone or in groups to share home news. They devoured the words and photos. "You'd see fellows with tears rolling down their cheeks." And if they didn't get a letter? "The unhappiest man alive was the one who did not get mail." That would start him worrying and brooding.

Letters soldiers wrote home were a source of valuable

information. With the discovery of one man's collection of letters and diaries, I realised their value. One thoughtful 2/2 man said: "Look up Woop Waters. He knew Charlie well, coming from the same Company; and he was his batman in New Guinea." I found Woop in an ex-servicemen's home. He was there because he could no longer walk — a result of his six years of continuous service. Otherwise he was fit and alert.

Woop, who was present at every one of 2/2 Battalion's campaigns, turned out to be an astute observer, with the ability to get right to the heart of the matter. Furthermore, he'd kept diaries, as well as his letters to his mother that he re-possessed when she died. They were all stored in a box he pulled out from under his bed. One valuable bundle, the story of the Greek campaign, had a mouse-hole through the middle, more's the pity.

When Woop joined up he was a baker and part-time boxer, of Irish ancestry. Old photos show a swarthy, handsome, tough little bloke with a Clark Gable moustache and a rakish tilt to his hat, whether civilian or slouch. He had an eye for the ladies, and "was in everything". In the army he was known for his boxing, and for always being in trouble. Perhaps no one in 2/2 Battalion, except a few close mates, knew the real Woop. But for his letters to his mother, his soft, sentimental side might never have been seen. His touching reverence for his "Mother of mine" dominates his letters. He did not miss a single Mother's Day church parade.

"A bit of a Hemingway," I thought, looking at him. He had a similar squarish face, a heavy sable and silvered beard, and an obvious toughness. I asked Woop to sum up his army experience in a few words. He did not answer lightly. He pondered for some time, then replied: "I learned to accept the separation and the authority, but I jacked up against rank. I hated being called 'Waters'. I was in more trouble over that than anything. It makes you feel like shit."

The unnatural quiet of the phoney war came to an end in April, 1940. First Norway and Denmark fell. In May, waves of German Stukas and 89 Divisions of Germany's Panzers and infantry speedily shifted the front back and back, through Luxembourg, The Netherlands, Belgium, driving the British army, like a hunted fox, to the beaches at Dunkirk. Who could have believed that 345,585 men huddled on the Dunkirk beaches could have been rescued by little boats under the fury of the Luftwaffe? It was probably sheer belief in themselves that made it possible. Chamberlain, humiliated, resigned and Churchill, the man for the hour, picked up the reins.

The soldiers in Palestine began to get impatient — perhaps a little embarrassed. They'd joined up to fight and here they were still waiting, with no "stoush" yet in sight. When the war in Europe got serious, the novelty of the Holy Land wore off. Living at close quarters in tents in a womanless world became more obviously unnatural. Their disquiet spilled into their letters: "We joined up to fight. The greatest fight we are having is the fight against boredom."

Woop Waters noticed what was happening. He wrote to his mother: "The life cracks them up, after the glamour wears off." And elsewhere he said, cryptically: "I know now why soldiers won't talk." I took this remark to mean that soldiers didn't like admitting to the unglamorous reality of service life, that ninety per cent of boredom.

In June, events took an unexpected turn. France fell and the Italians declared war. The Australians realised their first battle wasn't going to be against the Germans after all. It would be the Italians.

Julis Camp was prepared against possible air attack: tents were camouflaged and scattered. At night, the camp was blacked out.

Training began to change dramatically, the emphasis turning to speed, tanks and the desert. There were the new Bren guns, Bren carriers and anti-tank guns to learn about. As well, they had new uniforms — the famed Bombay bloomers.

Britain wanted to relieve the pressure on itself by taking the war to the desert. Anything that relieved the strain on Britain gave that nation a chance to survive. Churchill was determined to maintain British control of the Middle East —

Suez and the oilfields. That is why, in August 1940 the highly trained Australian 6 Division was given movement orders for Egypt. Egypt had to be protected, for in Libya, colonised by the Italians in 1911, there was a 250,000-strong Italian army ready to move into action to fulfil Mussolini's aim to make the Mediterranean an Italian lake, and the aims of his partner, Hitler, who wanted the whole of Europe.

The AIF was on the move. Just before 2/2 Battalion moved out of Julis, a lively farewell was held one evening to Ivan Dougherty, who had been promoted to Lieutenant Colonel, commanding 2/4 Battalion. Jack Boorer, on picket duty that evening, saw Charlie emerge from the officers' mess, very late:

> You'd know his form anywhere. I watched his progress. It took him hours to find his tent. He swung from tent pole to tent pole peering around trying to find his own tent. Suddenly, I was struck by the fact that his face looked funny. It was different. Then I realised that he had taken his teeth out and put them in his pocket. He was taking precautions!

The boys don't miss much, and they remember.

One dark evening, on the hill at Julis just before the bugles began to echo along the ridge, announcing stand-down, two young officers were walking near their mess, talking quietly. They knew they were about to move to the desert. They were wondering what it would be like when the time came. How they would measure up. Their waiting was over.

# 5
# The Desert — Consternation

> Horror of wounds and anger at the foe,
> And loss of things desired; all these must pass.
> We are the happy legion, for we know
> Time's but a golden wind that shakes the grass.
>
> *Absolution* by Siegfried Sassoon

The Australians went back the way they came, to Kantara, were ferried across the canal and put in trains for Helwan, a WW1 camp only eighteen miles from Cairo. A range of limestone cliffs separated the camp from the Nile Valley. Their site, a desert flat, was at the edge of the boundless desert where centuries ago armies had fought.

Desert training began. They learned how to use compasses. They learned to infiltrate whorls of wire, to make Molotov cocktails, to use new weapons such as their "diddums", as some affectionately called their Bren gun, and their Vickers. They also learned to survive on one water bottle per day.

Charlie Green, with a party of men went to the Nile Delta to reconnoitre for defence plans, should the Italians break through. Charlie's farmer heart, like Jack's, leapt at the brilliance of the emerald green growth that sprang from the Black Delta soil. Hospitable Egyptian farmers showered them with gifts. The party gorged on mangoes, grapes, pomegranates, guavas, bananas, dates, melon. It was like a picnic. Usual formality was dropped by Charlie and men got close.

What Tom Mawhinney wrote about C.H.G. was borne out:

> Everyone knew what a good soldier he was but it was not so well known what a warm-hearted and human man he was. He had

the capacity to unbend . . . He was a fairly strict officer, but then all the good ones were, but he was also intensely loyal to his men and did all in his power to get them any extras that might be going, be it a bit of leave or extra rations, or a spare bottle of beer.

Like their forefathers, the Anzacs, the 6 Division men took leave in Cairo. Cairo, with its extreme wealth and extreme poverty was, they discovered, even smellier than anywhere in Palestine. Somewhat compulsively, they followed their fathers' progress which they took either as a model or a challenge. Maybe they could outdo the originals. So they strolled around the bazaars, bought souvenirs, hassled the Arabs, cheated or were cheated, played pranks and had their pictures taken in front of the pyramids. (Charlie was snapped in front of the Great Pyramid on a little donkey, his long legs dangling in the sand.) Along the desert, homesick country boys galloped horses they had hired for five shillings. Of course they got drunk, and went to the infamous Wazzir (where they threw the piano and the British airman out of a window and started a fire). They brawled with Pommies and with Kiwis and could not resist the wrong sort of girls, despite the pictures and the warnings. Like their fathers, some got VD. War, it is said, electrifies the libido.

How amazing is memory. From its depths, this minute, has sprung a list of Arab words: *shufti, mafeesh, bucksheesh* . . . With them comes the living Charlie, full of fun and mischief. He enjoyed the slang, the dirty ditties, anything that reminded him of the lighter side of war.

A strange idea runs through World War 1 literature: that a man must be "pure" for battle. I wonder if this was the superstition in the mind of the soldier who noticed that Charlie looked "clean". The superstition that if a man kept himself "clean" for battle, God would protect him. Statistics give no credence to this. VD sufferers were as likely to survive as any others.

The Australian goings-on in Cairo did not go unnoticed. There was enough typical Australian lawlessness, reminiscence of WWI, to cause Field Marshal Wavell to sniff . . . Soon he would be obliged to re-assess the diggers. Out of the lines they might be hard to deal with, but at the front they were incomparable. "Diamonds", as World War 1 Germans described them.

2/2 Battalion men do not forget September 17, 1940. They were out in the desert on an exercise. A *khamsin*, a howling dust storm, was blowing. News came that the Italians had attacked and taken Sidi Barrani. Then a message that the brigade was to return to camp immediately. Through the howling wind they ploughed over the stinging, squelching sand for twelve hard, long miles. When they reached camp, they learned that the signal was intended only for the brigade commander to return, not the whole brigade. To compensate the troops for their long march, the canteen was opened. A soldier will forgive almost anything for a beer.

Certain they would soon be fighting the Italians, the boys began preparing their folk at home. The need for home contact grew, but they avoided causing worry. Woop wrote — oh, so typically: "Don't worry about the dagoes Mum; they are nothing." And: "You can't beat the boys of the bulldog breed."

Perhaps it was the increasing tension, but around this time Ernie Osbourne and Woop Waters, both boxers, were settling private differences with the gloves on. Woop reported, "A bloke got a bit fresh with me — I shot over the old right and down he went. Boys respect me more now."

Ernie had a problem with authority:

> One of our sergeant's got hostile with me. Soon took the sting out of him down behind the shit house with the gloves. He only went three rounds and said, "you win". While they have the stripes on, you dare not touch them, but if they have the guts, as this one did, well you can have it out.

Minor personal clashes there might have been but the Battalion, the Purple over Green, was being expertly moulded into a kind of being — a great body that moved, thought and felt as one.

Maybe it indicated excitement or a sense of responsibility — or even flash of the theatrical, but Charlie suddenly acts in a way that gets noted in the Battalion history. He was in charge of transport on October 8 for the 2/2's move from

Helwan to Amiriya, a staging camp. As every soldier knows, a staging camp is the last stop before the battle, the last safe place.

The troops were assembled at Helwan railway station, but there were not enough rail trucks. C.H., in a flash, untangled the red tape. He invaded the railway station and commandeered not only the necessary trucks but also an engine driver to shunt them on to the train. That's the kind of thing that the war historian C.W. Bean praised countrymen for. I too experienced Charlie's ingenuity. Once, miles from anywhere in the bush, our car broke down. With pieces of fence wire and even a scrap of rag, he got us home. As if it was the natural thing to do. It's a quality I admire; it makes you feel safe and secure.

Amiriya was bare and filthy. Woop described the camp as "bare as a badger's arse". Staging camps are like that. No one is responsible for a camp where men are in transit. However, it was only fifteen miles to the fascinating naval port of Alexandria. And only five miles from the surf.

The soldiers' first job was to dig trenches, not for drill but to protect them from stray bombs. Nightly now, the Italians were raiding Alexandria. Men watched the searchlights combing the sky and listened to the boom, boom, boom of bombs.

Some old hands, showing off in front of newly arrived reinforcements, nonchalantly disdained climbing into a trench. Until the night the bomb fell. Then they scurried smartly, one man finding himself leaping into a trench with a beer bottle in his hand. The reinforcements (needed to replace the loss of men through discharge, accident or illness) were untrained, and some last-minute hard training was essential. At Amiriya a five-day exercise was held on divisional scale. It was like a grand dress rehearsal.

By this time the troops were beginning to know the desert, which they needed to make their ally. It is a pity they had to experience it in war. A desert is alluringly beautiful. That spare gold and blue void can empty the mind the way meditation is supposed to. It is easy to appreciate its beauty from a tourist bus. Soldiers, however, found the desert awesome and pitiless, scorching by day and freezing by night. Perhaps they enjoyed it briefly, at dawn, or on evenings when it was quiet and they sat and yarned beneath a star-studded sky — or at its most spectacular, at stand down, when the horizon flamed crimson. Most of the time that sea of nothing was hazardous. There was no water, no cover, no landmarks. Mirages appeared and disappeared in the shimmering distance. In the deep, soft sand, vehicles bogged and marching was an ordeal. When the winds raged, the whipped-up sand penetrated everything, their bodies and their equipment. Their food gritted, their eyes stung, their guns jammed. With only one bottle of water, a man could not clean himself; nor could he slake his considerable thirst. At night, muscles straining, he would throw down his pack and slump to the ground, dead tired — and then, as a last straw, the fleas and lice attacked.

On those eerie black desert nights it was dangerous to stray, even to the next foxhole, so easily could one be swallowed up in the black nothingness. Over thirty years after the war this is how Woop remembered the desert: "The landscape was a mixture of sand escarpments and waddies. The only vegetation was a type of saltbush.

"Occasionally, we struck roaming tribes of nomad Bedouins with their goats and camels... How they survived was a mystery to us all... There sangars came into being. We gathered boulders and rocks and built up the lip of the hole as a bulwark. Stretched our ground sheet over the top to keep out the sand and wind and curled up with the fleas. When the *khamsin* blew, it was bitterly cold — like a mother-in-law's kiss."

Alexandria, by contrast, was exotic. The lure was not its fascinating history. They disported there as Antony did of old, desiring living Cleopatras. For soldiers waiting "for the push" time was running out. No wonder Alexandria has special memories still. It was a lively cosmopolitan place with its own peculiar smell, "like peanuts and tobacco". In the blacked-out streets, white-robed Arabs flitted to and fro. Horse-drawn

Above: Lieutenant Charlie Green, 1939.
Below: On leave in Palestine and riding an Arab horse, 1940.

Above: Charlie Green packed and ready for the move to Bardia, December 1940.

Below: Bardia township about the time of the Australian attack.

gharries carried pleasure-seekers to swell hotels, cabarets, salons or bars. In certain noisy streets, if you looked through the doorways, there would be melon-ripe flesh to tempt a wavering man. One street in particular, Sister Street, is a by-word... or a kind of password that some wear like a campaign ribbon.

Lofty Stafford, on duty, in Alexandria, was seen driving a Morris truck the wrong way down a one-way street. When he was accosted by an officious, gesticulating Egyptian policeman, he said: "It's all right Brother, I was only going one way." The perfect "fool".

Serious-minded Jack Boorer remembered that at about this time the Western Australian AIF vote saved John Curtin's Fremantle seat, that nearly went to the victorious conservatives in the elections. It was the vote of the 2/11 Battalion, that Charlie Green was to command, that saved Curtin for posterity. In 1942 he became Prime Minister and Australia's brilliant wartime leader.

Christmas was getting closer; so was battle. Letters written home reflected the soldiers' preoccupations:

— "the boys are rearing to go..." — "I had to come. It was the adventure feeling in me. Just like old grandfather." — "There'll probably be a few mummies left behind." — "... am camped in a sangar, a gunyah, built of stones and sandbags. I feel as dirty as a pig." — "You'd be surprised how bloody thirsty we get."

Most poignant of all was their homesickness: — "I suppose the house will be full at Xmas..." — "I wonder if my dogs still wait for me at the gate?"

It was just before they moved out of Amiriya that 2/2 Battalion lost their original CO, Wootten. One fellow described him as "the bloody boss who moulded us tough bastards". Before Wootten left the Battalion, he was given a send-off. Woop, the ex-baker, was involved in preparing the dinner. They had soup, curried prawns, fish, fowl, duck and black coffee. I wonder if that night, too, Charlie had trouble finding his way home.

Lieutenant Colonel F.O. Chilton became their CO, the man

to lead them into their first battle and through the ill-fated Greek campaign.

Colonel Wootten, as first COs do, put his stamp on the Battalion. He is remembered as tough, efficient, fair and down-to-earth, as his nickname, "Mud guts", suggests. His style was to teach lessons in ways that wouldn't be forgotten. Any young officer who heard this advice could not forget it: "If you bastards dip your pens in dirty inkwells, you can expect to blot your copybook." And what young, inexperienced officer was likely to complain again, after striking the boss's sardonic sense of humour? Certainly not the one who complained that the picks weren't heavy enough for the job of digging a hole for the mortar platoon. Colonel Wootten's solution: "Tie rocks on them."

The order to move up came on December 13. Before they left Amiriya for the front, they were heartened to hear that the British navy had thrashed the Italians at Taranto and that on December 7 the small British force, led by General O'Connor, had attacked the Italians at Sidi Barrani and sent them scuttling back to the defences of Bardia. The Australians were ordered to flush them out of Bardia, leaving the British to fall back.

December 13 was a terrible day. The *khamsin* that had been howling for seven days had reduced visibility to a gritty nothing. They went by train to Bagush and then by truck to Sidi Barrani — where Caesar had once chased Pompey.

Suddenly men were struck with the ugly face of war. The scene was enough to stir terror in men who hadn't yet been blooded. Sidi Barrani, fifteen miles from the sea, was an arid, shell-cratered, deserted battlefield, littered with grotesquely twisted and torn steel weapons and vehicles. It looked like the set of a battle for the moon. There were the spoils, too. From the dugouts the Italians had hastily abandoned, soldiers fished bottles of wine, as well as "scent", among other things. The diggers quaffed the wine, and laughed at the "pansy stink water" . . . until it occurred to them that the "scent" had a practical function — it deterred their fellow travellers, the fleas and the lice.

They continued by truck to the Salum escarpment where they bivouaced. After that they had to march. In the stony ground, dotted with clumps of camel thorn, they scratched their holes for shelter. After night fell, the cold crept into their bones. They were ready to take out those knitted balaclavas that their womenfolk had knitted and to don their issue of leather jackets. As they were now living on hard rations, there was no hot food, so the army issued a few primuses to make hot drinks — fuelled, dangerously, with petrol.

December 19 was another day men do not forget. They were ordered to march up the Halfaya, or "Hellfire" as the troops call it, to the plateau that looked down on their objective, Bardia. The 2/2 Battalion led the march which was for some unknown reason in daylight, even though they made a target for Italian aircraft. A couple of ineffective air raids did occur. As the Italian pilots characteristically flew too high, little damage was done. In one exciting incident a soldier reported: "We saw a Gloucester Gladiator shoot down an Italian. The boys cheered and cheered." From the heights of Halfaya the men looked down, in the fading light, on the beautiful green oasis that in peacetime was a holiday resort: Bardia.

After a descent and a rough, cross-country march, all in one day, the Australians reached the perimeter wire, west of crenellated Fort Capuzzo, on the Fort Capuzzo-Bardia road. It was just before midnight. They were only eight miles from the Italians, protected by concrete and steel in the Bardia fortress. Before the weary soldiers could slump to the ground, they had to dig-in. And there was work to be done before they could attack. The brilliant night-reconnaisance work of men like Harry Lovett and Archie McLellan located an enemy artillery post and the laying of what is called a "start line" for the moment of the attack. Patrols went so close to the Italian lines they could hear the enemy talking. Artillery shells boomed night and morning as they fell around both armies. Battle was imminent, as all men knew. It was a question of *when*.

For the waiting soldiers, conditions were miserable. Cold, dust storms and then mud. One man described the cold with bushman economy: "It was so cold, they slept in bunches like kangaroo dogs so they could share their blankets." Above all it was the sand that maddened them. Their meals, all eaten cold, were a paste of sand and tinned bully beef. Even worse, their one bottle of water tasted brackish, and aggravated rather than slaked their terrible thirst.

It was nearly Christmas. At home, there would have been plum puddings hanging in the kitchens, cold beer frothing in schooners in familiar pubs, pretty girls, curling green breakers rolling up on the sun-drenched white beaches, all around Australia.

Checking the postings for the Battle of Bardia, in the War Diary, I discovered Charlie's name was not there. There were, I noticed, nine new officers, indicating changes in the Battalion. But Charlie was not at the Battle of Bardia, the Battalion's blooding. What could have happened? I must admit I felt uneasy. After some searching, I found in another part of the War Diary the entry that on December 23 (three days before his twenty-first birthday) Charlie was evacuated to a Casualty Clearing Station with a septic foot.

It was fate once again, I told myself. Part of the design of his fateful life. But still I felt the need of an explanation, to satisfy myself and those who would question. Hours of talking with soldiers has taught me that an army pedigree depends on battle history. They say, knowing he was in 6 Division, "He was at Bardia?" "He was at Tempe Gorge?" I have always felt that a negative answer required an explanation. Such is the *noblesse oblige* of war.

Jack Boorer remembered that there had been an accident with a primus. One of those primuses fuelled with petrol, to make hot drinks in the cold desert nights. Jack remembered the news running down the line in C Company: "Green was on fire." That sparked a memory. I recalled Charlie talking about the primus that blew up, burning his foot. That was all I remembered. Until I got to know him, Bardia was only a name to me.

One of Charlie's fellow officers said he could understand how such an injury, unless the circumstances were known, could smack of a self-inflicted wound. And Charlie's close friend Adrian Buckley, who could not remember any details of the accident, said: "I remember his consternation."

When I questioned the CO, Sir Frederick Chilton, he firmly asserted, "If there had been any unusual circumstances, I would have been the first to have heard about it." That should have satisfied me.

The need to have an explanation bothered me. Not until I was revising my manuscript, did I realise one incident was still worrying me. This one. *Why* is it bothering me, I asked myself. He had an accident. There were plenty of incidents of men getting ill, having accidents or transferring. Why do we get the notion that when the bugle calls a man must be there? Was my response similar to that of the women in World War 1, sending white feathers to men who did not enlist? Or, in World War 2, shunning men who were in the wrong uniform — or, worse, not in uniform at all?

Like a bolt of lightning it came to me: "It's me!" I wanted Charlie to be perfect. Perfectionism is my terrible yoke — to wear, and to inflict on others. From official records, I learned that Charlie spent that Christmas of 1940 and his twenty-first birthday in hospital, apart from his comrades and his battalion. He never mentioned it.

It is a mistake, I've learned, to assume anything about matters Charlie deemed private. No one could determine when he was in crisis. If a crisis situation were obvious, there was no knowing what he was experiencing. At such a time you would observe only calm. Charlie's calm, that some people called reserve, mystery, or repression was his distinctive quality. It was a quality that aroused both admiration and, at times, an irritable protestation: "nobody could be that calm!" He took the big issues in his life to himself as his private concern, to deal with personally, in his way — a very confident way. This is the stuff of leaders; it was to stand out on the battlefield, and it gave his men confidence. However, in the long run his privacy left me with some unanswered, troublesome questions.

# 6
# Bardia — "Ripeness is all"

(*King Lear V, ii, 9:* Shakespeare)

> Let the boy try along this bayonet-blade.
> How cold the steel is, and keen with hunger of blood;
> Blue with all malice, like a madman's flash;
> And thinly drawn with famishing for flesh.
>
> *Arms and the Boy* by Wilfred Owen

> It is well that war is so terrible
> — we would grow too fond of it.
>
> Robert E. Lee

Although the Battle of Bardia is not part of Charlie's story, it becomes part of my quest. It is the story of his unit and his comrades, especially those who are telling this story. I can't turn my head as they go into their first battle — their blooding.

Churchill, always ready to push men into battle, wanted an offensive in the desert. He sent Wavell a cable quoting Matthew 7,7:

> Ask, and it shall be given you;
> seek, and ye shall find;
> knock, and it shall be opened unto you:

to which Wavell replied, more circumspectly, from James 1,17:

> Every good gift and every perfect gift is from above . . .

Wavell, whom Churchill later replaced, planned to strangle each Italian fortress in Libya: Bardia, Tobruk, Derna and Benghazi. The Australian 6 Division, a mere 17,000 strong, was ordered to attack on January 3, 1941. The Australians' battle plans and orders were made at divisional level by General Iven Mackay while the 2/2 Battalion commander, Lieutenant Colonel F.O. Chilton, took responsibility for the deployment of his battalion for its specific objectives.

The 6 Division objective, the 250,000 strong Bardia fortress, might have seemed impregnable. A military principle that superiority in numbers is not decisive was demonstrated at Bardia, alongside the maxim that "the offensive is the strongest form of warfare". Before it was fortified, Bardia was a seaboard town, with white cubist houses perched on a hill overlooking the wine-dark Mediterranean. Now it was surrounded by an eighteen-mile deep anti-tank ditch. Inside that was a continuous double apron of barbed wire. Within that again were two lines of underground fortified concrete posts, ninety in all, some forward of others. The posts were armed with machine-guns and in the area of the posts there were about 110 heavy artillery guns. These caused most of the casualties.

The attackers had to breach the fortifications and take the posts, which meant that they would face a long advance of heavy fire, point-blank. To give the advantage of surprise, the night patrols crept around in sandshoes determining the best place to break through for the dawn assault. Engineers would torpedo the ditch and build causeways for tanks to go through first, followed by the infantry battalions, who, once through the gap, were to fan out towards their respective objectives. The British 7th Armoured Tank Division was to support the Australians.

Colonel Chilton prepared the 2/2 for their job with a sand model, using all the data collected from aerial photos, maps and intelligence operations. The officers, NCOs and riflemen rehearsed their advance in relation to the posts they had to seize. They needed to know how many paces they should make and the number of minutes they should then pause, to synchronise with the supporting artillery which was to lay down a "creeping box barrage". There was no room for mistakes.

It was Jack Boorer who helped me understand this operation. Jack, though wounded, completed the action. He was forthcoming in his praise of their CO, Colonel Chilton, and the officers:

> Our training and preparation was thorough; it was brilliant. It gives a man confidence when he knows that so far as humanly possible we are prepared for what we have to do. If things go wrong, as they do, we have the confidence to use our own initiative.
> ... as for the CO (Chilton) he was special; a real gentleman. He was always a gentleman — even to the enemy.

Knowing how accurate was Jack's description of Colonel Chilton, that slim, quiet man, I was curious about one point. "What was his nickname?" I asked. — "Ah," Jack replied, "Sir Fred was above that."

So Christmas 1940 found the Australian soldiers in their foxholes some distance from the Bardia perimeter. Most had been overseas for one year. Without the Battalion's special kind of community, the disruption of their lives would have been intolerable. They call it mateship, a mateship that in battle is cemented into a bond that is holy. One man described the battalion, where this transcendence occurs, as "God's gift to man". And in Jo Gullett's book *Not As Duty Only*, he talks about this phenomenon that enriches men's spirit: "A battalion ready to fight implies a state of mind. I am not sure it is not a state of grace."

On Christmas Day they sunbaked, ate a dinner of bully beef and biscuit and wrote letters to reassure their loved ones. Secretly, they wondered if it would be their last. It is said that in the age-old way a man or two broke — and died before the battle began. War's barbarous demands were now apparent. Russian soldiers of bygone days used to knock their teeth out so they could not bite the bullet and so could not fight. Soldiers discovered their own ways of psyching themselves up for the battle. Woop wrote to his mother: "I've been patrolling in no man's land after d . . .s [censored]; but there were none about. It was exciting sneaking about in the dark; it is certainly better than shooting rabbits." Further on he explained: "One's blood does tingle when the bombs fall. Just like the first round of a fight. Wait till we get a crack at them."

In the cold, black desert night they huddled in the pits (like kangaroo dogs), gazed up at the glittering stars, and wondered. One man couldn't help thinking about the pill-boxes and trenches over there somewhere. Another, on the night before the battle, drank a whole bottle of gin.

At 0230 on January 3, they climbed out of their dug-outs and donned full battledress. No wonder they frightened the Italians; they looked like giants in their greatcoats that flapped as they moved. In their backpacks they had to carry guns, ammunition, respirators, rations, grenades and picks and shovels, in all a weight of sixty-nine pounds.

Lofty Stafford prepared himself for battle in a manner contrary to manuals and regulations. He didn't carry a rifle; he carried a Boyes anti-tank gun, a heavy thing about five feet long. To this he fixed his bayonet with signal wire. No one stopped him. Woop Waters carried with him a wishbone that his father gave him.

Quietly they moved to an assembly point, where they had "That Rum!" as someone described it. Lofty is recalled handing it on and whispering, "Take a swig, Brother". At 0535 they furtively followed the signal wire through the dark to their start line. There they had to wait, nerves taut, for the first glow of light and the artillery's signal. After all the waiting their moment had come. The tension was nerve-wracking in the chill silence of the eerie desert night.

The Italians, beside their guns in the trenches on the other side, were also waiting, not sure when it would start. The world had heard Mussolini's broadcast announcing that 40,000 bloodthirsty Aborigines were at the gates of Bardia like hell hounds, but that his General Borgonzoli (known as "Electric Whiskers") would vanquish the invaders. More propaganda was fed to the Italians in Bardia, with the intention of stiffening their resistance. They were told the Australians were wearing bullet-proof vests (leather jackets) and that if they caught prisoners, they would tie them to the front of their tanks. It was all counter-productive. The

Australians' World War 1 reputation was sufficient, without all the embellishments.

The Australian soldiers spent the longest minutes of their lives poised on the start line. As though on cue, as first light silvered the sky: "A bloody hare darted past the start line. That broke the tension, just as all hell let loose." Jagged yellow lights knifed the grey dawn, preceding the crash and bang of artillery and shells. The terrible din that marked the battle had begun. The ditch was torpedoed and in no time the great Matilda Tanks clanked forward through the gap. One nose-dived. The men of the 2/2 Battalion, bayonets fixed, went forward in a line behind the tanks, singing a ditty to the tune of *South of the Border*, "singing, always singing" as one of them said. Now they had to time themselves so many paces, pause . . . they had to keep going, keep thinking: "Must not stop for anything, until the barrage lifts." If a man fell, there was only time to stick his rifle in the sand to mark the spot for the stretcher bearers.

The Italian guns were answering.

Din and dust increased. They must not lose their direction. Bullets kicked up the sand and droned through the air like bees, tracers glittered overhead. The shells, most terrifying of all, flashed, wailed and soon came the boom, the crump. They were beyond fear now. Men screamed and cursed and leaders shouted the call to move their men "At the bastards!" They ran, they fired, sometimes they dropped to the ground, head buried in the dust, then up and on again, firing, throwing grenades, on and on, firing, jabbing . . .

Always they were on the alert for something going wrong or for a mate in trouble. Then the Australian soldier acts. He seems instinctively to know what to do. Through the din, through his straining mind, the soldier hears the cries that will haunt him all his life — of the wounded and the dying. Worse, he sees the bodies, inert, grotesque, contorted, erupting, gaping, smashed. He must go on and he does, for the sake of the others, for the honour of the unit. That is how the Australian soldier fights.

During the battle Lofty Stafford was seen looming over a

trench of terrified Italians, waving his anti-tank gun at them, drawling: "You'd better come out, Brothers."

Things went wrong here and there. Two companies got separated, a dangerous situation that was remedied by quick appraisal and hard fighting. Relentlessly advancing, the 2/2 Battalion and the other battalions pressed home the attack according to plan. By midday the fierce fighting was over. By evening Bardia was conquered. The 2/2 Battalion had reached their objective. They were astride the Bardia-Capuzzo Road.

They had done it. They had been blooded. They proved to themselves that day they were the best. With that comes initiation into the special few, and a strange exaltation.

The war historian Gavin Long, in the official war history *To Benghazi* credited the spectacular success of the battle to the personal qualities of the Australians: "... there is no fortress so strong in its engineering that men of determination and cunning ... cannot take."

Poor Electric Whiskers had some explaining to do to his boss Mussolini for his ignominious defeat. What chance had the Italians? Bergonzoli said that they were "like a flea against an elephant". A 17,000-strong giant had knocked out a 250,000-strong flea protected by a shell of concrete and steel. To keep the record straight, Australians point out that the first resistance was bravely fought by a crack regiment of Blackshirts who died at their posts. Most of the Italians, though, were simple home-loving countrymen who would have preferred to have been in their villages tending their olives or their vines.

Elated by victory, the Australians were quick to have some fun. They seized showy, gaudy Italian uniforms, dressed up, and clowned about. General Mackay disregarding their achievement, criticised their lack of discipline. Always the problem of discipline out of the lines — yet no soldier is more disciplined in battle. High-spirited they may have seemed, but who knows what dark spot lodged in their souls that day. What enduring and surviving a battle really means has been told by a 2/2 man. Anonymous, he probably speaks for them all:

> Battle changes men's relationship with each other. After battle they are close-knit in a way that is beyond understanding. They have upheld the unit's reputation, have acted on the only possible principle, which is not to let their mates down. In action when life is cleansed of bullshit, they learned terrible truths; for instance "the final culling when the individual's true character becomes known".

In captured quarters that night the Australians bathed for the first time in weeks and ate like kings. The quantity and variety of luxury goods that were available to the Italian soldiers astounded them. Don Fairbrother, in *Nulli Secundus Log*, says a life as soft as the Italians enjoyed couldn't produce fighters. The diggers were astonished by the toiletries, bath-salts, perfumes, colognes. They were more appreciative of the liquor. They had a choice of champagne, cognac or Chianti to wash down exotic items of food.

That night, the soldiers were not mindful of the magnitude of their haul in much needed tanks, vehicles, weapons and ammunition. And luckily, not many were required to guard the compliant prisoners. There has to be compassion for the defeated. Thousands of Italians were herded into compounds, frightened, hungry, thirsty, awaiting their fate. Piteously they held out pannikins for water and food, and beast-like accepted their helplessness. Too often callous victors seized private possessions such as watches. Worse, one man, it is quietly rumoured, not knowing how or when to switch off and maddened by the death of a brother, threw a grenade into the prisoners' compound.

The British press, according to Gavin Long, maintained that the Australians had had no real opposition. That was an unfair attempt to rob them of their achievement. Another instance of prejudice — or jealousy?

When the elation subsided and the clearing up had to be done, things looked different. Time then to wonder about the price of glory. It was not the time, surely, to believe Dixton Wecter's assertion: "War is the great lyric moment of their lives." That has to be an armchair fancy. After the battle there is time for the stocktaking. After the exhilaration passes there is time for truth.

Woop wondered about his boss. For some time he had been batman to Lieutenant Spud Jones. Every morning, among other duties, he used to clean his boss's shoes, a very special pair of handmade shoes, not army issue. Recounting what is a particularly haunting memory for him, Woop said: "I saw the truck pull in. I knew what it was because the two black corporals were on it. They were going round picking up the dead. They would wrap the bodies in blankets and put them in the truck. I felt peculiar, but I looked. What do you think I saw? I saw the boss's boots sticking out of a blanket. I called out to the fellows: "That's my boss" — "How do you know?" — "I know the boots."

The sorrowful batman who reflected "I was always losing my bosses" went to the burial service the next day. The men killed at Bardia were buried in the desert, up on Halfaya Pass near the famous fort at Capuzzo.

In another place, an RAP, an Aid Post where the wounded are taken, a boy was dying. An older soldier had been sitting with him off and on all night. He was so young. Just before he died, the boy whispered to his mate: "It's a pup for the footpath and a dog for the road."

Only they, the initiates, know the horror and the magnificence of that day, the day they became brothers. With a bond that passes understanding.

# 7
# Tobruk —
# The motley soldiers

> The man that makes his toe
> What he his heart should make,
> Shall of a corn cry woe,
> And turn his sleep to wake.
>
> *King Lear, III, ii, 31:* by William Shakespeare

On January 20, 1941, 6 Division captured Tobruk, their second battle within a month. Then 16 Brigade (2/2 Battalion's brigade) remained in Tobruk while 19 Brigade went on to Benghazi, captured it, then halted. Strategically, they should have gone on to Tripoli. Instead, 6 Division was withdrawn from Africa to be sent to Greece on a futile Gallipoli-like mission.

Into the gap in Africa came Rommel, the wily desert fox with his formidable Afrika Corps. He turned the tide of battle and would have overrun Africa and Egypt had it not been for the famous Australian 9 Division, the "Rats of Tobruk", who withstood a 242-day siege that stopped the Germans. The same Rats, later, at El Alamein, played a critical part in that mighty battle that finished the great Rommel. At El Alamein twenty-two per cent of British casualties were sustained by the Australians. It was their attack at Thompson's Post which forced Rommel into error.

The Battle of Tobruk was similar to the one at Bardia. It was a similar fort, similarly defended, in similar terrain. The Italians remained within, preferring not to come out and fight.

The battle plan was similar, too, to the one at Bardia, with some improvements to minimise casualties. The perimeter was breached, tanks entered and the following troops fanned out and bit deep. Their objectives were the guns that had done the damage in Bardia. 2/2 Battalion had a more dangerous job. Once through the perimeter, they had to fan out and knock out three lots of guns. They did this with fewer casualties than they had at Bardia. There were sixteen, compared with ninety at Bardia.

The troops found in Tobruk another large lucky-dip of spoils. A general (no names no pack drill as they say) took exception to the "picnic atmosphere" following the battle. But that did not worry the boys very much. They called him "Drip" — for a reason. In Palestine, the same general had earned a reputation for carping criticism. He would insist on a full turn-out of the guard and then find petty fault with them; he would complain if all sleeves weren't rolled to exactly the same height, all hats were not at the same angle. When the sergeant of the guard gave his present-arms as a final salute, the General would return it — in his habitual "most slovenly" way. So they called him "Drip".

The general's criticism after Tobruk wasn't only about "picnicking" and "dressing up like clowns". As well, the troops were guilty of "firing weapons indiscriminately" — or did he say "promiscuously" — and "they looked after dogs instead of men". This referred to the soldier's penchant for picking up stray dogs. As Jack Reedy of Charlie's C Company did. C Company's post-battle task was to guard the Italian prisoner compound. In the RAP station in the compound, Jack Reedy picked up a miserable, starving, white-and-dun coloured "wog dog" and took it back to the Company, hoping his mates would let him keep it. The pup made frantic efforts to win a home. They decided to enlist him in the AIF. He became NX-9, Bobby Tobruk, C Company, 2/2 Battalion, beloved comrade. "Wherever we go, he'll go," they vowed. Interestingly, I heard none of this from C.H. With Herc for a teacher Charlie had no sentimentality for dogs.

During its days as a rookie, the pup tried his comrades' patience; Buck said they all suffered. Jack Reedy was its undisputed master. While Bobby was still a pup, Jack would carry him in his greatcoat pocket. When he grew too big for that, Jack built a platform in his kitbag and waterproofed it. That was how Bobby travelled to Greece, where he served with some distinction.

I happened across an item in a letter of Ernie Osbourne's that in part fills in the complaint about "indiscriminate firing of weapons". Ernie's letter of January 23 tells laconically how inexperienced reinforcements went a bit silly after the battle: they "got amongst the guns and ammunition, firing everything. Five blew themselves up." Orders soon came down from Headquarters that the firing should stop forthwith. It didn't. Why? Who else but Lofty.

Lofty Stafford, who had fought with an anti-tank rifle at Bardia, was shuffled out of C Company after that battle. According to Adrian Buckley, Lofty then seized the opportunity to raise his own "army":

> C Company wanted to get rid of Lofty. Lofty was trouble. He was so . . . so "It's hard to put your finger on it" . . . so "irregular".
> When Bardia was over, Brigade Headquarters called for truck drivers. "Ha. Here's an opportunity to get rid of Lofty." He was approached.
> "Like to be a truck driver, Lofty?"
> "Sure, Brother."
> He was given his marching-out papers and he went down to Brigade HQ where an officer took one look at him, and smelled a rat. His unsuitability was so obvious. For one thing, Lofty wouldn't fit into a Morris 15cwt. The OC wrote out a new set of papers and sent him back where he came from.
> Lofty went into limbo, just as the Battalion was going into Tobruk. He was though, I remember hearing, seen again on the battlefield shouldering his anti-tank gun — fighting, no doubt, a one-man war.
> After the Tobruk battle, C Company had the job of guarding the prisoner-of-war compound. The cage that the 27,000 Italians went into was one they had built themselves, for the Australians. They must have regretted its poor sanitation. As luck had it, a terrible *khamsin* blew and the prisoners, lacking food and water became very distressed. In fact they became quite mutinous, making C Company's job very unpleasant.

Some of the officers with whom Charlie Green served.
Top: Frederick Chilton (L) and George Wootten (R).
Bottom: Cedric Edgar (L) and Ivan Dougherty (R).

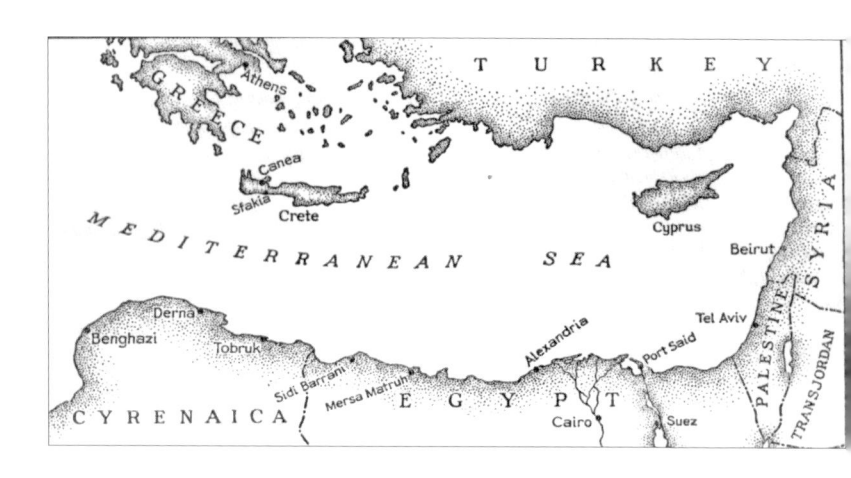

Above: The North African battle grounds.
Below: The famous dog 'Bobby Tobruk'.

Suddenly, through the dust, emerged a big diesel water-truck. It was driven by an Italian and beside the driver, directing the operation as he lay back, was . . . Lofty — smoking a cheroot. With him, he had a staff of four more Italians. Lofty had done something the whole army couldn't do: provide water for the Italian prisoners. Lofty's irregular methods were overlooked.

The order that "promiscuous" firing of weapons should cease was not heeded. Everyone noticed. There were so many really big bangs that Brigade sent down the following direction: "If the firing and explosions aren't policed, we'll send the provosts." The trouble was located. In a bunker, in a Wadi, they found Lofty and his "army". This was his HQ. It had store-rooms, stretchers, quantities of food, plonk and an arsenal of weapons. For his staff, he had recruited an Italian mechanic, a cook and two offsiders. He would send the Italians to collect weapons which they then taught him to use.

Knowledge of the incident was kept within the Company. Lofty, up before Buckley, reasoned: "I was helping, Brother. I got water. I delivered it and I've kept some Italians busy." — "Listen, Stafford," Buck said, "You've got something good going. We'll strike a deal. You carry on, but while ever we are on this job, I want two loads of water a day, and a case of goodies. Remember, though, if there's one more explosion, you lose the lot, and you go into the boob."

There was some rest and relaxation in Tobruk on the shore of the Mediterranean before the boys got a job salvaging all the equipment lying around. Then rumours began flying. Something else was on. It was puzzling. They had put on a big push: now, suddenly, they were being pulled out.

On March 7, the Battalion found itself in Mersa Matrah, another seaboard town of little white houses by the shining Mediterranean. At Mersa there was the luxury of being billeted in barracks. When it was found they were being re-equipped, especially with Tommy guns, it was obvious something serious was afoot.

Nature, as though it knew the calamitous next act, provided a foreshadowing atmosphere: "While we were there we had one of the worst sand storms to date. We ate, drank and breathed dust. To go to the latrines, there were guide ropes. Even the dysentry flies couldn't survive. In fact it was the opposite. Can you imagine passing sandpaper?"

Here, at Mersa Matruh, Charlie Green rejoined his unit. When he marched in, he was wearing three pips. He had been promoted to Captain.

# 8
# Greece — "A terrible beauty"

> Must we but weep o'er days more blest?
> Must we but blush? — Our fathers bled.
> Earth! render back from out thy breast
> A remnant of our Spartan dead!
> Of the three hundred grant but three,
> To make a new Thermopylae!
>
> *Don Juan* by Lord Byron

Greece must have been a momentous experience for Charlie militarily and personally. At a recent 2/2 Battalion reunion I met Steve Scott, batman to C.H. in 1942. Steve was very forthcoming:

> After Greece, he was the greatest bloody man that ever lived. Before that he was a bit bumptious. He was only playing. In Greece he had his baptism of fire. After that he was a different man.
>
> You know, I still have things of his I keep and treasure. I've got a pair of shorts and a razor. I keep the shorts to wear when I am painting around the house. As for the razor, I wouldn't part with that for worlds.

It wasn't only Charlie who changed and matured. The Greek Campaign had tremendous significance for the 2/2 Battalion and for the Australian Army. After the "Grecian Disaster" the 2/2 could not continue as a fighting unit. It had to be reinforced, re-equipped and re-trained. They learned a lot in a short time. They went to Greece fresh from the elation of the chase only to learn the indignation of being the hunted. In neither role did they tarnish their reputation; they were admirable in defeat as they were in victory.

The campaign was an inevitable disaster. The defenders of Greece, 56,000 British Imperial Forces and the Greeks themselves had not the material nor the men to resist Field Marshal von List's fifteen divisions and four Panzer Divisions — half a million men, and a combined German/Italian airforce of approximately 1000 planes. Yet out of disaster a bond developed. There are Greeks who still remember the Australians who came to help, the famous Aussies. There are misty-eyed diggers who remember, too: the beautiful country and the wonderful, self-sacrificing, grateful Greek people.

When the German push came, it was the Anzacs who resisted it. They had little support from tanks or artillery and almost none from the air. They had their rifles, some Bren Carriers, some anti-tank rifles men called "a joke" and mortars which were merely "burdensome toys". At the crunch, they had what was bred in them: indomitability, ingenuity — their inimitable Anzac spirit.

How did such a debacle occur? It seems that the few were sacrificed for the perceived greater cause. Greece had requested help from Britain against the Axis powers. It was promised. But the only troops available were those engaged in North Africa.

It was Churchill's idea. He wanted to aid Greece in her fight against the Italians and, in case of a German invasion, honour his promise. (Greece and Germany were not yet at war with each other.) Above all, Churchill wanted to inspire the world, especially the Americans, whom he was courting for help. As he informed his generals in confidence, it was to be done with as little loss as possible. Dunkirk losses in men and material had already dangerously wasted British resources.

History is beginning to uncover other motives. Churchill's real purpose was to thwart Hitler's plans. The Enigma Cipher machine had revealed to British Intelligence that Hitler planned to attack Russia in May. Apparently the imbroglio in Yugoslavia was a *ruse de guerre* that Britain and America had stirred up. (The agency involved is supposed to have spawned the CIA.) Hitler retaliated by brutally bombing Belgrade at

Easter, 1941, killing 10,000. It remains a fact that Operation Barbarossa, the plan to attack Russia, was delayed for five vital weeks. Churchill, trusting the lessons of history, had ensured that Hitler would be defeated as Napoleon was, by the Russian winter.

The role of Australia's 6 Division was determined in Britain, not in Australia. Churchill and his generals, fully aware of the impossibility of the undertaking, decided to commit the Anzacs. At the risk of jeopardising the just-won forts Bardia to Benghazi, the Australian 6 Division was pulled out of Africa and, complemented with New Zealand and British troops, sent to Greece. Australia's Prime Minister, Menzies, was consulted and he concurred, although with misgivings. Australia's Army chief, Blamey was ignored even though the AIF charter demanded his concurrence. Although Blamey was the natural choice as commander of the Anzacs, it was a Britisher, Maitland Wilson, who got the command. Maitland Wilson thought Australians were undisciplined.

The odds against the force were great enough without the mistake Maitland Wilson made in dividing the command with Blamey and a Greek general. The result was confusion and lack of unity. The Greeks, instead of reinforcing the defence line that the Anzacs established, went up to the Yugoslav border and formed the Metaxas Line, named after the Greek Premier who died in January 1941. Germany's von List capitalised on this. When he attacked, he outflanked the Greeks and captured Salonika in just two days.

That left the Anzacs sacrificially naked along their line in the mythical Mt Olympus area, which in the battle for Greece was named the Aliakmon Line. The wonder is that in situations like this men will unquestioningly obey, will stand and fight, knowing the dice is loaded. When a man dons a uniform he takes on with it the whole mystique of the Army — its sense of might, and right. The key to the mystique is the desirable blend of discipline and morale an army can engender. Australian soldiers appear able to produce their own special blend that includes an unusual degree of autonomy. The British seem to think it is lack of discipline.

From all accounts the Aussies at first knew little of the nature of their impossible mission. They were going to "another show". And they were going with high hopes. For hadn't they just had a glorious victory? Their belief that "we are the best" had been reaffirmed. According to their letters home, men were excited at the prospect of Greece and of the possibility of testing themselves as their fathers did, against the formidable "Jerry". It was an exciting prospect to travel to yet another country so important in their consciousness. After all, Greece was where democracy, what they were fighting for, was born. Already they had walked after Christ in Palestine; they'd seen those amazing edifices the pharaohs built to proclaim their immortality. Now they were going to the place where men had created their Gods and aspired to states of excellence in thought, word and deed. There was no time in Greece for soldiers to be tourists, to search for the places where heroes had once walked. They went straight up to defence positions. But from them they could at least see where the gods dwelled. When the weather cleared in Northern Greece the Australians could see Mt Olympus.

Charlie wrote an article on the 2/2's role in the Greek campaign: "Grecian Disaster": it was published in *Nulli Secundus Log*, a journal of articles written by 2/2 personnel after they came out of Greece, probably late in 1941. In "Grecian Disaster", an essentially military article, C.H. shows his clear grasp of the manoeuvres. Tactics, as Jack Boorer observed, was his forte, the expertise that ensured his potential as a leader. Yet it is not a lifeless article. His exclamation on the beauty of Greece has often been quoted. His humanity is revealed in his recognition of what some men contributed in bravery or excellence. Occasionally his quiet sense of humour shows. Most of all his writing glows when he speaks of the Greek people. His tribute, at the end, is also much quoted.

When I began selecting quotes from this article, I noticed Charlie's usage of "Hun", the term the troops used for the Germans. It reflects the continuity of Anzac thinking about their historical enemy the "Hun", the "Boche", "Jerry" or occasionally, with a bit of affection, "Fritzy". Having no precedent for Italians they were simply "Ities" — and Japanese were "Japs" or "Nips". (In Korea and Vietnam, Australians assumed the usage coined by the Americans, "Gook" and "Charlie".)

To bring C.H. closer, I am going to base the account of the Greek experience on his own words and thoughts, with selections from the only other complete personal account I have access to, the diary of Woop Waters, as counterpoint. For clarity's sake we need the context in which they are speaking.

In mountainous Greece, in 1941 devoid of modern roads and railways, an aggressor had to move through the natural passes, the obvious places to defend. Von List's army came down through the very same passes that Xerxes, leader of the Persians took. Von List, also paying attention to history, did as Xerxes did: he found secondary passes to outflank the defenders.

So it was at the passes that the Anzacs tried to stop the Germans, first at Verria and Servia and then in the east at Tempe. When this was not possible they withdrew to Thermopylae, hoping to stop them there.

The Germans' classic pincer movement down through Monastir in the centre and Salonica in the east nearly trapped the Anzacs. In the east there was only the New Zealand 21 Battalion trying to stop the Germans. The problem was that the east coast drive, if it won the town of Larissa before the Anzacs could withdraw, would trap the Australians.

The Germans had to be stopped on the east to allow the main force to move down to Thermopylae, the last pass where a defence could be made.

It fell to 16 Brigade, which came to be known as Allen Force, after its Brigadier, "Tubby" Allen, to rush to the aid of the New Zealanders at Tempe and to stop the Germans. If they didn't, at least until the withdrawal was effected, they all went in the bag, as the saying goes.

There was no transport for 16 Brigade. They had to march. Time was running out. That meant they marched non-stop for three nights. In snow and rain, in the freezing cold, they marched seventy miles over four ranges of mountains, carrying their gear, to do battle.

It is an epic that belongs to the Anzac mythology. That is why it is called "The Long March" or, with true Australian pith, "The Memorable Hike".

Charlie's and Woop's stories begin in Egypt, as the troops set out on their next adventure, full of cheer and high in morale. They had to be rounded up in Alexandria, where they were on leave. Provosts went into cafes, bars, all the likely places. All night C.H. heard them arriving back at camp in taxis, gharries, even on foot.

Woop: *"Leave in Alex was short and sweet."*

The battalion was moved to the quay but there was no boat as expected. After a while they "saw a small tramp manoeuvring among other craft". To their astonishment it berthed at their quay. It had a crew of lascars who ran about the deck in bare feet, jabbering with excitement as they lashed their mooring lines. Colonel Chilton, surprised at the nature of the craft, went ashore to check out the orders. The English captain of the craft was no less surprised. He didn't expect "mad" Australians; he expected 300 mules for Greece. And that was what the tub smelt and looked like. After confirming the orders, the CO organised a fatigue to clean up the *Bankura*. It was so small the men had to travel in the holds and live on hard rations.

At full speed of seven knots, the shuddering little boat couldn't keep up with the convoy; the escort "hovered like sheepdogs around their flank". Charlie adds here that Lord Louis Mountbatten was captaining HMS *Kelly* in the convoy, the ship that inspired the film *In Which We Serve*. Concerned about their vulnerability, the Australians set about mounting Brens on deck as anti-aircraft defence and then warmed up with some rounds. This displeased the British captain, who complained that the terrible Australians were brandishing guns near his cabin. Some guns were removed.

Two days later, an Italian spotting plane came out of a

murky sky and pinned their location. Within a few hours, eight planes dive-bombed the *Bankura*. C.H. couldn't believe that the pilots were Italian because they flew so low, not an Italian practice. With what Brens were left, the Australians fired as fiercely as they could. They were credited with two planes. The captain, somewhat subdued, asked for the guns to be returned to the deck.

Adrian Buckley recalled that Lofty Stafford was holding a two-up game on deck when the bombers came. After the raid, he was still there, alone. — "Had to mind the money, Brother."

On March 22, Greece was sighted; it was a glorious sunny afternoon.

Woop: *"The harbour echoed with coo-ees from our boat. British planes escorted us into the harbour where we were greeted by crowds of Greek people who had come to welcome us."*

It was noted that amongst the welcoming crowd, Germans from their embassy were there to report back on the troops' arrival.

The Australians couldn't believe that they could be welcomed in the way of the Greeks. "People didn't turn up to sell things" as they did in Palestine; they turned up to cheer them, to shower them with flowers and to press gifts and glasses of wine into their hands. C.H. wrote: ". . . it made us feel somebody really did care for us." The children looked at their hats and thought a contingent of cowboys had arrived. Very soon a few words of Greek were learned: *"Zeeto ee Australia!"* (long live Australia).

Once ashore, the troops were sped through the darkness in trucks to their camp at Daphni, silvered by the moon and perfumed by pine trees. It was magic, they all thought.

Charlie's enthusiastic impressions are the ones quoted in the war histories:

What a contrast! Instead of awaking with eyes, ears and noses full of sand, we breathed pure crisp air with the scent of flowers. Flowers! We hadn't seen them since leaving Australia. After months of desert glare the landscape at Daphni was a dream come true. The troops stood and gazed at the natural gardens full of shrubs and flowers which scented the breeze; at the grasses that made a swishing noise as you walked through — I'm sure many men that morning actually pinched themselves to see if they were really there. We saw civilians dressed as we used to dress before the war — civilians whom you could trust, in every way a contrast to the Middle East. Daphni was a pretty place. From the hillside one could look into the valley below and see Athens. The historic Acropolis added an ancient background to a glorious panorama.

Woop: *"The smell of the pines and a cool breeze from the mountains made new men out of us. The camp was an Aussies dream, plenty of beer and song. Close to camp were numerous wine bars which we made good use of."* To the unexpected announcement that there was to be leave in Athens, Woop wrote: *"Looks like a decent blue next time when the CO lets his head go like that."*

It was Jack Boorer who told about their leave. Interestingly, there are no accounts of any riotous behaviour in Athens. Already they seem old soldiers, quieter, more restrained. Or did they react so respectfully because it was Greece, and around them were the ghosts of men like Socrates, Pericles, Plato, Homer? Soberly they visited the Acropolis, gazed on the Parthenon, sat in Omonia (they call it Pneumonia) Square and joyfully fraternised with the friendly, grateful people. It was the Evzones that Jack remembered in particular. They put on a march as a gesture of welcome and acclaim. The Australians were thrilled. And not one quip was made about their skirts, stockings and boleros.

That leave was short and sweet too. C.H. goes on to describe the move to northern Greece. It began on March 26 on a primitive train. "The troops had to be packed in more like sheep than humans." They were headed for Larissa, the critical junction they were to fight for. Soon it would be April, T.S. Eliot's "cruellest month". They passed green forests, villages, hamlets. Clusters of people in "curious costumes" took their eye. They saw shepherds as the train wound through hills that were sometimes splashed with red poppies. Wheat and oats were greening in the fields, telling of regeneration as they travelled to their mission of death.

Above: Captain Adrian Buckley (in the civilian disguise he used when escaping from Crete).

Below: Men of 2/2 Battalion at the Aliakmon River crossing, during the withdrawal from Veria Pass

Above: Lieutenant Bruce 'Effendi' Brock.
(Alice Brock)

Below: Brock in the guise that earned him the 'Effendi' nickname.

Charlie had a keen, appreciative sense of humour. I treasure this warm, almost fatherly view of Greek naivete. It is another sight from the train:

> Approaching Larissa at approximately midday March 27, the troops were mystified to see coming in the opposite direction a long line of moving bushes (à la Birnam Wood). As we drew close we laughed at the Greek idea of camouflage — it was a train covered by bushes.

Woop noted another oncoming train: "... *a crowded refugee train stopped to look at the famous Aussies.*"

At Larissa they were taken by truck to a pleasant position just south of Verria, in sight of Mt Olympus.

On April 6, the peacefulness was shattered by the news that Germany had declared war on Greece. The next day, 16 Brigade moved north to "misty Verria Pass", and the Battalion went farther forward to take up defence positions high above the village at the pass. This often meant a 3,000-foot struggle up rocky, slippery tracks, carrying gear. When all the companies were in position, the Battalion was stretched so far out it took three hours to traverse it. This mountain is scored in men's minds. It is called "Panic Mountain". There, as Charlie describes: "... we dug in in frozen ground and lived in holes often half-full of water ... Reconnaissance was difficult. Only for about one hour at sunrise and sunset did the clouds clear. Then we got marvellous views. We could see as far as the mountains of Yugoslavia and the town and gulf of Salonica to the far north-east."

Woop: "*In the distance Mt Olympus stood out snow-capped and glorious in the evening sun. Little did we know that many pals would be killed around its slopes.*"

Mt Olympus stayed in men's minds. One soldier, Sergeant Jack Steep, wrote a lament, in which he charged Mt Olympus with the safekeeping of his comrades:

> Oh, mighty Mount Olympus
>   Ten thousand feet you soar,
> Where snows have lain ten thousand years
>   And will for thousands more.

We came to you as strangers,
 But our name had gone before,
And through your lofty ranges
 It will live for evermore.

And you, O Mount Olympus,
 Will you guard those lonely graves . . .

At Olympus, Charlie noted "food was scarce; and the cold weather made us eat like horses."

Woop recounts that the Greek Battalion they were relieving were amused at *"us boiling a pot of tea"*. He described a typical breakfast high up in the mist, rain and snow: *". . . filled our dixies with snow, opened up bully, boiled this and added the famous dog biscuits to thicken it. A tin of curry came to light and helped make it tasty."*

At Verria, after all their toiling to prepare their defence line, the Anzacs learned it had been in vain. On April 11, they received a startling message: the Germans had broken through on their left. This was followed by an order to withdraw immediately. There was no transport so the men had to march. Then came the most memorable of orders (as it turned out). They should destroy everything they did not carry away and blow up all bridges and roads.

This is how Panic Mountain got its name. Officers supervised the scorched-earth procedure. One officer in D Company zealously had his men urinate on all their blankets before burying them in the snow. Then came a countermanding order that not all were to withdraw immediately. Of course, it was D Company that had to remain on Panic Mountain another night. They dug up the blankets again. It was that cold.

Woop: *"We were told we had to march up hill and down dale to beat the Hun across the river; otherwise Mafeesh us all."*

It was Jack Boorer who told me of the men's horror on Panic Mountain just before they set out on the Long March. April 12, Easter Saturday, was the day Rommel recaptured Bardia. They who had been so triumphant in Bardia were now being chased by the Germans. They didn't like it.

Charlie tells how the great trek began. Donkeys were

"secured to transport heavy weapons but because of their poor condition were of little value. They had to be pushed along by their attendants. Through the moonlit night, while snow fell, men marched, stopping every hour for ten minutes, trying to find their way along ill-defined snow-covered tracks."

Woop (He is now a donkey attendant): *"My Donkey had a taste for dog biscuits which I had a good supply of."*

When daylight came, the marchers halted. This is the day Charlie Green walked his marathon. Brock Effendi records it: "While the Battalion hid and slept, Charlie went on to find a track over the next range. This he did, returning later in the day to lead us all back in the dark to the banks of the Aliakmon River, just east of Servia . . . This in my mind — the act of going twice over the track by Charlie — was easily the finest piece of endurance I saw in the whole war. To make matters worse for him, and for us, it snowed as we passed over the range."

The second night, the 14th, the moon shone so brightly and memorably, that it is noted in histories. After hiding all day the marchers tackled another 3,000-foot range while snow fell, blanketing the ground.

Woop: *"What a sight it was to see us all strung out, winding up to the summit of the mountain. The moon was out. What a grand sight it was . . . three hours later we descended to the river."*

An advance party of engineers had blown the bridge so the crossing "was another hazard". Undeterred, the ingenious engineers erected a flying punt. "The fore-end was attached to a wire rope. The stern was held towards the bank by a sweep; the rush of water striking the bows at this angle pushed the craft across the stream." The same engineers provided "the welcome cup of tea".

Jack Boorer told me how the soldiers swam in the freezing water to help "the tired little donkeys" across the river; otherwise they would have perished. Some had already slipped over cliffs in the mountains. I asked Jack where Bobby Tobruk was at this time. He said when he got tired someone carried him; mostly he was in his special place in Jack Reedy's pack.

By morning, they were once more at Servia pass, lying low because the sky was full of German planes. From their height they looked down to the plains north of the Aliakmon to see an artillery duel booming away between the New Zealanders and the Germans, hot in pursuit of the Anzacs. Though the bridge was blown, the Germans were getting across the river on floats. Then an infantry skirmish was seen between New Zealanders and a German patrol pushing after them. After the battle the New Zealanders were seen burying their dead, the dead that Mt Olympus watches over.

That same morning, from their positions of concealment in a pine forest, the men were horrified to see the charming village by the river, where they had bought eggs and chickens, flattened. About 100 German planes, JU88s, came in a flock and began the dreaded peeling off over the village. C.H. said it was an example of German "torture of the civil population, for Servia did not contain one single soldier or piece of army equipment".

The sky seemed to be always full of planes. And that is how Bobby Tobruk came to be an active soldier. Jack said he became "air sentry No. 1". He could hear, before anybody, the first whine of German planes. "And he was second to none in getting to cover." I suppose the pun is legendary, too.

At Servia, Nulli Secundus heard fateful news. The German drive down from Salonica was mauling the defenceless New Zealanders at Pinios Gorge. The Anzac Corps was threatened. If the Germans got to Larissa it was "mafeesh them all". 16 Brigade, Allen Force, was ordered to rush to Pinios Gorge in Tempe Vale to hold the Germans until April 19. That would give the rest of the corps time to withdraw through Larissa, to form the line at Thermopylae. Yet another "weary march" was made to meet up with motor transport held at Brigade HQ at Elasson, north-west of Larissa, to rush them to Pinios. It took ten hours.

Woop: He tells of his preparation before setting out. "*Got*

# Greece — "A terrible beauty"

*fowls from a village and eggs and bread, packed it in a kerosene tin and loaded it all on the donkey."*

Trucks took them to Larissa. Once through the congested, bomb-devastated town, German planes were "like flies" in the sky turning the narrow, unsurfaced road into a "bombers' paradise". The road was crowded with army vehicles and fleeing civilians, some riding in carts, some on donkeys; some were even pushing perambulators. "Our convoy became split owing to bombing and strafing runs. Trucks were burning beside the road and the dead were being buried in improvised graves beside their wrecked vehicles as we passed by." C.H. goes on to deprecate the absence of British or any other supporting planes.

Nevertheless, so Jack told me, and Woop noted it too, a lone Hurricane came out of the sky and shot down a German Air Ace who, Jack told me "was wearing an Iron Cross". To my astonishment, Jack said: "We felt sorry for him."

By the evening of April 16, they were at Tempe. C.H. tells how "on the night of April 16, we contacted the NZ 21 Battalion, beaten by the Hun at the northern end of the Pinios Gorge ... in the face of terrible dive-bombing and superior forces". German spotters continually hovered overhead as 16 Brigade prepared for their obviously impossible task. As C.H. summed up: "It was evident that the Germans were going to make an all-out effort to push down the gorge and take Larissa." It was their job to stop them, at least for one day. Everyone knew it was not going to be a picnic.

Woop: *"Tomorrow looks like being lively. Sat up till the chooks were cooked. Then at daylight* [the day of the battle] *ate the chook — the last square meal."*

Before their stories continue, here are the defence positions at Pinios Gorge. Bear in mind that the Australians were at a considerable disadvantage. They were poorly equipped, on the defensive, not dug-in and outnumbered. They had no chance. It was simply a feat to delay the Germans.

The New Zealand 21 Battalion, with their own artillery and anti-tank support, had fallen back west to the exit of the five-mile narrow gorge near Tempe village. At "Evangelismos, but most people call the place Tempe", the New Zealanders blew the rail and vehicle bridge; and east of Tempe, near a railway tunnel, they had built a road block. The 2/2 Battalion came up behind the New Zealanders. Their right flank was near Tempe and their left was strung in a long line along the south bank of the river.

As expected, the Germans struck down the gorge through Tempe and at the same time across the river from the foothills around Gonnos, which was across the river from the 2/2 Battalion position. At the rear of the 2/2 was 2/3 Battalion, in support.

It was Adrian Buckley's C Company (Charlie was his second-in-command) that covered the exit at Tempe not far from the New Zealanders; consequently, when the New Zealanders defence collapsed, the 2/2 took the force of the German onslaught.

Lieutenant Colonel Chilton, who was the CO again in this action, drew my attention to the site of the battle. Guarding the pass at Tempe, the same pass that Xerxes used, are the two famous mountains Ossa and Pelion. According to myth the Gigantes, in an effort to dethrone Zeus on Mt Olympus, heaped Pelion on Ossa, to scale the walls of heaven. But they were defeated, and imprisoned in the earth. It was in this valley, too, the Vale of Tempe, that mythical Apollo pursued Daphne until she turned into a laurel tree. In remembrance of her he always wore the laurel wreath.

Ironically, it was April, truly the cruel month. The great plane trees were budding and the famous Judas trees were erupting with red blossoms, as though to signal the blood about to be shed. There is a famous painting, *The Battle of Tempe Gorge*, by William Dargie, hanging in the War Memorial, Canberra which captures the atmosphere.

Charlie told how patrols brought back information on April 17, the eve of the battle:

> The Huns were now observed moving down the mountains on the northern side of the Pinios River with pack animals carrying heavy mortars and machine guns. And it was from this direction

the next day that one arm of the Pinzer move turned into a three-pronged push to get across the river.

Early in the morning of the 18th we fell for a clever trick by the Germans. German patrols drew fire in two places. In that way the Australian positions were pinned — for the German artillery and for the Luftwaffe.

Early in the morning two New Zealand artillery batteries, supporting Allen Force, shelled the gorge, forward of the 2/2 Battalion, to harrass parties of enemy moving down to attack. The New Zealand Forward Observer gamely remained forward to direct fire until the last minute. He didn't come back.

At eleven thirty the Germans sent forty-five planes and an escort over to silence those few New Zealand guns, before beginning their all-out attack. The planes flew down to 1000 feet overhead and began to circle. C.H. said that the common thing to say by now was "I wonder who is going to cop it this time".

Woop: *"Once we had a near thing when they copped our range with their long-range machine guns. Whew, how we grovelled for cover beneath our rock. Old Jim looked at me, laughed and said, 'A near thing, mate. Better keep low'... Lots were drawn for the beer ration."*

The all-out German pincer attack began to take shape at 1400 hours "down the gorge and across the river". D Company engaged as the enemy crossed the river on its front. C Company, facing the gorge, drew blood but C.H. rather proudly asserts: "not one crossed the river on C Company's front." The third prong of the river attack was the one met by A and B Company supported by the mortar men, led by "Punchy" Coyle, who extended the Anzac legend that day.

Woop: *"Wasn't the blue on full swing! Mortars, machine guns and bombs all together... What a relief it was to get a big Hun under one's sights. Bang. Cop that, you square head. That is how one became bloodthirsty and callous... One of the officers asked his batman to wash his socks. 'Go to hell' he said, 'There's a war on.' He washed them himself in his tin hat while he was being machine-gunned. Little did he know he would never wear them again."*

At the height of the battle Lofty Stafford was noted

extending his individual legend. Captain John Blamey wrote: "I must mention old Lofty, so called because of his height of six foot seven inches. He went to the top of the ridge and took cover behind a pile of rocks. The only trouble was that the rocks were three feet high, and he stood up to his full height despite the bullets whizzing about his head." According to the oral tradition, Lofty went into the Battle of Tempe as he did into Bardia, with his long anti-tank rifle with the bayonet attached by signal wire.

It was C.H. who drew attention to the feat of the mortar platoon led by "Punchy" Coyle, who gave a fine display of Australian ingenuity at Pinios River that day. C.H. called it "a grand bit of work". At least a battalion of Hun infantry began to ford the river near A and B Companies. Because of the fast flow, they were wading in about twelve abreast for support against the current. After contemplating the situation, Punchy coolly said: "Not a bad target." In truth, the target was way in excess of the mortars' capacity. Punchy was undeterred. He got his mortar men to drop extra primary charges (methylated spirits) into the barrels. C.H. reported that the base plate almost disappeared into the ground but the rounds fell where they wanted them. As a result of this bit of improvisation, the Germans suffered severe casualties. Sergeant Coyle, always known only as Punchy because of his prowess with the gloves, was mentioned in despatches and commissioned in the field.

Woop: *"On the river the mortars had chopped the Huns to pieces and the river was choked chock a block with dead bodies. No doubt Jerry had guts. Repeatedly they walked into our fire to be mown down."*

C.H. paid a tribute, too, to the heroic Bren carrier personnel. They "used the carriers in text-book fashion". Gunners leapt from their vehicles and rushed forward to occupy positions from which they fired on the crossing places. For their parts, Corporal Allan Lacey and Private Angus McQueen each won the Military Medal.

Aussie strength of will, initiative and courage held the power of the German Mountain Division at the bloody Pinios

River. "Battles are won in the minds of men", so Churchill said. The battle that day was not won, but the objective of holding the might of the Germans was achieved. The Australians had to resist with their minds and their hearts. They had little else. Only pitiful rifles, straining mortars and a few heroic Bren gunners. There is no knowing how long the Australians could have held out, but suddenly the situation changed. The sound of heavy machine-gun fire on C Company's right flank alerted them to serious trouble. Up till then their right flank covering the gorge had been defended by the New Zealand 21 Battalion. Obviously they were no longer there; they had been routed.

The great pincer trap was positioned: one steel arm was pushing across the river; the other was now moving down the gorge. In a long menacing line came steel monsters of the German Panzer Brigade, a modern mechanised phalanx. Suddenly the tanks were in the Battalion area. Everyone knew it was all over. For a couple of men crushed by the German tanks it was too late to make that individual decision that each man, now out of communication, had to make for himself. Escape — or else. As Charlie wrote, their position was untenable. The 2/2 Battalion could no longer operate as a fighting unit.

Towards the end of the battle, Lofty Stafford decided to wage another one-man war, or make a grand exit. Lieutenant W.S. Ward wrote: ". . . his final act was characteristic of him in the Battalion. He still had his anti-tank rifle when he decided to attack. Corporal Almond was distributing bully beef and ammunition when he was approached by Lofty, who demanded enough bully for two days and tank attack ammunition. He got what he wanted and was last seen with the tank attack rifle over his shoulder advancing on the Hun tanks." Lofty was taken prisoner. (After the war, he became a fisherman on his boat, *The African Queen*. He died of a heart attack, aged fifty-five.)

Woop (describing the last stages of the battle): *"Tanks came around under us and opened up. Did that lead fly and so did we. Everything was haywire. We were cut off. Our only hope was to retreat to the hills the* (foothills of Mt Ossa) . . . *We had no ammunition left. Tanks were in a fixed line up the gully giving the Australians hell . . . Under fire, men managed to make a climb that was normally impossible."*

Most of the 2/2 Battalion, especially Charlie's C Company, were cut off from the rest of the Brigade, who were to make an orderly retreat. Those cut off had no alternative but to take to the hills behind them. After that, though they tried to rejoin the retreating main force, the Germans were always blocking them. Their last hope then was to get to the sea, pray they be picked up by the RAN or failing that, acquire a boat. As it turned out, those who were a little late taking to the sea had to dodge the fast moving Germans already in occupation of the islands off the Greek east coast.

When they had time to reflect, men were bitter about the futility of it all. Their North African victory was wasted. In Greece they "didn't have a dog's chance". For the moment, though, they felt justly proud of their magnificent deploying action.

Woop: *"There was the might of Hitler's army battling against the Aussies. What odds! The Defence was Grand."*


Charlie Green, summing up, proudly recognises the achievement: "Our battalion plus some disorganised Kiwis and two splendid batteries of New Zealand artillery held a Mountain Division (1200) and a brigade of Panzers (250 tanks) for one day." Charlie and his party were among those struggling up into the hills.

The main body of the Anzac forces did get out of Greece, thanks to the 16 Brigade stand at Tempe and to the RAN. Just as Greece, in a sense, saved Europe, so did Allen Force save the expeditionary force in Greece.

It wasn't until about 7 a.m. on April 19 that the Germans took Larissa. On the evening of April 18 the Germans had reached the outskirts of Larissa on the Tempe road that the Australians had fought for. The road block they set up prevented some of the retreating Australians from getting through, so they had to circumvent the Germans across ploughed fields or take to the hills. It was every man for himself.

The Greek forces, independently commanded and out of communication, were cut off in the west and in the north by the tactics of von List. Realising they were surrounded, they began to capitulate. The British commanders, who had at first hoped to make a stand at Thermopylae, concluded there was no hope of saving Greece at Thermopylae or anywhere else. It was over. They had the task of planning a rearguard action that would save as much material and as many men as possible. Some commanders, like Admiral Cunningham of the RAN, had from the outset made plans for a retreat by deciding on evacuation points around the southern coast. The evacuees, in the main, were to be hurried to Crete, a critical naval base, for its defence. — There, too, they "hadn't a dog's chance".

Fortunately Australia's army chief, General Blamey, was put in command of the retreat and evacuation of the Anzac Corps. Credit is given to Blamey, his officers and the men themselves for their exemplary textbook operation. As is often pointed out, retreats can so easily turn into routs.

The withdrawing army leapfrogged down through Greece and spread out to designated evacuation points on the beaches of Attica and Peloponnesos while the Luftwaffe patrolled the sky, preying like hawks ready to peel off, divebomb and strafe the convoys struggling along Greece's primitive roads. With a sense of betrayal men turned their eyes heavenward, hoping for an RAF plane or two that might chase the German demons out of the sky.

At Thermopylae, where Leonidas and his brave 300 combed their hair in preparation for their battle against the Persians centuries before, the retreating Anzacs fought another delaying action against the Adolf Hitler SS Motorised Division. Again they proved worthy of that venerable company of heroes. Charlie wrote that they fought there "one of the finest rearguard actions of the war".

Just before Anzac Day, 1941, the survivors of the battle

were lying hidden in olive groves near the beaches, waiting to be lifted off by the navy. On April 24 and 25, all the troops were evacuated. As at Dunkirk, their last act on the beaches was to destroy their equipment or roll it into the sea. One report says that their horses had to be shot. The irony of a beach evacuation on Anzac Day was lost on no one.

But that was by no means the end. For half of the Anzacs there was worse to come. They went to Crete — the Isle of Doom as diggers call it, after the poem of that name written by a digger, identity unknown. Its value is historical:

> And then they landed us on Crete,
> And marched us off our ruddy feet.
> The food was bad, the water crook.
> I got fed up and slung my hook.
> Returned that night filled up with wine,
> And next day copped a ten bob fine.
> My paybook was behind to hell,
> When pay day came I said: "Oh well,
> They won't pay me I'm sure of that."
> But when they did I smelt a rat.
> And next day when rations came
> I realised their wily game.
> For sooner than sit down and die,
> He spent our dibs on food supply.
> And now it looks like even betting,
> A man will soon become a Cretan;
> And spend his days in blackest gloom,
> On Adolf Hitler's Isle of Doom.

Adolf Hitler successfully attacked Crete, with the world's first airborne army, because it was badly defended. All over again, men fought, retreated over daunting mountains, hid on the beaches and were evacuated — if they were lucky.

What the defeat of Greece did to the Greek psyche can be guessed from the action of its Premier of only three months, Alexander Koryzis. He committed suicide on April 18. On April 23, the Greeks formally surrendered. On Hitler's birthday, April 20, some young Nazi soldiers, elated at the news of the Greek capitulation, climbed Mt Olympus and flew from it their ominous distorted cross. On that most sacred of places it was audacity and hubris. But what Nemesis when it came! The gods are only sleeping. The Greek tragedy deeply affected the Australian participants. Something happened to men in Greece that defies words. It needs Yeats' paradoxical "a terrible beauty is born" to explain the magnitude of their experience. Was it the odds of the fight and the elation that comes from the daring and the surviving? Did it come from the inspiration of the brave, generous Greek people who risked their lives for Australian escapees, by feeding them, hiding them, guiding them? Or was it the country itself? Did they sense its glorious history, feel the presence of the heroes of its golden age? For a long time I pondered over William James's claim that "society would rot without its mystical blood payment". It makes more sense now.

One British writer, Compton Mackenzie, recognised the mutuality of the experience that united Greek and Anzac:

> The British and Imperial Expeditionary Force gave with recklessness of self which won from the heart of the Hellenic people a warmth of gratitude, a tenderness of comprehension and a dignity of regret beyond the power of expression in words.

I have heard of some of the ways that cathartic Greece captivated men — just as Byron was captivated and motivated to fight for it, write poetry about it and die for it. One soldier, for instance, spent his life's savings on building a temple in the likeness of a Cretan one. It is near the sea, in Western Australia, all blue-and-white and beleaguered by the sun — and memories. Another 2/2 man, Tom Harvey, M.M., laboured with classical Greek so that he would be able to read Homer in the original. Some didn't even try to get home. They disappeared into the hills of Greece or Crete, were classified "missing", and have never been heard of since. One veteran of Nulli Secundus sent me a letter not long ago. Of the move from Africa to Greece he said: "Goodbye, desert. Greece was short and sweet, but what a paradise." Yet he was at Tempe, in a rifle company.

Charlie Green's words of tribute to the Greeks contain the

sense that no matter what they endured, the shared experience had in some mysterious way added to their lives:

> To relate the stories of how these parties finally did make their escape would be incomplete without a mention of the magnificent Greek people. Those who did make their escape owe it chiefly to the Greeks. In the tiny villages tucked away in the mountains, the Greeks, although short of food themselves, gave what they had to our men. There were many touching scenes. Some of our wounded still trudged along as best they could. Greek women in tears would do what they could to relieve their pain. Other times they would mend torn clothing, cook food for us and always bid us *"Thies Kalos"* (Goodbye, good luck), as we got our feet to wearily continue the trek. Boots were worn out, clothes were often in shreds. The troops were tired and hungry — but never would they give themselves up to the Hun. Frequently the Greeks insisted that we stay with them and that they would guard us should Germans enter the village.
>
> Often the escaping parties had to make cross-country treks to avoid capture — and there was always a Greek to guide us. Greek fishermen undertook to take us across long stretches of the Aegean Sea to remote islands. During the latter stages these waters were patrolled by German craft, and had Greeks been caught with cargoes of Australians they would have most certainly been shot — but their friendly nature and sense of duty never failed us.

This passage of his is another that has been much quoted.

Steve Scott says Greece changed Charlie. I sense more wonder than horror at what he underwent and witnessed in Greece. A few brave men pitted against a great force of steel in a setting more fitted for fable than reality; individual acts of skill, ingenuity and compassion; the human spirit refining itself in its struggle into a pure white light, a perpetual flame.

But it wasn't a totally positive experience — that is, unless one believes in the purifying theory. Casualty lists, though difficult to interpret, show the cost. The British Imperial Force lost 15,000. Too much blood was sacrificed in a perceived stand for freedom. Nulli Secundus itself lost fifteen dead, while forty-six were wounded and 118 taken prisoner . . . a remarkably light payment in the circumstances. The

overall casualties of 6 Division were 239 killed and 784 wounded. The Greeks' own blood payment amounted to 15,700 killed and missing, 218,000 taken prisoner. Later all but officers were released.
It was a lot of blood to drain away in one futile campaign.

> The earth is all too narrow for our dead,
> So many and each a child of ours — and Thine
> This flesh (our flesh) crumbled away like bread,
> This blood (our blood) poured out like wine, like wine.
>
> from *Sacrament* by Margaret Sackville

Whether any boys from Ulmarra district were killed in any other force or any other war zone before April 18, I am not sure. The casualties in Greece were the first ones I remember. I was seventeen when the red-bordered envelopes first started to arrive. Among our first casualties were the two boys of the tennis courts, the ones I had always idolised: Bill Sullivan and Jack Ulrick. They were on the Bren carriers; it is little wonder they were hit. Bill was killed; Jack was wounded and taken prisoner. The two who always stood together. Their bond didn't end there. After returning from a POW camp in Germany, Jack married the girl who was once Bill's sweetheart. Two other Ulmarra boys were casualties: Ron Pattemore was wounded and taken prisoner and Bill Wright also became a prisoner.

Bill Sullivan's death threw Ulmarra into shock. Bill's mother gave to the community as fully as Bill himself had. Nearly every youngster in the town was taught to swim by Mabel Sullivan, or "Sully" as we called her. I think of her as Irish, burning with causes, big, jolly, red-haired and fiery. After school she would be down at the wharf dangling a length of rope in the river. Tied to the end would be some kid thrashing and gulping in the water until he could manage by himself and eventually learn to swim like a fish. After she lost her son, a kind of weariness sapped her vitality.

I am sure that is the day the town began to die. The grass gradually grew over the tennis courts and they almost disappeared. A way of life had died. The tennis court image never leaves me. We were happy then. The immaculate white figures leaping around on the courts. Baskets laden with cakes. Great pots of tea. Bouncing along rough gravel roads, idling along the road by the river, or stopping to open paddock gates on farms to bump along tracks through knee-high paspalum paddocks, past large, staring cows to another white-lined court. Our simple carefree world of nescience. A sweet memory.

Everything had begun to change.

# 9
# Greece — Escape

> Where we tread 'tis haunted, holy ground;
> No earth of thine is lost in vulgar mould,
> But one vast realm of wonder spreads around,
> And all the Muse's tales seem truly told,
> Till the sense aches with gazing to behold
> The scenes our earliest dreams have dwelt upon;
> Each hill and dale, each deepening glen and wold
> Defies the power which crush'd thy temples gone:
> Age shakes Athena's tower, but spares grey Marathon.
>
> *Childe Harold's Pilgrimage, II* by Lord Byron

Charlie, who hardly ever talked about the war, would occasionally mention his escape from Greece. Contented after a good meal, he'd remember he once ate raw sheep, he was so hungry. His big shoes that we'd joke about would trigger memories, too. The Turks, when they were helping the Australians escape, couldn't find a pair big enough for him.

From Charlie's article "Grecian Disaster" it is clear that the Greek experience, particularly the escape, was one of the biggest of his life. Sir Frederick Chilton and Jack Boorer were in Charlie's party for most of the escape journey, but I have based my retelling of the amazing adventure on Bruce Brock's account. It was like striking gold, again, to discover he, like Woop, had a diary and maps and an evergreen memory. The vividness of memory for some experiences is remarkable. The day they ate raw sheep . . . the day the German plane dived on their little defenceless boat in the Aegean . . . the day their boatman deserted them.

Bruce, an original 2/2 officer, was a schoolteacher by

profession. In his seventies, he remembered it all as if it were yesterday. His nickname "Effendi" came about in Palestine. To ensure his troops weren't robbed by the Arabs he used to bargain for them, and the Arabs would come to the camp looking for the chief, "Brock Effendi". I did not meet Effendi, and he has since died. I wrote to him for stories of the escape and got a fifty page reply. He'd always wanted to get it down, but hadn't the courage before. He was glad to do it "for Charlie's sake, a magnificent soldier and a fine friend", whom he'd have liked to have joined in Korea, had he been medically fit. He remembered how C.H. said once, during the Greek ordeal: "This would make a beaut story to tell the kids when we get home."

So Effendi began the story, believing it ought to be told. As he dreaded, the pain came. Early in the process he wrote: "Please don't ask me to re-tell any of it. It has stirred up intense feelings and given me sleepless nights." As the story came out, Effendi wondered that so much came back, at how some things were indelibly stamped in the mind, how, once the gates were opened, things kept coming . . . There was joy too. That sense, as others have expressed, of having lived again, truly lived. The elation of success and "always the wonderful comradeship". On the other hand there was the release, the unburdening of stored-up emotions. Emotions never really understood, never really dealt with. They were too big. In the end there was relief. Effendi said: "I feel as though a weight has been lifted off my mind."

There are too many soldiers with such experiences locked in their heads and hearts. That's why the tears keep oozing out when least expected, least wanted.

In his story Effendi remembers things Charlie did and said. For the first time, someone sees Charlie as I saw him. So very much alive, with a grin, a joke, a bit of teasing and for the most, "taking it as it came", even enjoying the challenges. This is the intimate side of the cool, detached Charlie that men looking at him from a distance would not see. That view is a later one, however, when he became a commander.

In his "Grecian Diary", after escaping up the hill, Charlie describes the last scenes on the battlefield of Tempe:

> Thoroughly exhausted on the top of the mountains which overlooked our former positions we could see the battle still being fought out by our carriers and parties who could not make their escape. It was a grim scene. As darkness fell we could see the Huns attending to our wounded, whilst the remains of our carriers burned a red glow below. Three German tanks knocked out by New Zealand tank-attack guns were blazing in B Company's area, an indication that the Hun did not have the tank battle his own way either. Two companies of the 2/3 Battalion had arrived late that afternoon and had taken up a quick defensive position some distance to the rear of D Company — they, too, were now involved and during the night the enemy poured thousands of rounds of tracer in the direction of their positions.

In the remainder of his article C.H. tells what happened to the fragmented Battalion. Those not cut off reformed under Major Edgar ("Boss") later a CO and a magnificent one too. Edgar's men joined the withdrawing British force, fought "brilliantly" at Thermopylae and were evacuated to Palestine or to Crete, to fight again.

The others, cut off when the Germans broke through, escaped up into the hills in one's and two's, and in parties. Charlie's story and theirs are really one. They escaped through their own initiative, courage and determination — and with the help of the magnificent Greek people. All the accounts of escape confirm the appropriateness of C.H.'s much-quoted tribute to the Greeks' "sense of duty". The accounts also confirm his tribute to the Australian soldier for his "toughness and ingenuity".

Most of this escape story is extracted from Brock Effendi's diary and maps. Into it he breathed life from his memory. It is shortened, only to keep a balance. The concluding phase of the escape comes from written and oral accounts of Colonel Chilton (Sir Fred). Adrian Buckley was with Charlie the whole time. What an oversight that I didn't prod his reluctant memory. Assuredly Buck would have had some fascinatingly different facets to add to the story.

*Effendi's story:*
Before he escaped up the hill, Effendi himself had an encounter with a German tank, and a shell explosion that threw him to the ground. When he came to, he scrambled up the hill vomiting. He also had an infected foot.

On the summit, from where C.H. described the closing battle scene, Effendi joined Charlie's group, mostly C Company men. It comprised Captain Buckley, Captain Green, Captain Brock, Lieutenant Bosgard, Captain Honeywell, Corporal Shanahan, Private Sanders, Private Whitton and Private Schofield. There is no record of those who joined or left this group.

They agreed to move quickly south, along a track. They wanted to get to the main force which they knew had to move down the road to Lamia. Interestingly, the group had no leader. Nobody pulled rank, no one assumed leadership and nobody asked for a leader; although the other ranks assumed from the outset that the others would lead them; and were happy that they would. Later, a leader did emerge, naturally.

It was dark and it had been a long, hard day. Not to mention the long march of only a few days ago. They had to get away so quickly they had no food and very little equipment. They had a Bren and some rifles, both necessary and a burden, because they could betray them.

Suddenly, ahead on the dark track, a voice boomed out, too loud for comfort: "Halt Pig!" Obviously a password, and as it wasn't a 2/2 pass word, it had to be New Zealand. After some quick thinking, a reply was given: "Islander", as Kiwis were often called. The challenger was the CO of the 21 NZ Battalion with a group of Kiwi escapees. They conferred. The NZ CO fortunately had some spare maps, a local one and an adjoining one, which he handed over.

The group, now swelled to about twenty, moved on, leaving the New Zealanders deliberating there, a bit undecided.

Despite their fatigue they plodded on in the dark, feeling their way with their feet along the goat tracks, as they had learned to do on the long march. They thought about the long march as they walked and they discussed Charlie's lone walk, his solo reconnaissance over the range to the Aliakmon river, something that men do not forget. Effendi recalled his stamina. They all needed that kind of stamina, now. It got very cold and the stars disappeared. Their desperate tiredness demanded they stop. Most hadn't slept for at least forty-eight hours. It was two thirty. A roster for guard duty was agreed upon. They slumped to the ground, that was so damp they felt for rocks to keep dry. Some muttering could be heard about large juicy steaks. Maybe "with onions", or "with eggs", or "with oysters". Then silence. The guard squatted with his rifle between his knees.

Daylight woke them. No one had moved. Fallen snow covered the inert bodies, camouflaging them. But the guard was also dusted with snow. He hadn't moved. Squatting there, he had committed the sin of falling asleep on duty. Understanding, no one complained.

After an imaginary breakfast of "bacon and one dozen eggs" and a drink of snow, they reviewed the situation. They decided to keep a small amount of emergency ration of chocolate they had and planned what they'd do, should they meet an enemy patrol; how they'd march mostly by night and hide by day, to avoid detection from the air. And, most importantly, how they would care for their feet. When they came to streams they would wash and massage them. Their very lives probably depended on their feet. They shared around what cigarettes and matches they had, and started out.

Needing food and information, they had to contact a Greek village, their first test of their ability to effect an escape. They couldn't speak Greek. Effendi spoke French, as did some educated Greeks, so he was one of the scouts who first entered a village while the others spread out, under cover, should there be trouble. Germans could be anywhere.

It was on April 19 or 20 that they approached their first village, Spelia, in the mountains. It was typical, built around a square where habitually villagers gathered under trees or in the cafe, the *Kathenion*. This day a large number were gathered. Atypically, a lot of women were there too.

A hush fell as Effendi walked into the square. No doubt the Greeks were considering news from the battlefields, and suddenly this man in the strange uniform had appeared. Was he German?

It soon became a noisy encounter. The rest of the Australian escapees joined in. The confusion didn't end until a red-headed woman appeared. She was able to communicate — she was the schoolteacher and could speak French. She explained the situation to the other villagers before she went to the schoolhouse and came back with a map of Greece and the Aegean. It was, however, a Greek map, with perplexing Greek lettering.

At Spelia they had their first experience of Greek kindness and extreme generosity, if not self-sacrifice. Food appeared — as it would everywhere they went, even if it were merely a piece of bread. Often it meant the Greeks themselves went without. Invariably they were given either *psome* (bread), *teeree* (a partly matured and smelly sheep's cheese), *avgo* (eggs, hard-boiled); *yaoulte* (a kind of yoghurt that was for some "particularly hard on the bowels") or olives.

Very soon they learned there was no paper in Greek villages; neither to wrap the food they are given, nor to use when the alien food ravaged their bowels. Some suffered diarrhoea all the way. The food they wanted to conserve they carried, unwrapped, in the pockets of their jackets.

When they were ready to leave the village, the Greeks excitedly conveyed that they had only to get to the coast and there they would find a submarine waiting for them. Already a mysterious all-knowing grapevine, a kind of underground movement, had automatically sprung into existence, ready to help with information and guides. The submarine promise was to haunt their escape.

After leaving Spelia, it was agreed that to go to the coast, and the submarine, meant traversing an exposed valley where patrolling German aircraft would be able to detect them. So they stuck to the hills and headed south, to try to reach Lamia and the main retreating army. Because they were well in the hills now, they could move by day.

April 20 was to be a long and tiring day. As they passed through some villages they were given the coloured eggs of Easter. Every Easter men remember the coloured eggs they saw in Greece. Especially the red ones, the symbol of Christ's blood. Jack Boorer told me he thought the dye had some preserving quality. That day the men began to exchange their uniforms for Greek clothes. There was the need for disguise. Villages they passed that day were Dogane, Kermenie and Kokorava.

Then their route took them along the shore of long, narrow Lake Voiveis, towards the village of Kalyria, where, they were told, they could get a guide to take them to the coast . . . because there was a submarine there! The men were walking along in single file, admiring the beautiful lake and vowing to return one day. Suddenly they saw, across the lake, that German planes had begun operating from a newly-established air-strip. That was an example of why not only numbers of planes, but speedy efficient organisation gave the Germans such air supremacy in Greece. A plane from the strip must have spotted the long line of men. It came to investigate. Aware of their foolishness, and frightened, the fugitives raced for a large, spreading tree and hugged its trunk for some kind of cover. The pilot swooped down, rose, turned and swooped again several times. He didn't fire. He must have been uncertain of their identity; otherwise they would have been strafed. The hunt for escaping British, and especially Australian troops had begun.

Jack Boorer told me how in the villages the terrified Greeks would tell them what Lord Haw Haw had been broadcasting. Daily he issued warnings. To the Australians he said they knew they were skulking in the olive groves and they would be caught and "castrated". To the Greeks he said they would be shot if they were caught helping the soldiers escape. It is no wonder the Underground was so readily conceived. There was another side to the movement. For the betrayers, the *Pente*, there was instant death or a mysterious accident.

Soon men were feeling the physical strain exacerbated by shortage of food, by diarrhoea and in Effendi's case an infected foot. Some felt anxious, knowing they had all agreed that as many as could were to escape. Those who couldn't keep up were to drop out to avoid jeopardising the successful escape of others. It was their duty, as soldiers, to escape.

C.H., it was observed, showed no signs of strain at this stage. "He was the fittest of them all. He even seemed to be enjoying it," Effendi observed.

On the evening of April 20 at Kalyvia, they got their first guide. He was to take them to another village, Kanalia and thence to the coast — and the submarine! They had been able to obtain some food in Kalyvia, the usual *psome* topped with *teeree*. The prudent ones reserved some, putting it in their pockets.

Their first guide was an unforgettable, wizened old peasant, eighty years of age. At first they had doubts about his usefulness. Until they got onto the tracks. There they couldn't keep up with him. They had to tug at his jacket to indicate he should slow down, so tough, sinewy and quick was the old man. C.H. said, "What age do they retire here?" In the dark the old peasant led them farther into the hills. Their feet began to tell them the country was changing. Tracks disappeared; they had to feel their way through rocky country with their new expertise won in the Greek hills.

Unexpectedly the guide slowed down and began to make gestures. Something was wrong. He stopped. To the horror of the Australians, he cupped his hands and shouted: "*Jobani*, Hi, *Jobani!*"

"This is it," they thought. "He's betrayed us." In his agitation, Effendi wrote the time on his map as 24.30. He should have written 00.30.

What the old Greek had in fact yelled was "Shepherd", because he was lost. As no one answered, they were forced to stop for the night and sleep amongst the sharp, jagged rocks.

The next day, April 21, the party reached Kanalia. In the village square, the tough old Greek, having got his pay, drank a cup of coffee and set out for home immediately.

In the cafe, the Greeks were only too ready to tell the Australian soldiers about the submarine that was waiting for them at the coast, at Volos. But there was a problem: the Germans were also at Volos. The villagers, aware of actual incidents of reprisal, were obviously nervous of their presence, and were clearly relieved when the Aussie soldiers departed . . . with the inevitable present of hard-boiled eggs.

Again, the group avoided the temptation to look for the submarine. They thought it was a myth anyhow. It was better to play safe and keep to their plan of going south to get to the army. The way south, as the Greeks told them, was "the uphill track". But there was an obstacle to the route south. They had to cross the one big road that led into Volos, along which heavy German traffic was moving. On the other side of the road was a flat with little cover. Once beyond the road and the flat, they could get back into the hills, the friendly, secure hills.

Near the road, they waited for darkness to spread out and attempt a crossing when there was a lull in the traffic. They watched the headlights of an approaching convoy. Near Effendi and not far from C.H. and Buck, the head vehicle stopped, leaving its lights on. Germans went to the left and right of the road. It was a comfort stop. One German walked off the road, almost stumbling over Effendi lying flattened out, motionless. "I was nearly soaked," he reported. "It was probably because of the lights that I wasn't seen. You'll note how little concern there was for British planes, that they should leave their lights on."

Over the road, past the dangerous flat and into the hills they fled. They could relax a little but their detailed army map that the New Zealanders had given them was by now redundant and they were relying on the Greek one, a fairly simple classroom map.

They looked out for someone who might act as a guide. A likely looking fellow did appear, bearing on his cap the letters A.A. from which they deduced he was a forestry worker. He led them three and a half thousand feet up the mountain before noon on April 22 in weather that was decidedly warmer. They had neither water nor food. As they walked they crushed under their feet wild thyme that threw up an agonising aroma. Thoughts turned to roast chicken, baked potatoes, *home*. Lumps came to their throats. They exchanged ideas about what they thought the folks at home would be doing now. It was here they used the emergency ration, the chocolate they had kept. Each portion allotted was so small that one man held it in his mouth and let it dissolve.

Almiro, their next destination, was yet another small mountain village, overlooking a grassy, flat valley floor. This they had to cross before attempting to pass between two villages which, they were told, were occupied by the Germans.

At Almiro, during daylight they needed to get a compass bearing. As they prepared to spread out for their routine village approach, a man wearing a suit came along a path. He was asked the usual first question, as they pointed to Almiro. "German *tho*?"

In reply, to their absolute horror, the fellow pulled out a .22 revolver and fired it in the air. Then, in the only English he knew, as well as Greek, he cursed the Germans. He seemed oblivious to any danger of alerting any German who might have been around. C.H. promptly christened him "Hopalong Cassidy".

When he was ready to listen they conveyed to him how desperately thirsty they were. He went away and returned festooned with bottles and water. He was very helpful except for his dangerous habit of reaching for his pistol and cursing loudly every time they spoke the word "German". He said his name was Dimitrion or "Jimino". Charlie still preferred "Hopalong". With Hopalong's help they got their compass reading, ready to tackle the night's task of crossing the grassy flat and then passing between the occupied villages.

When they descended the hill that evening and reached the flat they found the grass had deluded them; it was in fact a swamp. Crossing it in the dark was a nightmare. Sometimes they were up to their armpits in water. Men weakened by illness, lack of food and anxiety were gravely tried. They wondered how they would make it. But once through the swamp and the German-controlled villages, they enjoyed the thrill of success, of pride in their skill. Their compass work, learned so thoroughly in the desert, had preserved them.

By dawn, they were back to some foothills where they sighted a likely looking place. A shed, filled with sweet smelling meadow hay. Gratefully they nestled down for a day's rest, hoping no owner would come along with a pitchfork. One man, not too tired to quip, wondered about where the pitchfork might strike.

The day in the hay, and probably lack of food as well as stress seemed to have dulled Effendi's memory. The date becomes uncertain. There is a dreamlike account of another night in the hills and, as usual, hunger. They heard the sound of bells tinkling. That meant sheep or goats — and possibly milk. The sound led them to shepherds who were preparing cauldrons of milk for cheese-making. In return for warm milk, the Greek shepherds were handed money. They looked at it curiously and returned it. In the same district a householder was offered money for eggs. Similarly it was examined and returned. It was uncertain whether the Greeks were signalling that they didn't want payment or whether in those remote places they did not understand money.

The strain began to take its toll. Athol Bosgard, close to Charlie, who later often mentioned his name, became ill. He said, "I can't keep going." It grieved the others but they stuck to their agreed plan. Those who could, must get out; those who could not keep going were left behind. In case any other escapees were in the area, the group decided on their route before going on so that Bosgard would inform them. Sadly they moved off again.

By April 24, they were getting close to Lamia, north of Thermopylae, where it was known that the withdrawing British force could make a stand, as all defenders of Athens had done, ever since the inspirational Leonidas and his Spartans. Perhaps they'd be able to get through the German lines to their own army and take part in the last stand. That night they lit a fire, high in the hills. They had been able to buy a sheep from a shepherd and risked the fire for some warmth and to give the sheep a bit of a cook, at least.

Into the firelight, to their joyful amazement, walked a man. It was Bosgard. Knowing their route and with some determination, he had been able to catch up. In their hearts the men paid tribute to their comrade for his guts. (Some eighteen months later, Bosgard died in the Owen Stanley Range, New Guinea.)

Effendi noted how Charlie's stamina became more evident. "When so many seemed to be flagging, he seemed to be thriving on the sheer physical effort."

On the eve of Anzac Day, about midnight, after chatting late into the night, they were awakened by a colossal artillery barrage. They could see the flashes from the guns in the direction of Thermopylae. The guns thundered for a few minutes. Then there was silence. The next morning, they learned from a Greek that those had been the last shots fired before the British pulled out. The Germans held the pass.

Had they known it, on April 25 the last of the Australians were being evacuated from the beaches.

Hope fled and spirits sank. For days they had held to the hope of rejoining the main force. What should they do now? Should they retrace their steps north to try to get to Turkey by land, or would they make for the east coast and then try to island-hop to Turkey? They decided to make for Euboea — or Euvoia, as the locals call it. That island looked like a possible springboard to the Aegean.

Nobody was laughing or joking much the day they changed direction and headed for they knew not what. At least walking was easier. Along the tops of hills, the rises and falls are not so steep. When they came to a creek they halted to treat their feet and wash themselves and their shirts.

It turned out to be a day to remember. They were waiting for their shirts to dry a little when a group of Greek girls arrived. They had been studying in Salonika. When Salonika fell, they escaped to Lamia. When Lamia fell, they set out into the hills, where one of the girls had relatives. The girls, understanding the Australians' plight, insisted on giving them their own *psome* and *teeree* to carry with them, in case of emergencies. "Wonderful girls. What spirit," each man voted, not without emotion.

A sylvan scene for a Greek urn, in other times.

The men moved off silently, thinking about their encounter. A few miles farther on Effendi put his hand to his tunic pocket. Something strange. One of the girls had slipped a folded packet of money equivalent to about one pound sterling into the pocket before he put his shirt and tunic on again.

That night, several thousand feet up in the hills, they came to a tiny little stone church, no more than fifteen feet by twelve. Someone had recently been there. A few flames were flickering, not from candles, but from wicks resting in oil-filled glass containers. There was, too, a smell of incense. There they decided to rest. The stone floor grew so bitterly cold, some of the boys lit every possible wick, for a bit of extra warmth. In the soft flickering light, they fell asleep. Who knows what they dreamed of. Girls by a mountain stream?

On April 26 they pushed on urgently towards the coast and their new goal, to secure a boat to take them to Turkey. As they neared the coast they had to be more careful. Villages had to be approached with caution; the Germans could already be in occupation. That day they came to a village a bit larger than usual. A lot of people were gathered, talking loudly and waving their arms about. News had obviously arrived. It could have been about the fall of Greece, or the proximity of the Germans. Effendi, acting as scout as usual, had difficulty in convincing them he was an Australian. Learning his identity, they were nervous of reprisal, and wanted them all to move on quickly. Before leaving, in a small shop where the only food for sale was honey and salted anchovies, he chose a block of candied honey, knowing how everyone was craving for sweet things. Before Effendi left the village, one kind Greek, seeing the state of his boots, hastily obtained pieces of old car tyres to augment the thinning soles.

They were to spend another memorable evening on the 26th. They call it "the night of the miller's hut". They came upon a little stone-and-sod hut, no more than four feet high, straddling a stream. In it a frightened miller sat by candlelight. So terrified was he of Germans, he set his water-powered mill working to cover the noise of talking. While the escapees questioned him for information, a trickle of grain gathered in a vessel. He relaxed after a while and allowed them to sleep in the hut, but he had no spare food. The honey was shared out. For some its effect was such that they had to spend much of the night outside the mill. Dysentry plagued Effendi all the way. Charlie, he observed, escaped this problem.

On the move again next day, they learned the Germans were on the coast. The incredible grapevine also maintained there was a British submarine waiting to pick them up! They were almost beginning to believe it.

Farther on. Another village. Another square and a lively gathering. Feeling a bit lighthearted, the wandering Australians viewed the scene and joked about what would happen if they rammed the priest's stovepipe hat down on his head. They joined the gathering. Then, when they made a move to leave, they were pushed back onto their seats and told, *"Kathiste, kathiste"*. (Sit down.) Again they were afraid they had been betrayed, for usually the villagers were pleased to see them leave. They didn't believe their eyes. Suddenly a number of women appeared bearing bread, cheese, eggs and above all, coffee, black and sickly sweet.

"Leave it to the women's committee to organise things," Charlie said. Apparently he was given to saying this. On this occasion, as Effendi pointed out, the women actually did come into the picture. Charlie! Always so home-conscious. And female-conscious.

Before they left that village they remembered so well, they acquired, of all things, some tins of bully beef which had been taken from an army dump at Lamia, no doubt abandoned by the retreating British. For once they welcomed bully beef. With hope low and a fear they would inevitably "go in the bag" — be captured — some reserves of bully were a consolation.

Eventually they found their way to Pachis, at the coast,

Above: Greek mountain terrain similar to where 6 Division fought.
Below: A loaded donkey similar the one used by 'Woop' Waters for transporting equipment.

*The name's still Charlie* 121

Above: The escape party near Euboea in Greece.
Below L-R: Frederick Chilton, Charlie Green and Bruce Brock.

where they hid during the day in a huge box thorn tree; its branches swept the ground and a man couldn't move without being pierced by a long spike. Not far from the tree was a spring to which they crawled to drink and fill empty water bottles. Near the tree, too, was a mysterious find. On the ground, laid out on a piece of newspaper, were thirty-two black olives! They were never to know who put them there. The olives were divided up and they held a conference. The group, which, except for its nucleus, had changed along the way, with some soldiers joining and others dropping out, had now to split into smaller groups to avoid detection. The Germans were too close now.

Green, Buckley, Bosgard, Honeywell, Brock, Corporal Shanahan, Privates Sanders, Whitton and Schofield, most of whom had been together since April 18 when they escaped up the hill, remained in one group. They intended to get to the island of Euboea.

Others made different plans. One man, against advice, headed back towards a village known to be occupied by Germans. "Don't go that way", he was told. "To hell with the Germans. I'm hungry," he replied. The irony of it. He was the man who daringly joined a German mess queue, allowing the Germans to believe he was under escort, got himself fed and then escaped to the coast. At the coast he was picked up . . . BY A SUBMARINE!

Who would doubt the word of an officer and a gentleman.

Until now, there had been no recognised leader of the group, but it was decided that from then on Charlie was to become responsible for strategy. As Effendi and others have repeatedly said, "he was a born leader". It was automatic. Effendi explained:

> He had an infallible sense of what it was safe to do. At times he would advise something. We would disagree. Invariably he was right. He had another exceptional quality. He could always anticipate difficulty or a problem before it arose and had a solution ready, waiting. Or, he was able to avoid the problem before it arose. It was uncanny. That infallibility was one of the major factors that made him the brilliant leader he was.

On April 30, at midnight, the group were hidden on a beach waiting, as arranged, for a boat or boats to row them across to the lighthouse on Euboea. (They surely could not all have gone in the one trip.) They were there long before the appointed time. When they heard the splash of oars and a keel grating on the sand, they knew the Greeks had once more taken risks to assist them with that "sense of duty" C.H. hailed. They took off silently, the boatman rowing standing up, facing the direction in which he was going. It seemed hours later when they felt the bump as the boat hit the sand. By the time they paid the boatman, there was hardly any money left in their pool.

Once on Euboea, their Greek map was too undefined to be of any help, so they headed for the island's northern shores. At the first village they were very unwelcome and were hurried on their way. "Go to the monastery," the villagers said, pointing in its direction. By now hunger had begun to weaken them considerably. There seemed no end to the effort they must make. The strain was beginning to show "even on the face of Charlie Green". They headed expectantly for the monastery. When they got there they gazed on a beautiful stone building behind forbidding walls. The massive gate was locked. The weary men cursed. Later they learned it was in fact that monastery which had helped to coordinate submarine pick-ups. So the grapevine did know.

Despite their hunger and their exhaustion, they pushed on. At about midday they stopped to rest. Charlie and Buck cut up their pistol holsters and laced them around their boots, where the soles had worn through.

That night, May 1, they were in luck again. They came to a small isolated hut. The shepherd owner invited them in. Inside, he had a fire burning that rekindled their spirits as they sat around it with the shepherd's offering of *teeree* and *yaoulti*. Most of the *teeree* was slipped into their pockets for the road. A flagon of *retsina* appeared too. Only one man stayed awake to finish it off with the shepherd. Some were surprised to find that sleeping on the floor by the firelight was not as comfortable as they would have thought. They had become accustomed to sleeping in the open, where they could make a quick escape into the dark if necessary.

Next morning, they headed downhill to Aidhipsos, a small town lying in a large bay at the top of the island. Unsuspectingly, as they turned a bend in their track they met a narrow road and heard a motor cycle. Germans! Quick thinking sent them diving into some barley growing by the track. The German bike and sidecar passed. With true German discipline, the German cyclist stared stiffly ahead, as did his passenger in the sidecar, holding his *schmeisser* gun across his chest.

They darted across the road and headed for the hills again, where they felt safe. While they looked down on beautiful Aidhipsos, blue-and-white, inviting them back one day, they were surprised by someone who suddenly appeared and addressed them in French. He indicated that if they hid there till evening, he would return with food and assistance to get them off the island.

Warily they waited, spread out defensively and removed from the arranged place. In the dusk, they watched two figures approaching. One was their benefactor. They gathered around as the Greeks lit a fire and began to cook up a tin of broad beans, pods and all, with wild aniseed and olive oil. Then they were given a wonderful spinach pie, bread, olives and cheese — an unbelievable feast.

Getting down to business, they were told where the Germans were and to make for Pili. At Pili they could get a submarine!

Between their present position and Pili there was a wide treeless plain to cross, an uncommon feature in Greece. It was not the lack of cover that bothered them so much as the need to use different leg muscles. Their up-and-downhill muscles, so well developed, were not much help; they found the flat ground hard, painful going. "Even Charlie had to slow down," Effendi said.

Their Greek map did not show the tracks that led to Pili, so they sought guidance in a house. The occupier was a villainous looking old seaman. Charlie said of him: "He'd cut anyone's throat for two bob." Villainous he might have looked, but he gave them tea and set them on the way to Pili, where, he conveyed, there were more Australians, hiding in the scrub near the mine manager's house.

As they headed for Pili, plodding along in a light drizzle, they wondered whom they would find there. To their astonishment and joy, whom should they find but their own CO, Lieutenant Colonel Chilton and his party, comprising Sergeant Dick Smith, Corporal H. Hiddins and Private Tuffy Brown. Sir Fred and C.H. Green had got their parties to the same place by different routes. Was that remarkable coincidence — or that "infallible sense" they both possessed? Colonel Chilton, slight, quiet, scholarly, yet emanating absolute but just authority, led them the rest of the way from Pili. On the way he gathered to him another thirty-four members of the 2/2 Battalion.

A photo taken of the group at Pili on a camera carried by Private Hiddins is in the War Memorial, Canberra. The men's eyes show the ordeal they have been through. They have that strange stare, known as "Anzac eyes" or "the thousand-yard stare of battle". I think Charlie Green's eyes have that stare in the last photos taken of him in Korea.

Recently I was able to talk with Sir Fred Chilton about the escape, getting from him some details that were not in his written account. His memory for most of the incidents is, like Effendi's, still undimmed. The remainder of the story is based primarily on Sir Fred's account, supplemented by Effendi's.

Before the two parties met up, Colonel Chilton's group had similar experiences to Charlie's. They were shot at by German tanks at Tempe; they escaped into the hills; headed south east; wandered through the hills, sustained and guided by the local Greeks. They crossed the Volos Road, swarming with Germans, traversed the difficult swamp and were rowed to Pili. Colonel Chilton was having a wash in a creek in the hills near the mine when one of his men came to him, saying, "Some of our chaps have turned up here, sir."

While they were hiding, Greek people sent food up. This was organised by the courageous, self-sacrificing Greek family of John Mourtzakis, the mine manager. Luckily he spoke English. A friend of his, Dr Hatzis, would on occasion walk miles from another village to assist in negotiating with boatmen to take the Australians to Turkey. At Smyrna, Colonel Chilton expected he could get a substantial amount of money from the British consul to pay a boatman. According to Effendi, who had post-war contact with the Mourtzakis family, some reprisals were taken by the Germans on both the families Mourtzakis and Hatzis for assisting escapees. Colonel Chilton later gave assistance to a migrant member of the Mourtsakis family, now living in Melbourne. Sir Fred, forever grateful, has himself been back to Pili.

A boat was eventually secured. At 11 pm on May 9, a wet, gusty night, they boarded their small boat. Mrs Mourtsakis saw them off, giving them food and tearfully wishing them good luck — *"Thias Kalos"*.

After all the talk about submarines, it did occur to some men on that dark wet night that they might encounter one, but that it might very well be German instead of one of the mythical ones the Greeks kept talking about.

At Skopelos, where they nosed in next morning, to spend the day in hiding, they caught and killed a sheep. That might have been the one that Charlie used to remember. For Colonel Chilton "it was the toughest meat I've ever tasted".

The next night's journey brought them at "picanniny daylight" to an uninhabited island, Skandura. There they rationed out some of Mrs Mourtzakis' bread and some of the bully beef they had held in reserve, at the rate of one tin to four men.

It was at Skyros, the next island they reached, that they ran into trouble. The Germans were there. This was too much for the boatman. He landed them, took off and did not return. With him went their reserves of food and money.

They spent the day hiding in a marble quarry, where workers in ancient times had created an underground cistern to provide water. In the heat of the day the quarry was like a furnace but there was plenty of time to study the beauty of the marble. Not far from where they were hidden, a couple of men who ventured out of the quarry looking for food found Rupert Brooke's tomb in an olive grove.

While trying to find another boat, they met another sixteen escaping soldiers. Most were 2/2 men, including Sergeant Pierce. Others were New Zealanders. Apparently the New Zealanders had secured the only boat left on the island. They were willing to take everyone. Altogether now there were twenty men. However, the boatman, when he turned up, said he couldn't take all of them. The only solution was to draw lots. Those who lost the draw would undoubtedly be interned, eventually. Knowing this, the 2/2 men all said that Colonel Chilton should escape, so they fixed the draw, even though he demanded that he take his chance like all the others. In the end, the sympathetic Greek said he would take them all. They crowded aboard cautiously, placing themselves so that those men still wearing uniform would be least conspicuous. There was only one more island to hide out on during the day — Antipsara — and then they should be able to make it to the safety of neutral Turkish waters. There, however, they knew they might be interned.

It was a long run to Antipsara and they knew they could not make it before daylight. At 5 am on the morning of May 14, with Antipsara in sight, a German bomber suddenly dropped out of the sky. Blankets were pulled over crouching bodies, huddled anxiously waiting for the swish of bombs as the plane skimmed over them. The Greek stood at the wheel silently crossing himself. Every man held his breath. Nothing happened. Then the plane took another run, to machine-gun them as they believed. Again nothing happened. The plane flew off. "It will always be a mystery whether the pilot turned a blind eye," said Sir Fred.

On Antipsara there was no shelter and they had no food. After landing the boatman left; all day they feared he would not come back. Colonel Chilton remembered that he borrowed a Bible from one of the soldiers, Private Fuller, and read *Exodus*. Some men drew a draught-board in the sand and played with pebbles. It was one of the longest days of their lives: hungry, thirsty and possibly marooned.

Dark came. All was still and quiet as ears strained for the sound of their boat. Suddenly they heard the most wonderful noise — the put-put-put of their craft. That evening they set out again for what they hoped was their last night at sea. "Could they make it?" was what they each wondered. North of Chios, which was occupied by Italians, they ran out of fuel and could not resort to sail because of strong headwinds. The skipper changed course. Most of them had fallen asleep, Effendi reports but they were awakened by a flashing light. When they realised it was a lighthouse they relaxed.

At dawn on May 15 they found that the skipper, using sail, was passing a small promontory and was headed towards a village. Men say some shots were fired, or a shot. Whichever, it was a warning. They had arrived at Mordhan, a Turkish fort, where a jetty ran into the sea.

Turks were there when they landed. They bundled them out of the boat, confiscated their weapons and took them to a mosque in the village where they were sheltered. On the way to the village, Colonel Chilton remembered, one man collapsed from thirst and hunger, demonstrating their dire need for food and water. Not long after, a string of Turkish soldiers came from the fort with food. The Turks had sought a medical opinion and staggered the supply. After the meagre first course and during the long wait for the next, Charlie is reported to have said: "Right. Now bring out the dancing girls and a pound of steak!"

Colonel Chilton stressed that once the Turks learned they were Australian they were well-treated. Colonels came down from Smyrna to interview them. The men were checked over by the medical officer; they were given food and beer and a barber was provided to tidy them up.

Colonel Chilton, using French, had an interesting exchange with one of the Turkish colonels who had come from Smyrna. The Colonel, a veteran of World War I, explained that he had fought the Australians at Gallipoli and again in the Sinai. He showed them a wound to confirm this. Even so, he was keen to convey how much he respected the Australian soldiers, "Brave!" he said. Colonel Chilton conveyed that the respect was mutual. The Turks decided to put the Australians on a boat for Smyrna and there they would be billeted at the Army barracks until an official decision was made about them.

At the barracks in Smyrna the Australians were wonderfully treated by the Turks. The men, with money given them by the British Consulate, could buy from the mess the beer and cigarettes they had missed for weeks. Often the Turks would not allow them to pay but insisted on treating them.

In Smyrna, eighteen more 2/2 Battalion men turned up, making forty-eight in all, gathered again under Colonel Chilton's command. It seems quite remarkable that so many independent decisions led groups to Smyrna.

The Turks, ignoring the international rules of war, instead of interning them provided them with a means of completing their escape. Each soldier was fitted out with civilian clothes and a bag of rations. Charlie, whose boots were worn out, could not be fitted with civilian shoes and indeed they had trouble finding at short notice any boots large enough. He often laughed about this.

On May 18, the Australians were put on a train at Smyrna for a three-day journey to Alexandretta. This meant they were to enjoy more travel, through the spectacular Taurus Mountains, precipitous and snow-capped. Travelling through the plateau of central Turkey, where the grasslands were studded with grazing cattle made the likes of Charlie very homesick. During that memorable journey, Turks, guessing their identity, showered them with food.

At Alexandretta, on May 20, they were put on a Norwegian tanker, the *Alcides*, headed for Port Said. It was crowded with a couple of hundred escaping Norwegians, so the Australians were billeted on the bare deck, blazing hot by day and cold by night. On May 24, they landed in Port Said to be put on a train for Julis, Palestine. On May 25, they were "back home" at Julis, the camp where they started in 1940.

When Colonel Chilton marched his forty-eight men into camp there was a reception party of Second Seconders to greet them. They were mostly those who had been evacuated from

Greece on April 25, as well as a few escapees... the sad remnants of a fine Battalion, mauled in battle. In their incomparable way, they communicated their joy, their sorrow and their banter. They shouted out the old familiar call: "You'll be sorry!"

Everyone understood.

NOTE:
Maps used during the escape were donated to the Australian War Memorial and should be available to future researchers through the Collections Curator.

# 10
# After Greece — "A home thought"

> The tide of battle ebbs away,
> but will return
> and the green-draped caverns will resound again
> to the bitter drums of war.
> Now, in this pause,
> in which the very world seems to suspire,
> the soldier slips his safety-catch,
> eases his stiffened limbs
> and, relaxing all but the well-trained brain's
>     unsleeping eye,
> unbars the door to his imprisoned mind.
>
> *Soldiers Look Homeward* by Peter Middleton

After Greece there came another period of inaction for the men of the 2/2 Battalion. It was a period charged with emotion, with grieving for the dead, the missing and for their wounded Battalion.

It was in this emotional period that Charlie Green wrote his fateful letter to me. Another step down a long road, to lead him still farther from his roots.

Most escaping parties, leaderless, seemed to know what to do to get back to their unit at Julis, a testimony to their ingenuity, training and discipline. Discipline — that complex and hard-earned quality. Some took up to three months to get back. Some died on the way from typhoid. One man walked all the way through Turkey. It took him eleven months.

When the count was eventually taken, only about 300 originals were left in the 2/2. Those 300 became true veterans, with the inevitable marks of battle: the silent tongue, the blank stare, the soul's dark spot and the deep well of tears. What irked was that they had been battered in a campaign that was ill-conceived and then bungled. That's what had happened to their fathers. And even when they did shine in battle, as in Bardia, their achievement was belittled by the British press. Between May and June 1941, morale plummeted to its lowest ebb. The late Sir John Dunlop, writing as recently as 1982, said they "lost confidence in the judgment of higher command because of being given fronts too wide to defend, and negligible weapons or support against the might of the Panzers and the Luftwaffe". It was a view no doubt generally held at the time.

But the spirit of the 2/2, like that of most great fighting units, was immortal and unique. It had taken on its own indestructable essence through men submerging their identity in that of the Battalion. In battle they "fought like tigers for it". Eventually, after rest and recuperation, given new blood by reinforcements — disdained though they might be — the Battalion retained its identity and its power, so that it was ready to answer the next bugle call.

The next call came in New Guinea in 1942, on the testing Owen Stanley track. There the Battalion was battered again, this time to shreds, on another impossible mission. At the end of that campaign, unarguably their worst, a mere seventy-odd men walked out of the jungle. Yet the morale was not so low as it was in 1941. Jo Gullett, in *Not as Duty Only*, accounts for this indomitability, that engenders the "state of grace" he talks about. He said, a battalion reaches its full state of grace "if among other things it is near but never quite mutinous. We were that in New Guinea. It became a matter of our belief that MacArthur was mad, was asking of us the impossible, but that we would show the so and so that Australians could do it."

A foolish Army decision that other ranks — ordinary ranks — should get a mere one or two days' leave after the Greek campaign didn't help morale. Soldiers registered anger. Some expressed their feeling in an understandable way: they went absent without leave. Was this undisciplined? It seems their understanding and caring CO, Chilton, didn't think so, from the way he pleaded their cause. This is recorded in the War Diary. Eventually, in July, more generous leave was given.

In the meantime there were some outbreaks of rebellious behaviour. Discipline is not something that can be automatically demanded, least of all from Australian soldiers. It arises from giving them a fair go; from knowing the delicate balance between demanding too much and too little, between the important and the trivial.

In Woop Waters' letters home at this unsettled time there's a lot of grief and a lot of anger. On hearing leave was "knocked back", Woop wrote: "What sort of treatment is this?" He mourned "the old faces missing". There was a hint of rebellion and certainly no remorse for having "shot through", "pulled up the kellick" (gone a.w.l.) and for being "put under open arrest when I got back". During this period he played two-up with extraordinary intensity as he admitted in letters that became strangely confessional: "While I am playing I watch the spinner as though my life depends on it." At another emotional time he expressed his resentment of "reos" (reinforcements). It is fairly characteristic of originals, at any time, to give reos a rough time — until they prove themselves. At the cost of a few bloody noses or some wicked practical jokes, no doubt. Woop, from the stance of a veteran, refers to the reos as "being blooded". In calmer mood, with a weary and moving sadness he wrote: "The rude new men are not the same as the ones gone." Contained in this may be the explanation of his earlier expressed resentment. Reos replace the good old hands, because they have been killed. Then, in this same emotional period, a new leitmotiv enters Woop's letters. "You've wondered why I've changed. Perhaps one day I'll be able to tell you all about it."

I doubt if that day of telling ever came for Woop, or for any other veteran. It didn't come for Effendi, until forty-two years after Greece.

Some of "the old faces missing" were Bill Sullivan, killed in battle, and Jack Ulrick, Bill Wright and Ron Pattemore — all prisoners of war. Lofty Stafford, so unforgettable, had gone "in the bag" too. That left his mates wondering how the rigid German mind would cope, if it did. I wish we knew. But there were familiar faces back in Julis as well. Jack Reedy was back in the Q store, and his "wog" dog, Bobby Tobruk, was miraculously back from Greece too. Jack always stuttered, and now his stuttering was worse than ever.

Someone asked him why this was so. He said: "Mmmy fffather ttttold me once thththat if I eeever hhhad a ggggood fright it would ggggo away. It's wwwworse thththan ever." It is common knowledge that the dog, Bobby, had changed too. He took a liking to the booze, Jack Boorer told me. So did Woop, who, he confessed, became "quite a booze artist".

Bobby was Reedy's comfort and consolation. "Jeez, he loved that dog. We all did." One night there was an incident involving a refo, still innocent about Battalion ways and Battalion identities. Bobby was drinking his beer, as usual. The bloke kicked him. "All hands leapt to. Boong. It was on. They nearly killed that bloke." A lot of steam to let off.

Not long after coming out of Greece, Jack Reedy and C Company lost their mate, Bobby, when he was hit by an Arab truck. Like the strange chance of some soldiers who survive several battles to die in some unheroic way, so it was with Bobby Tobruk. Jack Boorer was moved at the memory: "He was a little dog who led a man's life." Watty Barratt wrote a diggers' epitaph for Bobby. As such it is a masterpiece of the laconic. It gives, too, a lively picture of the army routine the soldier dog shared with his mates, and reveals the often unsuspected sentimental streak in the tough Australian digger:

> He was only a stump-tailed poodle,
> He had no pedigree,
> He was born in a Libyan dust storm
> Near an Itie RAP.
> He would do his share of line guard,
> And share of picket as well,
> And never a crime had Bobby
> And never went AWL.
> He saw his share of fighting,
> And fought like a soldier, too,

For we taught him concealment and cover
In the barracks of Mersa Matruh.
He barked at the planes of Olympus,
And fought in the thick of the van,
The boys of C Coy loved him
And voted young Bobby a man.
For Bobby was born to battle,
Though with none of a battler's luck,
And he who dodged dive-bombers
Had to die 'neath an Arab truck.
So we gave him a soldier's funeral,
'Twas all that we could do,
For Bobby Tobruk was a cobber of ours
And helped us see it through.

In Palestine they were not getting much news of the war, as usual. Had the 2/2 been able, it would have been fighting in Syria with the 2/3 and the 2/5, who, because they came out of Greece more intact, were attached to the 7 Division, AIF.

The world was not very aware of the Syrian campaign. Eyes were on Russia. On June 22, 1941, Hitler attacked Russia, a campaign that finally cost Russia some 20 to 22 million dead. June-July 1941 saw things getting worse. Rommel was master in Africa. That was read by Churchill as the need for another change of generals and Auchinleck got the unenviable job. Russia was besieged. There was worse to come.

If the world news didn't help cheer the 2/2 Battalion, a sudden move on August 18, 1941 did. They were sent to El Arish, near the Egyptian border, right on the Mediterranean coast. They had the job of guarding the railway line and resisting a possible paratroop attack. Their other task was the now familiar one of policing the Arabs, who had intensified their raids for weapons and ammunition.

El Arish is a beautiful oasis. Once Napoleon bivouaced there. In World War 1 the Light Horse made its HQ at El Arish because of its natural water supply. Many glowing descriptions have been given of the majestic palms dominating a typical "wog village", of the soft sandy beach and the enticing blue water. Of how 2/2 Battalion swam and sunbaked and grew strong again.

It may be because it only happened once in El Arish, or it may have been because the 2/2's beloved band was involved, that one night there is well remembered — the night the bomb fell.

Army bands don't function simply to play inspiring music on the parade ground. According to a tradition dating back to Waterloo — where so much army tradition seems to have been born — bandsmen act as stretcher bearers during battle, a job as dangerous as a rifleman's. On a railway embankment close to the barracks, one beautiful moonlit September night, the band, led by Albert Lee, set themselves up on the railway dais to give a concert. They were playing a medley from *Bitter Sweet*. Romantic music for a romantic night. Suddenly, over the strains of "Love will find a way" the dreaded drone of a plane was heard. "The railway bridge, the train nearby", they all thought, and scattered as one. They say it must have been an Italian plane. It flew high and missed its target.

Charlie's fatal impulse. That's what I would call Charlie's spur-of-the-moment decision to write to me about two years after our first brief contact in my father's shop. It undoubtedly determined the course of his life and possibly his death. Why did he decide to write? It might have been a romantic, balmy El Arish evening that turned his mind to girls; it might have been a mere flash of memory. When I eventually asked him, he said: "I remembered the little girl who sold me my pen." It might have been fate.

Charlie's first letter was not destroyed, as so many of the hundreds he wrote were. On one tour of duty, when we were numbering our letters, I remember marking "167". He wrote daily. His first letter is dated September 18, 1941 — three days before my eighteenth birthday:

> Please do not faint or do anything drastic when you see who the author is.

Perhaps you will be wondering why I decided on writing to you after being away so long. Well tonight I happen to be in a position where I have nothing at all to do and I couldn't think of a better way to fill in time than to write a few letters.

Well, Olwyn, a lot of water has passed under the bridge since I last saw you, or for that matter anyone at home.

If my memory serves me correctly the last time I saw you was my last day of final leave when I had a shave at the shop.

No doubt you have been kept rather well-informed of our moves by other people that are over here so I will not bore you too much about where I've been and what I have seen . . . [Speaking of the Greek campaign] all weren't as fortunate as myself and a number of casualties resulted. Very hard luck indeed about Bill S and Jack U; both were excellent soldiers.

How's Ulmarra? I couldn't imagine it changing. I have heard of several marriages, deaths and births etc, but that is about all. Do you still play tennis? How I'd love to be able to put on a pair of "creams" and have a hit of cricket or tennis — it will come some day, I suppose.

We are at present camped very close to the sea and needless to say we do much bathing and sun-baking and everyone has a lovely colour up.

I hope this hasn't been too much of a shock for you. I must close and would be glad to hear from you some time.

    Yours truly,
    Chas H. Green

Charlie's letter was addressed to Coldstream Street, Ulmarra. Everyone knew everyone in Ulmarra. Someone brought it to me in the store where I was working.

I was no longer working in my father's shop. Because of man-power shortage, I'd been offered a man's job in the Clarence River Pioneer Co-operative Dairy Company in Ulmarra. I was the sole employee, acting as jack-of-all-trades: manager through to storeman. To the Co-op manager's credit, I received a man's pay.

I've never forgotten the store and the butter factory adjoining. I can remember vividly the smell — that creamy smell when I walked over the wet concrete platform in the butter factory, where cans of thick yellow cream were clanged around by men in rubber boots. The store itself was no more than a wooden shed.

We stocked everything a farmer might need. In the back of the store were bags of fertiliser, potatoes, corn, sugar, flour, onions. Of all the smells in the store, the blood and bone at the back wafted up to the front, where I usually stood scooping something or other into brown paper bags, and stacking them on open wooden shelves: rows and rows of sugar, flour, dates ... I remember the dates particularly, probably because I nicked a few, and dunked them in condensed milk. A luxury snack as rationing was already emptying the shelves of lots of things, especially confections. My customers were mostly farmers, in felt hats and flannel shirts, either too old to go to the war, or exempted because they were in a protected industry.

I am going to tell the truth. I was doing a man's job; it was well paid, yes. But I was doing it because I hadn't the courage to join the Forces when I turned nineteen. I had a great fear of war. I am a fearful person. Fear of violence of any kind has plagued me all my life. I think it started at school, when boys had fights. There's one sickening one I can't erase, between older youths. The terrifying fierceness of it, their oaths, the thumps, the blood. Even the memory can shock my body.

That's why I was imprisoned in myself in the store, in Ulmarra, the day Charlie's letter arrived, even though I wished I could have been elsewhere — doing something big. Like the servicemen. I looked at the envelope, the strange writing and then the signature, the formal "Chas H. Green". I felt the thud in my chest, just as I did that day I saw him in my father's shop when I was sixteen. Tall, handsome, exciting and different looking in his smart officer's uniform. And he had remembered ME.

I suppose that was when I fell in love. Not with the man but with a fantasy. Suddenly the world seemed full of miracles.

# 11
# Syria to Ceylon —
# "A strange interlude"

> Where Hiram felled his cedar-wood,
>   Where Saladin rode by:
> In sorrow and in solitude
>   Grave-hallowed mountains lie.
>
> *Song out of Syria* by R.S. Byrnes

"The strangest interlude of the War." "A nonsense." That is what has been said about 2/2 Battalion's period in Syria in 1941, and in Ceylon in 1942. Charlie Green and his co-author, Don Fairbrother, describe their stint in Syria in "Syrian Interlude" in *Nulli Secundus Log*. It is a wry, witty article showing a new, worldly note I am not sure whether to ascribe to Charlie or to Don.

The correspondence begun between Charlie and me in 1941 continued until he came home about eighteen months later. From the beginning we found it easy to talk on paper. We laid down the basis for our relationship in letters, where we conducted much of it during the next four years of the war. I do regret, now, burning so many of them. It was an uncomprehending act, which certainly didn't achieve the obliteration I desired. Early, we exchanged photos. I sent the most flattering one of myself I could obtain. The one he sent me, a sepia studio portrait, is etched in my mind. I looked at it for a long time before it became flesh. So I know every detail. His head is slightly turned, yet I look into his soft, brown eyes; his skin is smooth and clear; his short-cut, straight, dark hair grows into a widow's peak; there's the scar I can feel on his lip where the horse kicked him once. And there is the little smile lurking. Always ready to smile, wryly, knowingly, caressingly. In the photo, he was impeccably turned out in his officer's uniform. As I mostly remember him. Ignoring the unthinkable reality: his face tense, the boom of guns and the smoke and dust of battle . . . ignoring, too, the other Charlie, the farmer.

Charlie and Don's "Syrian Interlude" is solely about 2/2 Battalion's experience. It doesn't give an account of how Syria was captured from the Vichy French, who had been in control after France fell in June 1940.

At the behest of Churchill (and Australia's then Prime Minister, Menzies) Syria was invaded on June 8, 1941. It had to be captured before Hitler got there and threatened Palestine, the British "lifeline" Suez, and the oilfields of Iraq and Iran. Wavell, the commander in the East, hard-pressed by the loss of Greece and Crete and Rommel's victories in Africa, unwillingly mustered a mere "scratch" force for Syria. In the van he had put the Australian 7 Division, led by Sir John Lavarack, still unblooded because Blamey had declared them unready for Greece and Crete. Attached to 7 Division were two 6 Division Battalions that had not been badly damaged in Greece: 2/3 and 2/5 Battalions. Supporting the Australians were Indian and Free French units.

The Australian Labor Party once again objected to Australians being led by British Generals when their own General, Blamey, could have — indeed should have — done the job. The general in charge of the Syrian invasion was none other than Major General Maitland Wilson, "Jumbo", who led the Greek campaign without distinction — and who did not like Australians.

Sir John Lavarack did not like the battle plan. Right though Lavarack proved to be, the British ignored him and with their customary highhandedness proceeded with their plan, which ran the invading force into grave trouble. Instead of the little resistance that British intelligence had guaranteed, the Australians were to meet deadly, accurate artillery fire that cost heavy casualties. It took five weeks to capture Syria. The Syrian campaign has never had adequate media attention. It is said to have been pushed under the carpet; it was too embarrassing at the time. French were fighting French and allies were fighting allies. In his article Charlie called it "fratricide".

The AIF's 7 Division deserves its share of honour. At the time it was overshadowed by the famous 9 Division in the more spectacular war in the Western Desert. If it were not for the Rats of Tobruk, the brilliant Rommel might have conquered Egypt — which doesn't bear thinking about. That war of battling and racing tanks in the desert waste land, engaging one British General after another to get the better of the heroic Rommel, is the stuff of movies and war games. So was the advance into Syria, had it been so well recorded.

During the advance into Syria, the ingenious Australians, natural bushmen, needed to revert to the skills of their legendary fathers, the Light Horsemen. To effect reconnaissances, to protect flanks and to patrol generally, the Australians mounted a corps of horsemen, but without plumes, that became renowned as the "Kelly Gang".

Syria capitulated on July 11. A little while before that, Lieutenant Roden Cutler and Private J.H. Gordon won the Victoria Cross — the highest of honours. And towards the end of July, Wavell, a skilful soldier, a poet, a writer — yet not good enough — was relieved of his command. Churchill wasn't satisfied. Wavell wasn't dashing enough to provide the resounding victory Churchill so desperately wanted to boost people's morale. Sir Claude Auchinleck got the burdensome job.

Once again, one gets the impression the Australians did what was expected of them: to serve under the British flag and not to be singled out for any special mention. But the British were ever ready to criticise. Two serious allegations were made by Major General Spears and Major General Maitland Wilson about Australian soldiers in Syria. Australian Army investigations found the allegations to be "libellous" and unfounded. Maitland Wilson had declared that he was going to give Australians a sentence of "penal servitude" that might serve as an example. It goes to show how deeply ingrained was the prejudice against the so-called "undisciplined" Australians.

It was October before 2/2 Battalion and the rest of 6 Division got to Syria — to chip stone.

Charlie's and Don's article begins with their departure from languorous El Arish:

> ... when in late October the convoys began to roll north there was the usual sense of excitement in the prospect of a new land.
>
> But visions of surfing at Beirut and lounging among the Lebanon Cedars were quickly dispelled as the Battalion turned northeast from Haifa. It threaded its way through the mountain roads to the Damascus plains and came to rest near the village of Qatana. Once again we had the pleasure of meeting some of the cream of the British Infantry, for the Battalion took over from the 2 Battalion, Black Watch. The hand-over took a couple of days and for a period we had the pleasure of entertaining the Black Watch rear party officers in our mess — where many stories and experiences were related over the Scotch.
>
> After the shadows of the palms of El Arish, and the sea breezes which tempered the otherwise hot desert sands, the Qatana area, dry, rocky and barren, had little attraction for us. We had to console ourselves with the fact that age-old places such as Damascus, Beirut, could now be personally explored.

Why were the men of 6 Division in Syria after it had been won? The British, obsessive as ever about the oilfields and Egypt, wanted a defence line across Syria. Along the line, 6 Division had to build two defence positions: Qatana and the Gap.

Building the Gap position was 2/2 Battalion's job. This entailed chipping an elaborate defence position out of bare rocks, by hand, with picks. It also meant laying thousands of yards of wire and erecting various section posts where a group of men could hold out for days. Each Battalion company was camped in an isolated position close to their allotted job in the bleak, rocky hills. For a while they were no longer soldiers, they were navvies, chiselling away at the stone. General Blamey approached Auchinleck, complaining that navvy work was no proper use for a famous fighting unit that at least should be training. Auchinleck was persuaded to employ locals to do the digging.

Lord Haw Haw, who had hounded the men through Greece, started taunting them again, in broadcasts directed at them personally. He told them they were digging the tank traps the wrong way. He also asked them to keep the Nissan huts warm for when the Germans arrived to occupy them.

War histories refer to the boredom and isolation of the Battalion's role in Syria. Each company, in turn, went for a period of garrison duty to barracks near Damascus. There, according to Charlie in "Syrian Interlude" the boys discarded their dungarees and donned uniforms to appear in their true light, "big, bronzed *Australien*" before "the mademoiselles" of Damascus, in the oldest city in the world. (The War Diary noted an increase in VD.) British complaints about Australian unruliness may not have been altogether unfounded. The War Diary records that some 6 Division men did in fact rough up some Frenchmen in Damascus. There was no explanation of the possible provocation.

What Charlie Green described as the typical Middle East problem, thieving by the natives, was as bad in Syria as in Palestine. Someone described it "as a kind of war". An incident that illustrates the problem was recorded in the War Diary. It was Charlie himself who wrote the report. He, as OC of B Company, had to lead a search into a village suspected of thieving. They recovered a stock-pile that C.H. said "looked like Paddy's Markets". There were "guns, hand-grenades, bayonets, shovels, respirators, clothing, cable, etc".

Individuals are rarely singled out for mention in the War Diary, yet Charlie was mentioned for an article he wrote on "Mountain Warfare". This indicates that his talent for tactics was coming into prominence.

There's one Syrian story about Charlie that is told every Anzac Day; at least every man in 2/2 Battalion has heard it.

"Curly" was a reinforcement in Syria. He committed the grave offence — a very grave one, according to the Army — of losing a piece of equipment, for which he had to go before the OC of B Company, Charlie Green. Curly's punishment wasn't loss of pay, cancellation of leave, or time in the boob. He got 500 lines: "I must not lose my respirator." Curly still exclaims, incredulously, "I must be the only bloke in the Army who ever got lines. It could be a record for Guinness's."

I was curious. I met a platoon commander of Charlie's from B Company and quizzed him. He said Charlie had some definite ideas on discipline at the time. He told Dick Smith: "I don't like criming a man. You can't make soldiers out of them in the boob."

In October 1941, Australia got a new Prime Minister. John Curtin had definite ideas where the AIF should be: in Australia, preparing to defend their own country against what he perceived as the great threat of Japan, not chipping stone in the hills of Syria.

Who could forget that announcement on December 7, when Curtin's fears were realised? The voice on the radio said: "We interrupt this broadcast to bring you a special news bulletin. The Japanese have attacked Pearl Harbour." The Americans were at war. And we were well and truly at war.

Not many people realise how close invasion of Australia was in 1942. The fall of Singapore, thought to be impossible, changed history. It marked, it is said, the end of the British Empire. Australia was forced to turn to America (as Curtin in his famous speech announced) for its survival. Complacency and ineptness left Singapore "naked", unable to conduct a jungle war. As a consequence, Australian's 8 Division, AIF, was sealed off there for the rest of the war, captives in barbarous Japanese prisoner-of-war camps. Before Singapore surrendered, 1789 Australians died. Of the 16,000 taken prisoner, only one third were to survive the unspeakable horrors of Changi and the Burma Railway. But all that and more were yet to come: the bombing of Darwin, the shelling by Japanese midget submarines in Sydney Harbour, and the Japanese driving almost to Port Moresby, at Australia's front door.

In Syria, in December, the men of 2/2 Battalion were getting ready for Christmas. One big change had occurred. It is traumatic for a Battalion to lose a revered leader. Though every man regretted the departure of Lieutenant Colonel F.O. Chilton, awarded a DSO and promoted to Brigadier, they were lucky to have in his place one of their own promoted to that hallowed of roles. The new man, "Boss" Edgar, was a contrast to the courtly Chilton. He was bluff, in the Wootten style. And, like each of his predecessors, he was a first-rate leader.

For Christmas 1941 they vowed they would make amends for the previous one; then, "like kangaroo dogs" huddled in their pits, they had waited to go into Bardia. Now cold winds blowing off Mt Hermon were beginning to promise a white Christmas. C.H. relates how men concocted "strange brews of rum punch" and how officers "arranged with some difficulty a night at the French club . . . one could hardly forget the manner in which a vigorous bun fight ensued during dinner and the horrified looks given us by the more circumspect, distant French officers". (And I can confidently state that C.H. would have been throwing buns as vigorously as any.)

On New Year's Day, "Syrian Interlude" reports there was a big gymkhana at which one of C.H.'s B Company platoons (Dick Smith's) "won a cup large enough to hold sufficient rum to warm the whole platoon". The wind and rain that began that day developed into a raging sixty-two mph blizzard that lasted forty-eight hours, ferocious enough "to disturb an arctic explorer". It was the largest fall for twenty years at that rocky outpost. "Man, beast and vehicle were alike grounded; our world stood still. Communications ceased to function. The task of defeating frost-bite and hunger was paramount. We have vivid recollections of battling through a howling gale, stung by driving snow, of icicles which promptly appeared to glue the eyelids to blindness. Mittens and balaclavas caked with ice combined to give us an uncouth, ferocious appearance. Crawling on hands and knees to dodge the wind, feeling forward inch by inch as the only means of progress — thus were the rations issued and tots of rum delivered."

Another soldier remembered looking out of his tent on January 4, which dawned calm. All that could be seen was a glistening white coat over the rocky, unpostcard-like wilderness. One thing stuck out of the snow. The roof of a privy. With typical ingenuity, some soldiers confiscated it. On the privy roof they joyfully tobogganed down the slopes.

That Christmas, as C.H. wrote, "the Jap problem had no sense of urgency for us — we were far away in another theatre of war". Had they but known it, by the next Christmas many of those merry men would be dead.

Their strange interlude in Syria was nearly over, as they realised when British relief forces began to arrive to man the rocky fortress that was never attacked. They assumed they were going home.

First they went to Beit Jirja in Palestine; they were given leave to Tel Aviv and jabbed with needles — both warning signs. A big party was held in the officers' mess at Beit Jirja, reported in the War Diary as a "sad" farewell party. Every officer who had ever served in 2/2 Battalion was invited. So were nurses. And a band was hired, to make it a memorable adieu to the Middle East.

On March 7, 2/2 Battalion found themselves yet again at El Kantara, where they had disembarked in 1940 and whence they crossed over to Egypt later that year on their way to meet the Italians. This time? No one knew. They were ferried across the canal and marched to Kabrit, by the Bitter Lakes. After two days there they were transported to Port Suez and put on the *Orontes*. On March 11 they sailed for a destination unknown. Instead of going home they were diverted. They were to experience another strange interlude. Lieutenant W.S. Ward tells about it in *Nulli Secundus Log*. He named the article, appropriately, "Stand To".

After an uneventful but cramped squeamish trip across the Indian Ocean, the troops sighted what they thought was a tropical atoll, a fringe of white sand separating blue sea from a clump of palms. Nearer, they realised they were approaching land. Then they saw a huge sign: *Ceylon for Good Tea*. Once again they were in Colombo. This time a band played to welcome them; they had come as defenders.

Their next temporary home in Ceylon was Horana. The camp site was in the middle of a rubber plantation. Once again there was work to do, preparing defences against an expected invasion, this time from the Japanese.

Churchill, Machiavellian like, was determined that at least Britain would survive. Australia's peril notwithstanding, the AIF went to Ceylon. Curtin, who had stood up to Churchill, couldn't get the AIF home to defend Australia. A compromise was reached. Churchill promised to send 9 Division home, but according to the deal, two Brigades of the 6 Division should be diverted to Ceylon, even more critical to Britain after the fall of Singapore. At that time Churchill had no other troops to send there to repel an expected Japanese invasion from Burma. Part of the deal was that the Americans would provide a division of troops for the defence of Australia. As it turned out, 9 Division did not get home until February, 1943, after the crisis for the fate of Australia had passed. The Rats were critical for the battle against Rommel. The Australians were intended to defend south-west Ceylon, where a Japanese invasion force could have been expected to land. The only other defenders were a few British troops in the north of the Island.

2/2 Battalion had the task of constructing a defence line "east from Colombo and south to the Bentola River". Charlie's B Company was to defend the bridge at Kalutra over the Kalu Ganga River:

> This was a big bridge about 250 yards long which crossed a mud flat covered with mangrove trees in the centre. There was also a railway bridge running alongside it. Kalutra is on the coast and is an attractive native village, it had a club with tennis court and other amenities. The Government Agent had a nice residence on a small hill overlooking the river. Unfortunately, his garden was turned into a defensive position dotted with weapon pits. In order to secure an adequate field of fire for weapons, it was necessary to clear a great deal of timber and in many cases a lot of the houses would have to be demolished. The fire lanes through the timber were easily cleared, but a very accurate check had to be kept on all trees cut down — their type, map of reference, and whose property they were on. This was most difficult as fences were non-existent. It was quite easy to credit Mr Periera with an

areca nut tree, when, in fact, it belonged to Mr Fernando . . . It is on record that one tree had more than 120 owners.

Fortunately for the locals, the Australians marked the buildings that were to be demolished "and it was left at that".

In April, 1942 an attack on Ceylon was attempted. (Soon after, on May 4, the Japanese were to launch their attack in the Coral Sea. That famous battle temporarily saved Australia, for it prevented the invasion of Port Moresby and the isolation of Australia.)

The April attack on Ceylon was aborted by the RAF, another heroic, unacclaimed action. The RAF broke up the invading force of two aircraft carriers, two battleships and some troop transports. In doing so, all the planes that went out were lost.

The following day, April 5, Easter Sunday, Japanese Zeros dropped bombs on Colombo. There was little damage, but the terrified native stevedores who were still unloading Australian equipment scuttled into the bush. They could not be persuaded back to the wharves. So the Australians had to unload the ships themselves. The soldiers were extending their experience: from navvy to stevedore.

There was no more enemy action. The rest of the time in the jungle in Ceylon was not wasted. The Army saw to that. The intensive jungle training, a lot of it innovative, was to be appreciated when, a few months later, the men were struggling over the Owen Stanley ranges in New Guinea.

Ceylon, with its distinct British flavour contrasted sharply with the Middle East. The "natives", according to Woop, were "friendly and clean", quite unlike the "wily, scavenging, cheating, dirty Arabs". Soldiers took to drinking tea in little shanties that were scattered through the district. There was a local brew, too, that they called "hootch".

Steve Scott remembers the hootch. Steve was Charlie's batman in Ceylon. (Steve is the one who wears Charlie's old shorts while he is painting.) He said that after Greece, Charlie was "the best bloody man who lived". A reason for Steve's admiration was Charlie's care of him. Caring for his troops emerges as one of Charlie's notable characteristics. Steve says: "He looked after me; he protected me. I was very sick. The MO didn't know whether I had malaria or alcoholic poisoning from the local hootch." Steve, who had thought the young Charlie "bumptious", tells this story, too, showing how the maturing Charlie was learning to unbend: "Charlie who was still B Company Commander, had need to remind his men that he should be properly addressed. C.H.: 'You'll call me Sir'. — Soldier: 'What about when we are on leave?' — C.H.: 'The name's still Charlie'."

There's another incident, worth a thousand words, that tells about Australian soldiers with time on their hands. Dick Smith remembered it:

> One day one of the local gentlemen came to B Company Headquarters, asking for "Mr Green". To Charlie he explained he had come on behalf of his daughter. There was money owing to her that hadn't been paid. Thereupon he handed Charlie a list of his daughter's creditors (for services rendered).
> At the top of the list was — "Mr Green", followed by the names of all the platoon commanders, including Dick Smith's.

That's where the story ended, of course. I persisted. "What did Charlie say?" — "He wasn't amused."

The Army promoted Charlie to Major in June 1942. Soon after, he became CO of HQ Company, an appointment that signified he was moving towards the position of second-in-command of the Battalion.

But fate intervened again.

Movement orders came. Certain it was home this time, on their way to meet the Japanese, the troops stuffed their kitbags with good Ceylon tea, knowing it was rationed in Australia, and boarded the *City of Canterbury* on July 7. Charlie very nearly did not get on board. The night before the ship sailed he had an accident. A lively farewell party was held in the officers' mess. Some pranksters "doctored the whisky" and threw training bungers around. One bunger was thrown into the mess and Charlie put his big foot on it to extinguish it before it exploded. He was too late. It went off under his foot, breaking a bone. This was not detected immediately, as simultaneously he came very ill. He had contracted typhoid, as had another man who died before the ship sailed. Charlie himself nearly died at sea. In September 1942, C.H. was in the infectious diseases hospital at Heidelberg, Victoria. The rest of the Battalion was on a ship headed for New Guinea.

It was two and a half years since the returning Australian troops had seen their homeland. Of the original 809 men of 2/2 Battalion, 236 crowded the ship's rail as it pulled into the dock at Port Melbourne on August 4, 1942. A waiting crowd cheered and a band played "There's a Boy Coming Home on Leave".

Things had changed in Australia, the boys saw as they looked down on the wharf. A staff car pulled up almost at the gang-plank. The driver got out to salute the reb-tabbed passenger into the shiny vehicle. The driver was a girl, nattily uniformed, smart as paint. "You little beaut!" called a lusty digger. Women in the army was but a hint of the many changes that had occurred, that they found hard to adjust to.

Before a crowd of half a million cheering, excited people the 16 Brigade marched through the streets of Sydney. Eight days later they got orders to go to New Guinea. Leave was so short that a lot of plans went awry. Jack Boorer postponed his wedding and so did Woop Waters — who never married in the end. Fate again.

2/2 Battalion was destined to take part in the first land battle victory over the Japanese, a victory that saved Australia. Though the Coral Sea Battle had saved Australia temporarily, in New Guinea there was a threat to Port Moresby, both from over the Owen Stanley mountains and from Milne Bay. If the Japanese had taken Port Moresby, as they so nearly did, an attack on Australia would have been inevitable.

I wish more were aware of what men of 2/2 Battalion — and the others who were there — endured trying to save Australia. Then, perhaps, some who ridicule Anzac Day might think again. They might want to defend the veterans' right, and need, to remember and mourn those who didn't come back.

On September 13, while 2/2 Battalion was embarking in Brisbane for New Guinea, C.H. was in Heidelberg. On October 4, the Battalion arrived at Ower's Corner, a famous place on the Kokoda Track. Waiting there to urge them on were a lot of dignitaries. Even MacArthur was there. He said to Brigadier Lloyd, in command of 16 Brigade: "Lloyd, by some act of God, your brigade has been chosen for this job. The eyes of the western world are upon you. I have every confidence in you and your men. Good luck and don't stop."

MacArthur was the new war lord who replaced Churchill, to urge hapless soldiers on to do the impossible. When things looked bad, MacArthur changed his tune and sent insults down the line — the Australians were failing to do the job, he said.

The hell of the Owen Stanleys equalled the worst of World War I, though it was a very different war. In New Guinea there was a one-man front against a silent, invisible, tenacious enemy. The jungle was dark, eerie, stinking and dripping or pouring. On the near-impassable track, wide enough for only one man, a column was prey to snipers lashed into trees, machine-guns and ambushes. Down in the gullies they ploughed through mud. Climbing the ridges they slipped and sweated as they scaled up precipitous ridges that soared up to 1700 feet. Starving, because supplies couldn't get up or because aeroplane drops were lost in the jungle, and possibly feverish from dengue, malaria or typhus, men laboured like animals over the Kokoda Track. The lion-hearted "Fuzzy Wuzzies", their guardian angels, likewise battled over the track, bearing their supplies and carrying wounded diggers. Sapper Beros' poem, *Fuzzy Wuzzy Angels*, praises them.

Worse was the nature of the fighting. The Japanese would not surrender. There was no alternative but to kill them in hand-to-hand fighting. If not, they'd likely sham death so they could spring a surprise or an ambush. It was kill or be killed. Men call the ferocious battle in the Kumusi area "The Death Valley Massacre". Worst of all was the sight and stench of death. Bodies on the track would remind them of their likely fate. Sometimes these bodies were victims of "cannibalism". Flesh was stripped from them in a ritualistic way — the implement, a rusty razor blade, was left lying on the body.

On November 2 the Brigade's objective was achieved; they captured Kokoda. Only seventy 2/2 men were able to walk out of the jungle. The rest were killed, wounded or ill.

They tell it better themselves in these few lines:

> Prisoners few are taken
> In the jungle war we fight
> 'Cause we meet 'em first — you're right.
> But if upon the other hand
> He spots you creeping round
> 'Tis then another Aussie lies
> Sprawled out upon the ground.
> Those Japs are very hard to find
> The jungle is so dense
> So when you move 'tis slow and sure
> While every nerve is tense.
> You recollect how Panda died
> With his face half shot away
> But you never see that mentioned
> In the late communique.

I found this poem, *The Late Communique* by J.W. Davies, in 2/2 Battalion's Journal, *Nulli Secundus Log* for April, 1984. It had been printed to commemorate the author's death.

Two of the many men who died on the trail were brave Bosgard and the grand old "War Dog" Harry Honeywell, both of whom escaped with C.H. from Greece.

A salute for them.

# 12
# Home — Marriage vows

> By the spring I saw my love
> (All who have parted once must meet.
> First we live, and last forget),
> With the stars about his head
> With the future in his heart
> Lay the green earth at my feet.
>
> *The Spring* by Kathleen Raine

Though letters flowed between Charlie and me all the time he was in Syria and Ceylon, I remember nothing of what he wrote. Those letters were burned. All I remember is how long it seemed before I saw him in the flesh.

I recall 1942 — the critical year. The Japanese were fearfully close. The bombs on Darwin, the submarines in Sydney Harbour gave rise to jokes about people scuttling to the bush and jolted Australians into a full realisation of their peril. It was "all hands to", as the soldiers say. Every resource had to be directed to the war effort. And there were 800 regulations to ensure that we did: they told us how much petrol, beer, cigarettes, meat, butter, sugar and so on we could have.

So far-reaching was the war effort that in Ulmarra, you would see our own Dad's Army marching down the little street, on a Sunday afternoon carrying their wooden guns — the only weapons available to them. Women went into uniform and into the factories; never again were they so willing to give up their independence for the restrictions of unpaid domestic duty. So began inevitable social change.

1942 was the year MacArthur made his HQ in Australia. I can remember thinking that our future depended on this man alone. He appeared as some kind of god or miracle worker who with a magic wand could produce planes, guns and soldiers. The country was filled with his soldiers, "oversexed, overpaid and over here" as the saying went. The glamorous American dough-boys were to turn the heads of Australian girls and to make our men turn bitter and angry. The east coast cities, Brisbane, Sydney and Melbourne were like giant cocktail shakers. Young men and women from all over Australia and men from all over America were shaken up together — a heady mixture, that wartime cocktail. Sometimes the mixture boiled and brawls broke out.

In the cities, the wartime cocktail brought sexual promiscuity. By contrast, country life was enforcedly monastic from a shortage of petrol and the absence of young men. In isolated Ulmarra, to get to a dreary dance, or the movies, we had to ride bikes to Grafton, ten miles away.

Charlie's letters must have remained merely friendly and uncommittal, because at one dance I met M, to whom I became attached. He was called "Puppy". He was like a pup: sandy-haired, freckled, affectionate, playful. He was going on seventeen, I was eighteen. We cared for each other in an innocent, companionable, affectionate way — a loving way. I hurt him when I dropped him, the moment Charlie appeared. Had Charlie not swept into my life, I might never have had the courage to fly out of my cage of sweet dates and smelly blood-and-bone fertiliser. There is good reason for my never forgetting M. Jagged ends remain sharp.

That year of 1942, excitement, fear, courage, loyalty, patriotism, heroism charged our nerves, lifted us to another plane. We felt fully alive in those days when there was a cause. It was probably our finest hour. To use one soldier's words, confronting possible conquest, society shed its bullshit. Temporarily, too, society was streamlined into two noticeable castes. There was the hero class of warriors, fighting on land, sea or in the air. The rest were seen as the untouchables of those days, the shirkers, always justifying or rationalising. That's where I feared I belonged.

When 6 Division got back to Australia in August, 1942,

Charlie, because of his illness, did not come home on leave with the others. I don't remember if I knew why he was missing. The old soldiers astound me with the accuracy of their memories. I recall how I felt rather than what occurred. A few things never fade; the rest is black and impenetrable, like fumbling through a dark room.

I am balking, too, at going back to the point where I enter Charlie's life. But it has to be faced, mistakes and all; that is what I have undertaken.

There's a big difference between then and now. In 1942, I knew practically nothing of C.H.'s past experiences. Yet that wasn't how it seemed. We thought we knew each other from our letters. Then, after love struck, there was no need to question. We were one. Charlie, the anticipator, might not have been so carried away. I don't know. (Already, I have become conscious of how much I didn't know, and how much I assumed.) Effendi's words about a hidden Charlie that even I didn't detect might have truth. He said: "You are probably the only person who knew the real Charlie Green — you saw most of his facets. I knew there was another C.H.G. that few suspected existed but I never found out what it was . . . It existed, but it just didn't come to the surface with us."

Before we met each other again, a strange letter arrived that he had written either on the ship or from hospital. It was a disturbing, rambling letter I could not understand. I never asked him about it and he never mentioned it. Maybe he didn't remember writing it. In that letter he said he had won a decoration but he did not want me to mention it until it was official. I didn't understand decorations then, yet my memory says he wrote "VC". I knew it was impossible, for there had been no recent action. I believed it was a delusion from his fever, the kind of nightmare you would expect a soldier to have. Nevertheless, I had an uncomfortable feeling. Those uncertainties were quickly dispelled when I met him; he was so sane and so unpretentious.

I must have hoped for a phone call, because I can see myself in the factory store, working close to the telephone, a black box-like contraption fixed to the wall behind me as I stood at the grocery counter. It did come but I do not remember what was said.

He appears, somewhere, in no context, as he always does, as in a dream: tall, impeccable, handsome. Thinner than in the photograph he'd sent, I noticed. The same large, soft brown eyes to melt in, and the clear, brown, smooth skin. He asked me to go to dinner. Dinner! We only went to tea, at the Greeks in Grafton, to have pies and peas in the cubicles beside the wall mirrors under a shelf of Greek vases. Where do you have dinner? He took me to the posh Crown Hotel in Grafton, on the bank of the river, the most resplendent place in town. He came to my parents' home in the main street of Ulmarra to pick me up. There he stood, flowers in hand, smiling, wearing, I noticed, a Sam Browne belt, something I had never seen before. We went to his father's car, parked outside. He had trouble starting the gas burner, a home-made contraption. Gingerly he fiddled with it, to avoid soiling his spick-and-span uniform. He made a few jokes about the burner and quoted a song, popular at the time: "I don't want to set the world on fire". He did not quote the next line, "I just want to start a flame in your heart". That makes the lump come. How like him. Always that touch of humour.

We walked by the river on that late spring evening before we went into dinner. I remember I wore a white dress and that alongside my not quite five feet, he looked so tall and impressive. I could smell the river, hear the water lapping and see it shining in the moonlight. We went into dinner. At the door he took off his cap and belt and hung them on the coat rail. We went to a table by the window overlooking the river. There was a very white cloth and some red hibiscus and there was wine. Wine! I have no idea what we talked about. It all seems so incredible now. When we were leaving, he went to the coat rack to pick up his cap and belt. His Sam Browne was gone! Strange. It seems symbolic to me now.

He took me to the farm to meet Herc, Bertha and Alvan. Dot wasn't there; she, like Charlie, had deserted the dream to join the armed forces. We sat in the kitchen and drank tea, after which Herc, as he always did, lay on the couch and puffed his pipe — and thought. I am sure Herc thought I was not right for Charlie, and he probably told Charlie so. I didn't fit the dream. Nor did I fit his image of a wife. But Charlie had dreams too, big dreams. And at the time I seemed to fit them.

Charlie put on his old pre-war clothes and went into the dairy to help milk the cows. That would have made Herc the happiest man alive.

What happened seemed fated to happen — our falling in love. It felt so right, so made-in-heaven. For me Charlie promised big things. He gave that sense of being able to conquer the world, of being able to do anything. He promised, too, loyalty, security, romance and fun — everything anyone could wish for. It took C.H. a week to make up his mind. He asked me to marry him. There was magic in finding that fairy stories can come true.

Magical though it was, I felt the terrible seriousness of it; he did not do anything lightly. A "yes", bore, I instinctively knew, simple but profound obligations. He wanted a wife who would understand the commitment in the age-old Biblical way — loving and honouring unto death. To this day, I wouldn't like to think of the consequences of being unfaithful to him. Sensing all this, I gave an answer of utmost honesty. There was one thing I had to make clear, I realised, otherwise one day I might fail him. Before I said "yes", I told him: "Charlie, I want to make it clear I do not want to live on a farm. You must understand that." I do not remember him saying anything. Then I went on, as a kind of a joke, expressing a trivial desire: "Oh yes, and the other thing is, you must grow lettuce for me." (I have a strange passion for lettuce.) At that, he smiled.

So much hinged on those promises, not lightly made. We did not have any marriage date in mind then. I was only nineteen and we had no idea what lay ahead. His leave was over and he went away.

C.H. may have known he was going to New Guinea. He did not tell me. He flew to New Guinea on October 10, 1942 but was returned to Brisbane, to hospital, on October 31. His damaged foot, that was causing him trouble when he came home on leave from Heidelberg, presented a real problem when he tried to walk the Owen Stanley track. It swelled so that he couldn't wear a boot. It was then discovered there had been an untreated fracture. For months, he wore plaster and for the first time was obliged to be placed in a job apart from his Battalion.

Among his surviving letters is one he wrote on December 12, saying how pleased he was to "be able to get on with the job" — tutor in the Tactical School at the Pacific Hotel, Southport, that had been taken over by the army. "Fancy soldiering on in Southport," he wrote. He said he "felt confident he would be a success at something he had always had a flair for" and went on: "my morale has greatly improved over the last 24 hours". He felt despondent at being separated from the Battalion.

Shortly after that he suggested we should marry immediately, to take advantage of his six-month posting in Australia. It would enable us to be together in a fairly normal way, he explained, as he would be allowed to live out in Southport.

So quick a marriage had not entered my head. I was hardly ready for it. Charlie wrote to my father, explaining his reasons for the sudden decision to marry. It was only a month since we had met again. From what he says I, apparently, was stalling. I wonder now if I had given my real reasons. Charlie wrote:

> O's only worry appears to be that owing to coupons, etc, she would not be able to have all the usual paraphernalia in the way of bridal gowns or whatever they call them. I personally don't consider them an absolute necessity.

I was immature. One of my priorities was the wedding and the paraphernalia. I was marrying a handsome officer and it could have been an occasion. I was frightened, too. I was marrying, without any understanding of the basics of my anatomy. I don't know how, had I realised it, I could have been enlightened. I wonder if it is so different today. Our conditioning urges us to the altar, to connect, and there it abandons us.

What about the soul of marriage that we neglect? Where do we learn to admit it, value it, nourish it, expand it?

It is hard to realise now the strictures of the moral standards we faced then. In my understanding there was no thought of sex before marriage. Charlie's urgency was beyond my comprehension. He had just returned to society after a long, unnatural separation. In six month's time he did not know where he would be. Possibly dead — like his mates on the Owen Stanleys.

To C.H.'s credit, confident, mature young man that he was, he showed patience and understanding with my inadequacies. Never did he put any kind of pressure on me, not even eventually about the farm. Perhaps he ought to have.

Marriage meant leaving my tedious yet well-paid job, over which I had no regrets, even though I was giving up my independence. This is because Charlie never allowed me to feel that I was a dependent — one of his many gifts to me. "Dadda", the benevolent factory manager, found a replacement for me so that I could get married on January 30th, 1943.

The wedding. That image never dims. I left for the church while it was still dusk that summer evening. I'd been going to that little church on the Pacific Highway, near the butter factory where I used to work, all my life. Crowds of people waited outside and along the path to the porch. Some were prepared to stand on stools to watch. I wore a lace frock I had borrowed and a beautiful trailing lace veil that belonged to the family. In the porch I looked down to where I knew Charlie would be standing, waiting. There he was. I saw his tall uniformed back, directly in line with the splash of colour from the stained glass window. Beside him was another uniformed back, that of his former CO, the man who struggled out of Greece with him, Frederick Chilton. He had come a long way to be there. Walking down the aisle is the longest walk you ever take. So many faces seemed to be turned, watching; the church was crowded on that hot night. The perfume that rose from the trails of frangipanni I carried was sickly and overpowering. I was by his side, trembling. When he looked down

Olwyn Warner.
This is the picture that Charlie received at Qatana in 1941.

*The name's still Charlie*

Wedding day for Charlie and Olwyn Green, January 1943.

at me and smiled, I felt calm. That was the beautiful moment, to hold forever. The pale, gentle clergyman shook, too, right through the service. I thought he would lose the ring when it was placed on the Bible he held. It was as though he was overcome by the special mystery of that perfumed night.

Vaguely I remember somebody taking photos. Something went badly wrong with them. The young inexperienced photographer stood me on a box, as I was so short, and draped my dress and veil to hide it. The pictures were so horrible I have never wanted to look at them.

Despite ration coupons, my parents were able to put on a wedding breakfast in the School of Arts. I can remember being frightened by then. I had had time to realise what had happened; until then, I had not thought beyond the wedding. For after weddings come wedding nights, at least they did in those days. In a hotel room in South Grafton, by the river, we unpacked, sending the hidden rice, pounds of it, scattering all over the floor. Some giggles from me and curses on the culprit from Charlie. We put down the mosquito net. I never forgot the mosquito net that went down on my wedding night, that unfortunate consequence of ignorance and unmatched anatomy. I felt like crying, though I didn't, I am proud to say.

Next, we went to what is now called the Gold Coast to have a seaside honeymoon before C.H. took up his post at Southport. We had time to adjust to the intimate presence of each other, time to lie on the beach, for him to lift me over the waves in the surf, as a game and as an act of protection I enjoyed giving myself up to.

(Except, sometimes, he saw to it, mischievously, that I went under, not over the waves.) He was the leader, the innovator, the protector; it came naturally for it was the role he was born to. With him — not with anyone else — I enjoyed being the follower, though sometimes I could be an obstructor, more out of fear than inclination.

One of the things I learned to cherish with C.H. was the sharing. Beautiful things became more beautiful, experience more pleasurable and pain less painful when shared, producing that sense of our mutuality. Another of his gifts to me.

Consequently, when he died, all experience was diminished. That's why I miss him most, feel most pain when I see beauty like sunset over the water or a child winning its first race. For then I want to turn to share — but there's only the void. The poet Frank Sidgwick has captured that particular ache:

> Is it because the lad is dead
>   My eyes are doing double duty,
> And drink, for his sake and in his stead,
>   Twice their accustomed draught of beauty;

The flat in Southport was our first home. I starched his drills, cooked our meals, and felt married. We would sneak into the bath, laughing quietly so that the prim landlady with her ear to the wall would not hear as we frolicked in the way of lovers discovering each other.

Another thing that arose from our closeness was our private language. The word "happy" is like a command code to call up our past together. It carries, as well as its own special meaning, many precious memories. When we were leaving for our honeymoon, my mother, in C.H.'s presence said, "Make him happy". With glee, he seized on this, to keep reminding me: "Remember what your mother said. You've got to make me happy." He would use it in a very special context. The word immediately acquired its new meaning and changed its function; it became a noun. C.H. could use it in telegrams as a code. He was witty and mischievous. Only his intimates would have discovered this. He had also a beguiling spontaneity. He would stop in the middle of an activity to embrace, sometimes when walking somewhere — provided no one was looking or he was not in uniform. Then he was more circumspect.

Memories of Southport are otherwise blurred, except for a few scenes of parties at the school, reminding me I had, as an officer's wife, social responsibilities: learning to keep my end up at a cocktail party or to ensure the wheels of a dinner party turned smoothly, even learning how to take a drink. Here lies the clue to why C.H. might have seen some possibilities in me rather than in a farm girl, as Herc would have wished. If anything I was over-concerned about doing the right thing in the right way.

Some 2/2 men turned up at Southport, visiting. Those who survived New Guinea were on leave. It was at Southport I met the much talked about Buck and his wife, Barbara. You could sense the bond between these two similar young countrymen. To my knowledge they did not once talk about war, though Buck had just got home from the Kokoda Track. And there must have been much to talk about. Unless, as they both understood, they wanted to forget that hell and get on with living. Perhaps, too, they wanted to spare us, for the day would come again when we would be at home waiting and wondering.

Buck was to achieve his dream after the war, on his farm, tinkering with his beloved machinery, with Barb always beside him, among the sheep or on the tractor. Charlie had a dream like that and I denied it to him. I think Buck knows. He has never said anything. Just as they never talked about war. I hope he forgives.

The Southport appointment soon drew to an end. Because we knew our time was limited, we were able to live fully. There was no need, then, to face conflicting expectations or preferred ways of life. Or imperfection. C.H. sought to return to his unit. The insidious imperative, as I call it, was at work, infecting me too. Where does the sense of guilt arise in wartime that does not permit a man to be away from his unit, especially from a combat unit? C.H. indicated he would have preferred to have been able to get on with a normal life, but he had a duty: he wanted to be with his own Battalion. Southport had been a gift of fate. If it had not been for the explosion at Colombo and the typhoid, he could have been dead, as he was probably aware.

At Southport, I felt our seedling love begin to grow. Despite some bad seasons it was to survive.

# 13
# Anticipation

> I think continually of those who were truly great.
> Who, from the womb, remembered the soul's history
> Through corridors of light where the hours are suns,
> Endless and singing. Whose lovely ambition
> Was that their lips, still touched with fire,
> Should tell of the Spirit, clothed from head to foot in song.
> And who hoarded from the Spring branches
> The desires falling across their bodies like blossoms.
>
> *I think continually* by Stephen Spender

Retracing Charlie's life has brought surprises and shocks. His letters are a shock. I expected they might be, otherwise I would have re-read them years ago. (The final letters from Korea stayed in a separate bundle; I was unable to read them again until I began the chapters on Korea.) On the yellowed pages of those I did not burn, in ink that is fading, there is Charlie's soul bared. He joyously believed he had found the only woman in the world and that was enough to ensure a happy-ever-after.

It is not going to be easy seeing what happened to his dreams. Especially for me. I am hoping to find absolution, if not through more understanding, then by confession.

In June 1943 after that brief period of what Charlie called a "normal life" in Southport, he returned to his Battalion, a somewhat changed man. His Battalion had changed, too. There were all the new faces to adjust to, replacing the ones who had gone.

The Battalion was now in North Queensland. After the critical battles in New Guinea, the 2/2 Battalion and the rest of the 6 Division were stationed at Atherton, to regroup for future operations. At this time 2/2 Battalion was obliged to face an unexpected crisis, out of battle. They talk about it as though it were a campaign.

What caused the crisis was the considerable losses that the AIF and also the militia battalions had sustained during the fighting at Milne Bay and over the Owen Stanleys. The only way to solve the problem was to combine battalions. That is how the 2/2 Battalion found itself having to absorb a militia battalion. They had to take into their hallowed ranks conscripts or "Chocos", as they called them. Worse, their new CO, to replace their beloved 'Boss' Edgar, who had taken them over the Owen Stanleys, was also a "Choco". That was the crowning insult.

In 1981, the trauma still felt, still raw, Frank Burley of 2/2 Battalion wrote: "One of the tragedies the Battalion suffered was that he (Charlie Green) did not follow 'Boss' Edgar as CO. He was the logical successor."

That comment made me understand Charlie's desire to be with his unit. It underlined, too, the depth of a soldier's emotional commitment to his special family — his Battalion. Though Charlie wasn't appointed CO, he was given the job of second-in-command, a difficult job in a Battalion charged with conflict. It astounds me how often, to this day, you will see anger emerge over the trauma of having as a new CO an outsider "who discriminated against the old hands". Yet — and here's the wonder — they will proudly claim that despite this, Nulli Secundus never lost its identity, the identity forged by Wootten, Chilton and Edgar. Nothing, not reos, "chocos" or anything else, could harm its spirit. Its mystique triumphed; that mystique fed by the blood of its own. The "rough new men" eventually succumbed, honoured to be included in that special band. Unified, they were to fight "like tigers" again in New Guinea in 1945.

The 6 Division were isolated for 18 months in North Queensland after the Owen Stanley campaign. Discontented because they were inactive and so far from home, they developed a complex. They were "the mugs", they complained. The rest, the "chocos", the Yanks and the shirkers, were down south having a good time or making money on the black market.

They were to put in eighteen months of training at Atherton. How discipline was maintained is a mystery. But there was now a lot of new equipment provided by the Americans, so that exercises were mounted on a scale they had never experienced before, in the jungle and on the beautiful North Queensland beaches, where landings were rehearsed.

Charlie fell in love with North Queensland. He loved the beaches. But he saw no future in beaches. Now that he was married he was beginning to think a lot about the future. His imagination was sparked by what he saw as the potential of the tablelands: "Things grow while you look at them," he would tell me, describing Atherton. He would see crops, not soldiers, marching over the land; and corn, oats, potatoes and who knows what, parading in the paddocks. He had, always, this great urge to grow things. If I had been of a like mind, I might have moved there, found a plot and started it for him. As it was, I did not respond. I ignored all the hints. I was, naively, confident in our future because I believed Charlie was one of those people who couldn't be stopped. He could do anything. I did not anticipate any problems. I believed our love was special. He apparently thought so too. Those close to him noticed how he embraced it. Only a short time ago Buck said, not unkindly: "God, he used to bore me talking about you."

There were the flowers. I still wonder at all they had to say. Not only to me but about him. The ritual started in September, 1943. A long, rather large box arrived in Ulmarra on my birthday. I'd not seen one like it before. Inside were velvety, wine-red roses resting on a bed of flowers of all kinds. *From your loving husband*, the card said. Every year after that, no matter where he was, the jungle of New Guinea or the icy hills of Korea, the flowers came, until . . .

Recently I discovered in army records something I didn't know then. In October 1943, Charlie was flown to New Guinea on a brief, secret mission. At that time there were a lot of rumours that 6 Division was embarking for a battle zone. If it were, the plans were aborted. Instead, the whole division got Christmas leave.

Charlie and I went to Yamba, the place he came to think of as the symbol of his happiness, so his letters suggest. There he indulged his craving for fish that his deprived body must have needed, and he revelled in the sun and water. I always associate him with clear light and water: he was honest, simple, clean. Noel Murrell, whom we met honeymooning at Yamba, never forgot that Christmas either. I visited him in 1981 in Brisbane, where he was hospitalised for a terminal illness. Suddenly, at the mention of Charlie, his faraway look was replaced by animation. He sat up, face bright, reliving this incident in the dining room of the guesthouse in Yamba, where we were staying. The waitress was taking orders.

Waitress: Soup? — C.H.: Yes, thank you. — Waitress: Entree? — C.H.: I'll have the fish. — Waitress: Main course? — C.H.: Fish, thanks. — Waitress: Dessert? — C.H.: Do you mind if I have fish instead?

The memory of C.H.'s vitality, fun and his goodness gave Noel a brief surge of energy. He died a few days later.

Back in camp, C.H. reflected on his leave and his life:

*January 5, 1944*

My precious darling wife,
Although it is not yet a week since we had to part, it really feels like a month. I miss you terribly . . .

Did you hear the broadcast of the 16th Brigade's march through Sydney? I heard it and by the cheering I would say there must have been a large crowd present . . .

Darling, I pray for this war to end so that we can have a normal life and settle down in happiness.

R.M. has been discharged from the army. He applied for release to return to industry. His people own a sheep property . . . I don't blame him a bit for getting out the way things are. He has been in since the beginning and has done a good job at all times. I envy him. Buck and I are of the same opinion.

Our band, still under the baton of Albert Lee, should be better than ever when the "mob" arrive back; they have purchased quite a number of new instruments and a large quantity of new dance

numbers for the jazz band. I'd love you to hear them; they are really good . . .
My heart aches for you whenever I think of you.
Goodnight and God bless, Charlie.

He envied the man who had gone home to his property. Another way of indicating what he desired?

There was a problem surfacing, a problem of irreconcilable dreams. What I do not know is whether life on a property was always his hope, or whether war weariness and desire for a "normal life" turned his heart homewards to the familiar. Or was it Here's old dream, another unconscious imperative? He may have concluded, realistically, he had no real alternative in civilian life, something I didn't realise. Or was Sir Frederick Chilton right when he said: "after his war experience had broadened his horizons so much, he would never again have been satisfied with the narrow life of a dairy farm."

Hindsight now enables me to identify this problem of Charlie having expectations and plans for the future that I seem not to have been aware of. Perhaps I didn't want to see. There was this difference, too, between us: Charlie, the anticipator, I the sceptic. He planned ahead; I, superstitiously, believed the certain way not to get something was to want it badly. Nowadays I would call that negative thinking.

In our pen and paper marriage, we usually avoided too serious subjects. We tended to deal in dreams rather than reality. Not fully aware, we allowed words to lead us into flights of imagination and aspiration. We spun a beautiful, romantic web, sticky with high expectations.

In 1944 Charlie was justified in thinking about the future. There was every reason to believe the end of the war was in sight. That year the Allied counter-offensive in the Pacific rolled back the Japanese and it seemed the tide was with them. The island-hopping strategy took the South Pacific drive under MacArthur from the Solomons along New Guinea's north coast to Morotai, ready to honour MacArthur's promise that he'd return. In the Central Pacific, Admiral Nimitz's drive reached from the Gilbert Islands across the Pacific to Guam and Saipan in the Marianas. From there, Japan was within range of B 29 bombers.

In Europe, June 6, 1944 was "D-Day"; 5,000 vessels crossed the English channel to land troops on the beaches of Normandy. It was the biggest military operation in history, an enormous gamble that heralded the end of the war in Europe.

In Atherton, the 6 Division were preparing for the last push of the war. C.H. was acting as CO of 2/2 Battalion, preparing for his big test. In August, he was sent to the Senior Tactical School at Beenleigh, in Queensland, as a student, to hone his already considerable skills for a battle command that was imminent.

Quickly, as usual, C.H. made it possible for me to join him at Beenleigh. This was another happy interlude, another promise of future bliss. We lived at Webster's cafe-boarding house. To reach our room we climbed the tall, wooden steps of the typical Queensland building on stilts, walked around the wide veranda and climbed through the low window. I had a 21st birthday tea among the palms and ferns in the cafe. A memory that lingers.

The weeks sped. On December 19, 1944 C.H. was aboard the *Jane Adams* with the 2/2 Battalion headed for Aitape, New Guinea.

Woop Waters accompanied Charlie as his batman during the New Guinea tour. Woop summed up his job as unique: "A batman is mother, father, wife. You do everything but sleep with them." Woop, always in trouble for one thing or another, had some things in his favour. He was a good cook. And a compulsive jotter.

C.H. is next located in the 2/2 Battalion history: "On January 20 the Acting CO Major Green with 16 officers and 44 OR's moved out as an advance party to Matapau east of the Danmap River. The Danmap was rising fast and the vehicles had to be towed over the river. Major Green decided that the site for Battalion HQ should be at Suain on this side of the river and the Battalion would move to this location to take over the reserve role from 2/4 Battalion which would then move into action."

By chance, a letter C.H. wrote on January 20 survives to show me nearly fifty years later why I knew so little about soldiering. His letters told nothing of the action (but that is no real excuse for not appreciating his desire for a "normal life"). That he should air men's grievances indicated how strong feelings were running; complaining was unusual for him.

*20 January, 1945*

Olwyn, my darling,
... Despite the floods you have been doing an excellent job getting mail to me. The way you have taken the opportunity to get a letter through to Grafton by boat has been wonderful. Only for this I would have had a long dreary spell without word from you ...

I am a very weary person tonight — have walked the hills all day ... has resulted in a very sleepy person.

21st. Darling I actually fell asleep writing this ... didn't wake until 7.30 which is our breakfast time normally. I thought how you have done this for me when I have slept in on leave ... I have such lovely memories of all the little things we do for each other. My heart aches for such days to return again ... You are just the wife I always dreamed of having. I often wondered just how the girl I did marry would measure up to what I had hoped for. My dreams have all come true and you are more lovable and wonderful a person than I ever imagined ...

He wrote again on March 11 about letters he had been writing to Hawkesbury Agricultural College seeking information on courses and job prospects he could expect. He replies to some comment I had made. This excerpt is very important. It explains, I believe, the vigour with which he later attacked the problem of preparing his men for civilian life when the war ended. He wrote: "I agree with you that very few people can look back and say 'I have done exactly what I should have' concerning professions, careers, etc. This business has taught me a lesson, the hard way too, that my kids will have everything worked out for them long before they leave school."

I've noted, but never really understood what he meant by having everything worked out for them.

On March 12, while the 2/2 Battalion was already in action and men were already dying, Charlie Green's next posting was to remove him from the Battalion that had been his family for nearly six years. He was appointed commanding officer of the 2/11 Battalion, a Western Australian battalion in the 19 Brigade of the 6 Division. He was twenty-five. Someone believed in his ability.

Woop, on learning this, confronted Charlie: "I'm coming too." — "You can't." — "You ring up the Brigadier and ask him. If you don't I'll end up in a rifle company and that will be the end of me."

That's how Charlie took with him to the 2/11 Battalion a batman who was a self-appointed historian.

# 14
# 2/11 Bn, Perth, 1982 — The Battalion remembers

> The present CO, Lieutenant Colonel C.H. Green, assumed command in March, 1945 when the unit was resting in Aitape after its blooding in the Danmap operations. He created a precedent in the Battalion in that he is the first CO to be appointed from without the unit.
> A new CO's task is always difficult, particularly for a stranger, and Lieutenant Colonel Green very quickly won the respect and liking of officers and men by the quiet, unobtrusive manner in which he set about getting to know the Battalion.
>
> *"Commanding Officers of the 2/11 Battalion"* —
> David Arlon C. Jackson, M.C., O.B.E.
> *d* 8.7.1980.

Charlie Green died over forty years ago. Yet in a sense he defies time — and death. In April 1984, a young German immigrant, Dorothea Saaghy, was inspired to sculpt a bust of him, not for a fee, but because the subject appealed to her. It was suggested by Major Price, of 3 RAR. She worked from a couple of old photographs and a sense of knowing him from stories she had heard. He reminded her, she said, of the countrymen of her homeland, Bavaria. While she worked she talked to him, she told me. The resulting bust is not a close physical likeness of Charlie but it is alive with a sense of his presence. It captures his honesty, strength, tenderness and in particular his smile. In it she has captured, too, the mythical Australian soldier, in the uniform of an officer, not a digger. When Colonel Bruce Ferguson (Charlie's second-in-command in 3 Battalion RAR in Korea in 1950) saw the bust for the first time he said, "That's the little smile I remember so well!" It set Bruce reminiscing, recalling how Charlie would have that smile on his face when "he was taking you out of twist". He then, inevitably, spoke of his tragic, freakish death. "He was a great CO and a fine friend."

What a strange turn of events! When the citizen soldiers of the 41 Battalion erected a cairn to C.H. in 1980, they did so in the hope it would help towards bridging the divisions within the army, especially between enlisted and career soldiers. Without knowing this, the Staff Corps Officers of 3 RAR have built one such bridge. The sculpture they commissioned closed a gap that has historically been bitter, between AIF and Staff Corps Commanders. For Charlie Green was not one of them. As an AIF officer in the Regular Army, he was really an outsider. The more credit to the new young breed of career officer who recognise that irrespective of his background, it was for his ability that Charlie Green was selected to lead the Australian contingent in Korea when that war broke out in 1950.

It is provocative that Charlie is claiming attention nearly forty years after his death. Perhaps it is the tragic waste, the wonder that the potentially great should be cut down. The Japanese would see it differently: they would say he fell like a cherry blossom at the moment of perfection — a true warrior's death. Sometimes I think his spirit burns too bright for death to extinguish.


Charlie arrived at 2/11 Battalion, east of Aitape, New Guinea, on March 14. The picture never varies in the telling. The jeep drove up. Out stepped a tall, dark, slim, very stern man. He had one arm in plaster. That is never omitted in the telling.

At 10 am he held a conference to meet the Battalion officers and issue orders. One officer, Alec Matheson, arrived late at the meeting, without any qualms — until he saw the new CO. "Oh Christ," he said to himself. It was the same fellow that only a few days earlier he had "locked horns with" on a Brigade exercise. Alec said: "I knew he'd be a hard nut to crack." Apparently C.H. noted Alec's lateness and also remembered the earlier encounter.

Before the day was over the word ran through the Battalion like a bushfire that the new boss "couldn't crack a smile". Someone promptly dubbed the new CO "Chuckles". From that day, he has been known in 2/11 only as Chuckles. Sometimes, out of affection, they will say "bloody Chuckles".

It was little wonder Charlie couldn't crack a smile. He'd just experienced the same kind of situation in the 2/2 Battalion. He himself was now the unwanted outsider: he was not a Western Australian and he wasn't a "Legs Elevener". He probably knew that he had usurped the Battalion's choice for the command, Archie Jackson. As well, as doubtless he had been forewarned, the Battalion "was in chaos"; its "morale was very low".

It was from Woop Waters, Charlie's batman, that I picked up the hint that Charlie landed in a hornet's nest when he went to 2/11 Battalion. Woop, sitting on the veranda at the soldiers' home in Toronto, New South Wales, chipped away at a shillelagh he was making as he told me about those first days with the 2/11 Battalion. Woop, never one for formality or protocol, probably called Charlie "Boss", not even "Sir", in 1945. Now he calls him Charlie. Everyone knows Woop wasn't, as he said himself, "God's gift to the army". His remarkably comprehensive, accurate and touchingly laconic diaries have forced his critics to re-assess him. He left the army with a paybook full of black marks and a haversack full of incomparable writing.

For Woop, being batman to the CO was a new experience. It gave him a sense of power that he indulged fully, probably at times in a way that would not have advanced Charlie's cause. Charlie seems to have been lenient with Woop. He probably recognised his long service. Woop was a "thirty-niner" and he had not missed one battle. If Woop had overstepped the mark he would have known it. Woop himself said of Charlie: "He was fair, but he stood no nonsense."

The shillelagh that Woop was carving as he reminisced would join the assortment of sticks he kept to help him get

Above: Lieutenant-Colonel Charles Green at the time that he took command of 2/11 Battalion in New Guinea, 1945.

Below: The area of north New Guinea in which Charlie Green led 2/11 Battalion.

## The name's still Charlie

around. Woop's "anxiety gait" was his legacy of continuous active service. For a while, as he talked, he was young, aggressive and powerful again, throwing his weight around as the CO's batman. This is what he remembered:

> "Charlie told me to go to the armourer and get myself an Owen Gun. But when I asked for it the armourer refused.
> I said to him, 'If you want your stripes, you'd better look to it.'
> 'Who the hell do you think you are?'
> 'The CO's batman. Got it?'"
> 
> (Apparently he did, for Woop got his Owen Gun that he writes about in his diary.)
> 
> "I had a similar go-in with the tailor. I had got Charlie and myself fixed up with new jungle greens. As usual Charlie's trousers needed altering. He was hard to fit with issue gear. He had long legs and very big feet. When I took his strides to the tailor to have them altered he was very grumpy.
> 'Who the hell's this for?'
> 'Compliments of the CO,' I replied.
> 
> The old RSM wasn't so easy to get the better of. Before Charlie took over the battalion, the RSM, an old Scot called Mitchell, had been running the Battalion. Charlie's arrival put his nose out of joint. He began to challenge Charlie's authority, through me. The old bastard gave me hell. I had it out with Charlie. I went to him and said, 'Who's running this Battalion, Charlie, you or the RSM?'"
> 
> (No doubt Charlie had to make it clear to both of them that he, Charlie, was the CO.)

Woop's stories indicated that the Battalion was indeed in a state of chaos when Charlie arrived. In 1982 I went to Western Australia to unravel the story of the Battalion. The 2/11 then had no unit history. Before it was too late I wanted to retrieve Charlie's story and some Battalion history lingering in the minds of those soldiers who were still alive. As we all know, WW2 soldiers are beginning to fade away now. To trace the people I wanted to talk to I took with me a little note-book of Charlie's. In 1945 he had listed names and addresses of the next-of-kin of all men killed during his command, and of his officers.

In Stan Lenton's Fremantle Hotel I had a rendezvous with two 2/11 officers: Alec Matheson, 8 Platoon Commander and

Neil Wilkinson, the gentle Battalion Intelligence Officer. Out of respect for his stepfather's unit, the 2/11, Stan Lenton gave us the use of his private sitting-room. Later, I talked on the phone with other ex-officers who were unable to get to the hotel.

Some experiences are too big for pride or prejudice to distort. For the 2/11 men, there are events that very obviously stand out in each man's mind: the march through the sac sac swamp, the battle of Hill 710, the evacuation of the wounded. Otherwise, they remembered a kind of collective concept of Charlie, derived from their perception of him as their new, alien CO. When you first question 2/11 men the invariable response is: Charlie was stern, austere, unsmiling, reserved — and able. No one ever questioned this. The officers conceded Charlie had a very difficult, lonely job. As Bruce Ferguson, Charlie's successor as CO of 3 Battalion RAR, said, "It's the loneliest job in the world."

Once their memory was prompted, Alec and Neil began to reveal more personal and specific recollections.

As Neil was the Intelligence Officer, he worked closely with Charlie — as did Ted Byers, the Adjutant, whom I met later, in Adelaide. Neil confirmed that Charlie was at first very formal, a bit severe and obviously determined to make a success of his job. When I questioned Neil about Charlie having trouble in being accepted he surprisingly said: "It took him longer to accept us than for us to accept him!" Eventually Neil discovered how he became aware of the man behind the apparent austerity of the CO they called Chuckles: "When you got to know him, you discovered he was gentle and rather emotional. For instance, when Lieutenant Vern Chidgzey was killed on patrol, Charlie was very upset."

Neil told of Charlie's practice during action of doing the rounds of the companies, something I was to hear from many sources. It wasn't merely a matter of "having guts" as Neil called it. When Ted Byers later described the same practice he called it "caring". Charlie would say, "I want to see how the boys are." "Often," added Neil, "He'd go when it was dangerous and he shouldn't have. When he took these risks, he was casual about them to the point of being nonchalant."

Then he said: "It was when personal tragedy struck me that I witnessed his concern and his sympathy. I learned that my wife was dying of cancer. Charlie, though it was not regular, offered to secure my release from the army so that I could go home to be with her. He urged me to do that, but I declined. I would catch him watching me closely to see how I was handling my problem." (Neil told me that miraculously his wife clung to her life until he got home and he was able to spend some time with her.)

Alec, a more outgoing man, remembered differently, objectively — but not without the admiration, or perhaps the respect he had acquired: "Yes, he found it difficult at first, but he could handle any situation. For instance, everyone wondered how he'd handle one obnoxious big-head in the battalion . . . in fifteen minutes, he cut that big-head down to size." Alec must have followed Charlie's later career out of interest because he added: "He might have gone by the book in New Guinea, but in Korea he threw it away. In New Guinea he was a great CO. In Korea, he was magnificent. You ought to track down Bernie O'Dowd. Bernie was in New Guinea with us. Charlie got him a field commission. Bernie went to Korea with Charlie. In fact, Bernie adored bloody Chuckles. He thought he was terrific."

And it was the observant Alec who noticed how Charlie changed after battle, once he began to relax. Merriment appeared in the mess, especially at breakfast.

Alec clearly remembered the last time he saw Charlie Green. Because he was a thirty-niner, Alec became eligible for early discharge in September 1945. Knowing he was leaving, Charlie called him to his office to say goodbye. He invited him to sit down, then said: "Well, Alec, what went wrong between us?" They talked for quite a while. That gesture of Charlie's gained more than a healing of the rift; it won Alec's enduring respect.

In the hotel room at Fremantle our talk turned to the jungle, the Japs, the battle, and inevitably to Hill 710 and the evacuation of the wounded on that horrific wet, black night. We seemed to be back in the jungle, and painful memories were being unleashed.

I thought it would be a kindness to bring us out of the jungle, and back to Fremantle. Impulsively, to get confirmation as much as to sum up before the formality of farewells, I suggested: "C.H. didn't do too badly, considering he was an uneducated farm boy who left school when he was thirteen to work his horses on the road."

"What?" said the astounded Alec, "I don't believe it!" That flash of realisation pierced the usually breezy Alec in some unexpected spot. Suddenly a tear rolled down his cheek. In a second there wasn't a dry eye in the room, and the farewells were hastily mumbled.

Phone calls, later, were no less rewarding. I was getting to know the men and I was collecting background to the bare, dry details of the only available account of the New Guinea campaign, contained in the War Diary.

Captain G.E. Royce, the OC of B Company, described the jungle, over the phone, so accurately I could envisage the whole scene and appreciate the hell of the dripping, precipitous terrain they fought in. Ted Royce added another facet to Charlie's style of leadership by explaining that he remembered him gratefully for the clarity of his orders and also for his readiness to listen to a man if he said, "I can't do it".

Lieutenant Casper, fondly known as "Tropical Frog", was too ill to travel to Fremantle but he answered the phone. Immediately he related how Charlie first appeared among them, slim looking, with his arm in plaster, and how he got the name Chuckles. He dwelt on the extraordinary amount of energy Charlie put into an education scheme, after the war ended, in an attempt to ease the soldiers' transition back into civvie life.

Lieutenant Ryan was featured in the War Diary, I was to read later, for his trying ordeal when his platoon was ambushed on July 1. He recalled Charlie's arm in plaster, his quietness, and how one day when he was out in a forward position, Charlie suddenly appeared, much to their surprise.

"He just said 'How are you?' You know, he'd walked a long way to see us," Lieutenant Ryan said.

A picture, clear and consistent, emerges of a man adjusting to a big challenge in his particular way. It's consistent because he cast a solid image. The emphasis on his dourness is most likely a product of years of mythologising: old Chuckles couldn't crack a smile!

In Western Australia I met another group of 2/11 men, most of them thirty-niners, who were captured in Crete. The 2/11 Battalion was another example of the phenomenon of the infantry Battalion. For all the internal groupings — the elite originals as distinct from subsequent reinforcements — there was the overriding Battalion spirit. Men's ultimate loyalty was to the Battalion and its very gallant history, beginning with its ancestor, the 11 Battalion of the first AIF, which landed on Gallipoli and also won high honour in France. The baton was picked up by the 2/11 Battalion that was almost annihilated in the Greek campaign. It did not fight again until 1945. Its full history is yet to be written.

The following remaining reminiscences are from veterans who did not settle in Western Australia after the war. So we may suppose they are not affected by reunion mythologising.

I found Bernie O'Dowd in Melbourne, hoping that as he'd served under C.H. in New Guinea and Korea, he would be able to comment on his development from one command to another. The grandson of the Australian poet Bernard O'Dowd, Bernie himself had experienced a hard, deprived life. Bernie's background was much like Charlie's. He had little education and grew up on the goldfields, becoming a miner not an academic. Today he is a solid, tough looking man with a heavy black beard. Like the words that run in his blood, so does his Irish heritage. There's a sharp edge to his thinking that softens as his diffidence melts. In New Guinea in 1945, Bernie was a Sergeant Major in D Company, which fought the bloody battle on Hill 710 that every man talks about. Bernie, too, was an original. He had the AIF Number WX377. Like Charlie, he ended up in the Regular Army where he rose to the rank of Lieutenant Colonel.

When I talked to Bernie, I could see no evidence that he once idolised Charlie. He described him very objectively. Charlie, said Bernie, was not, like many AIF colonels, a personality man. He relied on his professionalism. He kept himself at a distance. In fact, he was a bit of a mystery. He didn't even have that common touch that Australian soldiers like, Bernard claimed. Several times he repeated that he found C.H. very intense, an attribute no one else had so far mentioned. He concluded with the sudden thought that C.H. could at times show warmth. Then he told a story to illustrate how Charlie got him a commission in the field. Charlie's recommendation was not sufficient. Bernard had also to be interviewed by the 6 Division General; in 1945, that was General Stevens. Bernie tells the story:

> "During the interview, Colonel Green was sitting very quietly, saying nothing. I thought, 'I've blown it', after the questioning, which went like this:
> General: 'What's your background?'
> Bernard: 'Miner, sir.' The General was not impressed.
> 'Education?'
> 'Left school at 13.' The General was not impressed.
> 'What courses have you done?'
> 'None, Sir.' The General was not impressed."

What Bernard didn't know, of course, was that if Charlie had been asked the same questions, he would have been giving almost the same answers.

> "Colonel Green could see that I had been discomfited by the interview. He called me to his tent, to see if I was feeling OK about what had happened. That was kind.
> Bernie: 'I blew it, Sir.'
> C.H.: 'Just wait and see.'"

The General, probably persuaded by Charlie, approved the commission. Who knows. C.H. might have told him that his own background wasn't any better.

His memory stirred, Bernie remembered one other positive thing about Charlie: "I clearly remember his inspiring speech at the end of the war in New Guinea. He said, 'Stick together at home as you did in war'."

There remained one more very important man who could extend the story of Charlie in the 2/11 Battalion. That was Ted Byers, a name I had heard on Charlie's lips and someone I myself had met years earlier, when the 2/11 Battalion disembarked in Brisbane in 1945 on its way home to Western Australia for demobilisation.

Ted's face was familiar when I saw him in Adelaide in 1983. He is still the same tall, sincere, merry, warm person he was years ago. Another gentle giant. There was no visible evidence that Ted had recently undergone major surgery — probably another legacy of the stresses of war, robbing his last years of the peace and comfort he had earned.

"Couldn't have missed you," quipped Ted. "Saw your photo often enough on his table. I'll never forget the day I said goodbye to C.H. on the steps of the Brisbane Town Hall. I could show you the very step."

I began checking with Ted the impressions I had gathered in Fremantle.

"They tell me that Charlie couldn't crack a smile, Ted?"

"*What?*" He registered incredulity. Having lived away from Western Australia for years, he had not had his views modified by group opinion.

What Ted remembered above all was Charlie's passion for his wife, whose photo was always on his table and whom he was always talking about. "I remember, too, he talked about a place called Yamba, where he apparently often went. He had a lot of happy memories of that place." Ted was the only person, except Effendi, who detected the romantic Charlie. And Ted also recognised Charlie's very human side: his compassion and his concern for his men.

Eventually, Ted got around to talking about C.H.'s qualities as a CO and his achievements. He said that C.H.'s first task when he took over the Battalion was to obtain cohesion. Fortunately for him, the Battalion's own choice for their CO, Archie Jackson, was an honourable man who overcame his disappointment and gave Charlie his support. Whatever other qualities Archie Jackson might have had, he certainly wrote memorably and accurately about the Battalion's situation and its dynamics. Quotations from his impressive articles on the commanding officers and the spirit of the Battalion preface these chapters on the 2/11 Battalion.

Ted did single out one quality of Charlie's that he thought a necessary attribute for a CO. C.H., he said, had that rare ability of being able to make decisions and give clear orders. The order was never delivered as a command, but as a request: "I'd like you, Captain . . . to take it if you can." But he preferred to talk about the jolly times and about Charlie the man. Ted would have been an excellent Adjutant, being a "people person", as they say. He enjoyed reliving his experiences. At one point, as the stream of memories poured out, he paused, smiled and said: "I could talk all day."

This medley of impressions of Charlie seems to vary in emphasis. There is no actual inconsistency, which is a measure of his personal integrity. Charlie is to be interpreted in layers, not in a hard-to-decipher conglomerate. Reflected in this medley is the interplay of the wide range of personalities that make up a community of men, each perceiving and reacting to people and situations in his own unique way.

A lot is said about the skill of a battalion commander able to win battles because of his technical and tactical knowledge. A more abstruse skill is involved in bringing into harmony and cohesion the vagaries of the human heart and the human head. As Bernie O'Dowd said, Charlie wasn't, like most AIF commanders, a personality man. How he got a battalion to cooperate and fight is something of a mystery and is a matter of interpretation. It has something to do with the respect in which he was held. And that boils down, I believe, to his honesty.

I think that rare quality that C.H. possessed, leadership, was not acquired; it was innate.

The other outsider in the 2/11 Battalion was the batman, Woop, so after my visit to Western Australia I went back to see him. I suppose I wanted to double-check. I told Woop that Charlie was known over in Western Australia only as Chuckles, who couldn't crack a smile. Woop was surprised that he, the eyes and ears of the CO, didn't know this. He turned it over in his mind a few times, and then pronounced the final authoritative words on his boss.

First, he recognised C.H.'s responsibility with a neat metaphor: "He was the hub of the wheel." In a few words he summed up what made him tick: "He was not hard, he was just fair; he took things as they came; he was deep, and sincere; he never pulled punches; he was not ambitious; he had a dry sense of humour; he was the white-haired boy of senior officers. But you'd know it if he had shit on the liver."

Then he told me this anecdote, illustrating either Charlie's consideration or Woop's final authority, I am not sure which. The story also illustrates how long-serving veterans start to get superstitious about their luck.

When C.H. went to visit the outlying companies dug into the hills in New Guinea he would be accompanied by Woop, part of whose duty was to act as guard to the CO and as a runner during battle. Nowhere in Woop's references to the "walks" with the "boss" does he specify who is with them. In fact, it seems as though there were just the two of them, but I am sure this was not the case. There must have been a fighting patrol. On one of the walks, they got ambushed. During the shooting Woop had his hat shot off. He was very upset about this and when they got back to camp he said to C.H.: "That's it boss, I'm not going again."

C.H.: "You've got to. It's your job."

Woop: "You go, that's why they pay you fifty shillings a day." (That's what he claims he said.) "I'm pushing my luck."

C.H.: "OK. You have a rest."

Woop mused on the walks for a while and then he reflected: "God, he could walk."

# 15
# 2/11 Bn, Aitape to Wewak — The Battalion fights

"On him, the Commanding Officer, rests the task of developing the soul of the Battalion. For a Battalion has a soul . . .

A Battalion breathes and lives and laughs and loves — and fights . . .

And all these functions of the Battalion are controlled perhaps unobtrusively, by that person in whom has been vested the honour of commanding the unit."

*"Commanding Officers of the 2/11 Battalion"* —
David Arlon C. Jackson,
M.C., O.B.E.
d 8.7.1980.

"Can you imagine it? You're twenty-five, you have a battalion of men under you, there's a battle going on, and you have to be able to tell a company commander, years older, that he's no bloody good." That comment, obviously from someone who was there, stuck in my mind for years. It crystallised Charlie's position when he commanded the 2/11 Battalion. He was young to have so much responsibility.

Another, Major General (Sir) Ivan Dougherty, talking one day about leadership, got to the crux of it. To any who question the criteria for selecting commanding officers, Sir Ivan says, "Who would you like to command the Battalion if your son were in it?" That would be the acid test.

From the outset, Charlie Green showed potential leadership, as men have witnessed. Soldiers noticed it; so did senior officers to whom Charlie was "the white-haired boy". Soldiers respected him for his ability and for his authority. It seemed a welcome bonus that he looked the part: he had that real Australian look, tall, brown, strong. He was one of them.

His talent was noticed too: his unerring instinct for coming up with the right solution to a problem. Effendi called it "infallibility"; C.H. himself once referred to it as something he "seemed to have a flair for". Not long ago Effendi added to his former remarks by saying that though Charlie had the "peculiar ability to make instinctive yet right decisions, this did not mean he neglected to plan. On the contrary he planned carefully and thoroughly".

At this stage of C.H.'s development the veterans began to use the word "professional" to describe his leadership. By professional they mean more than expertise; they imply he was objective and impartial. Even so, his main concern was always the welfare of the men. I believe he enjoyed doing things well, whatever he did. His reward was a sense of achievement.

The choice of Charlie Green, the young farmer from Swan Creek, as a battalion commander, the youngest in the AIF, was now put to the test in battle, in a Battalion that was run-down and at first unaccepting of an outsider.

To make the task more difficult, the New Guinea campaign, compared to Bardia, Greece and the Owen Stanleys was without a cause — in truth, without necessity. In some history books, the Aitape-Wewak fighting, where many Australians died, is not even mentioned. In May 1945 Charlie's Battalion was ordered to take an insignificant Japanese base in the New Guinea hinterland. Yet by 1945 the Americans were at the door of Japan; they had taken Iwo Jima and had landed on Okinawa, only 350 miles from Japan. The Japanese were defending Okinawa so desperately they were sacrificing men and planes in waves of kamikaze attacks. By July Okinawa was captured. The Americans were already planning their invasion of Japan itself and from their newly won bases were able to bomb Japan.

In New Guinea, in 1944, MacArthur had leapfrogged from Saidor to Aitape and farther west to Hollandia. From these two beachheads, the Japanese in New Guinea and the Solomons were encircled and, according to MacArthur, neutralised. The only two bases of any strength left unconquered were Rabaul in New Britain, and Wewak in New Guinea. The Americans regarded the operation in New Guinea as complete.

Australia was given the task of defending the beachhead at Aitape. The Australian General Blamey believed more was required: that the Japanese in the Wewak area should be cleared or, as they say, "mopped up". The Japanese were not prepared to give up one inch of ground, anywhere, no matter how insignificant. Nor would any Australian soldier, given a job, "back off". The battle the Australian soldiers undertook in New Guinea was fought with no less dedication than before. That is because, in the final count, the Australian digger fights for his unit, for his mates — for his own sense of honour. The plan of operations, drawn up by Blamey, required the 6 Division to make a two-pronged drive from Aitape to Wewak: one drive west along the beach, the other through the inland.

When C.H. took over the 2/11 Battalion on March 14, they had already seen some action, the particulars of which are missing from the War Diary. They did not do battle again till May, giving Charlie time to mould them, his way. Meanwhile, they were following behind the advance fighting its way to Wewak, some forty miles away.

A letter written to me on March 30 tells nothing of C.H.'s movements or his new, important job. He gives me his undivided attention as though there were nothing else of importance in his life except us, and his hopes for our future.

*March 30, 1945*

My Dearest wife,
   Here's your old pest again. I wish I could make a real pest of myself, don't you?
   I received two letters from you Nos. 100 and 103 . . .
   The "job" I spoke of is far from being completed yet . . .
   Regarding the house plans darling, I think if anything it's nicer

than the other one but I have a few suggestions to offer. One is in relation to the bathroom. I like a shower included in the bathroom. This has a shower at one side of the house and the bath the other. The one bedroom right at the back looks a little odd . . . Now if we could only own a nice big farm and have the means to build a home like that for ourselves it would make me the happiest man alive . . . Whilst on this subject you mentioned that with my recent promotion someone thought that I would be set for an army job. I can assure you darling that it would have to be something good and above all I wouldn't consider it for a moment unless I could have you with me . . .

Another hint. What he really wanted, at least then, was a big farm. And I wonder if, at the time, I noticed. I might not have noticed, either, his teasing criticism of the house plans I had sent him.


It seems that on April 7 the 2/11 moved to But, a beachhead captured on March 17 by no other than Charlie's old Battalion, the 2/2. The 2/11 remained for a few weeks at But, enabling C.H. to diagnose and correct weaknesses, to mould the Battalion into a unit prepared for action. He smartened up discipline and busied the troops with sporting activities, all aimed at physical and mental readiness.

Mail came regularly, as did newspapers; even ice-cream, dropped from aeroplanes. Sometimes aeroplanes brought important guests like Senator Fraser (not the Prime Minister), who couldn't give "satisfactory" explanations to complaints of shortgages of supplies, particularly of cigarettes, so important to the fighting man. Shortages angered the troops because of the low priority given the 6 Division, who according to MacArthur were supposed to be minding New Guinea, not mopping up. The supplies were going to the real war, which was obviously the American push to Japan.

A Western Australian, Sergeant L.J. Williams, regimental aid post, began recording the Battalion's experiences. He entitled his account "Action Again" and submitted it to 2/11 Battalion Association for their proposed unit history. Sergeant Williams was remarkably cognizant of what went on in the Battalion so his bifocal view — glorification of the troops and disapproval of officers — gives an interesting slant. His view probably mirrors that of the ordinary soldier. He mentioned Senator Fraser's visit, as well as that of Lord Wakehurst, who "did not grace the 2/11 with his presence".

Charlie wrote to me from But on April 20. Excerpts give a picture of the Battalion. His emphasis, as usual, is on pleasant memories and future hopes:

> ... things will no doubt be interesting soon ...
> [the only hint he gives that action is imminent.]
> I only hope darling that whatever we undertake we meet with a reasonable amount of success; actually I am not worried about this at all because I think we both possess sufficient common sense to make good at whatever we decide upon ...
> I can see C.H.G. will certainly be a busy person. When I think of this I have visions of myself hanging up curtains and goodness knows what else. Never mind darling I am just thinking how very much I would like to be doing all these things at this moment ...
> We are getting them [newspapers] again now and they are eagerly awaited every day. Yesterday we had a good supply of papers. They dropped three bundles in our area ... I believe some chaps have been lucky enough to receive a parcel of ice cream from the plane. You could imagine the mad bun rush for such a luxury ...
> We are having a swimming carnival of sorts today. I don't know how it will go but at least they should get some enjoyment out of it. It's really a surf carnival but the sea here is very calm, hardly any big breakers — not like Yamba where I have to LIFT you OVER the waves — you like me doing this though don't you darling. I only wish I could be doing it right now ...
> To think of Yamba. We have some lovely memories of that place haven't we? I'm sure darling that we will have an even more wonderful time there on our next leave ... Makes me very lonely when I cast my mind back to all those lovely times we have shared.

The soldiers' reaction to the events in Europe is not recorded anywhere. The newspapers that dropped from aeroplanes would have told them of the denouement on the European stage. All the leaders except Churchill and Stalin had died. Roosevelt was first on April 12. Churchill said he was "the greatest American friend we have ever known". On April 28 Mussolini was shot whilst fleeing; on the 30th, shortly after his birthday, Hitler shot his wife Eva and then himself. The war was virtually over. But this news did not alter the situation of the boys in New Guinea. They still had the job of clearing 50,000 Japanese out of the jungle.

On May 1 the Battalion moved, still behind the fighting advance, first to Boiken and then to the staging camp at Pus. "Staging camp" — that "last safe place", where the fighting man leaves all his belongings except what he needs in the line, and what he must carry in his pack. There they write their last letters before they march out to meet the enemy.

Near Pus, on their way "to the line" the 2/11 Battalion marched through Charlie's old Battalion the 2/2. Joe Ryan of the 2/2 remembers this day clearly. He said that the 2/2 men cheered lustily to honour Charlie Green leading his Battalion.

The 2/11 Battalion had a preview of action before they left the coast. At Cape Wom, their last bivouac before they swung into the jungle, some shells fell. But they were from their own artillery. Ted Byers, Charlie's adjutant, who recalls events with amazing clarity, laughingly related how on May 6 he and C.H. were standing in a bit of a hole, watching with satisfaction the artillery behind them plastering Wewak, the last bastion of the Japanese in New Guinea. At Wom they could look across the bay to Wewak: "We could see puffs of smoke on the hills near Wewak, indicating where the shells fell. It was exciting to watch. Suddenly there was a crack overhead and C.H. said, 'Jesus, it's fair dinkum, Ted' as we both sank into the hole."

Sergeant Williams wryly noted that six 75mm shells burst over HQ, which moved to a nearby crater with "only their dignity hurt". The sergeant did not record another incident next day. On May 7, six US Lightnings flew over and bombed and strafed the troops assembled in the Wom area. Though men ran out waving towels at "the silly cows", they didn't seem to notice. There were quite a few casualties; no one was injured in the 2/11.

May 8, the day the war ended in Europe, drew only passing comment from Charlie in his letter of that date. His "having fun at the moment" must have been a reference to the stray shells. It is a short letter, yellowed with age and spotted from rain or perspiration. It is given in full, for it is unusually short and was written just before Charlie moved his men into action:

> My own darling sweetheart,
> I am still as busy as — but must scratch a line before the day ends . . .
> We are really having fun at the moment and I am a very busy man. The battalion is going well though and all has been success so far. I hope it continues this way.
> The war in Europe is over. What a relief it must be for Britain — the poor devils have been bombed and Lord knows what over the past five and half years. I'm sure we can't realise what it means to them.
> No doubt the old Jap will be scratching his head now. The amount of equipment etc. that will be available for the Pacific now will be colossal, will certainly overwhelm the Japs. They should have sufficient brains to realise how hopeless it is for them to carry on. At least they will have to learn the hard way if they don't decide on surrender.

That's the way fighting soldiers kept the realities of war from their womenfolk. These days no one is protected: satellites flash the killing field directly to our dinner tables.

Following the 2/11 Battalion through the Wewak battle showed me how little I'd previously known about the campaign in New Guinea — and C.H.'s part in it. The orders for the 2/11's role in the clearing of Wewak are set out in the War Diary, the Battalion's official record and in the 19 Brigade Diary.

Charlie's orders came down from the General, through the Brigadier. He in turn had to decide how his Battalion was to tackle the job. It was his lone, awesome responsibility. They were first to cut the so-called "Big Road" (a misnomer: in reality the road was a track, but of great strategic importance, running south from Wewak.) Once across the track, they were to capture the Wirui Mission, roughly north-east, lying between them and Wewak, to the north. This was part of the Australian brigade-strength encircling movement of the main objective, Wewak.

Charlie, working from very inaccurate maps, as his intelligence officer Neil Wilkinson told me that day in the Fremantle hotel, began moving his men inland through the jungle, to get to the Big Road. Soon they were in trouble. They hit a sac sac swamp not shown on his map, and had to go through it. There was no way round. Each man, carrying eighty pounds, had to wade waist-high through the featureless swamp.

It is about this point that Woop Waters began his second New Guinea diary, written for his mother. He had waited until the action started. Woop, in his sixth year of service, was becoming weary and was now intent upon surviving. No man who crossed the swamp that day will ever forget it. Woop is writing in a tiny captured Japanese notebook. He has lost some spark and is perhaps projecting when he says, "What's left of the old hands are war weary and tired and they act like an automaton."

> Since my last letter to you we moved up in action. Had to carry our packs which consisted of the following: three days rations, bully and biscuits, toilet gear, half tent, mosquito net, canvas stretcher a couple pair of sox and a few odds and ends. Of course not forgetting my Owen gun and ammunition [the gun he got from the armourer with the CO's compliments]. I had to move with the "boong" train to keep an eye on the boss's gear. Our first stage of the trip was along the beach for about two miles. The going was not too bad and we made good time. The heat was terrific and we were soon a lather of sweat. Passing a YMCA hut we had a mug of coffee and biscuits which were OK. From here on the going was tough. Swinging inland we struck a jungle track. Mud and more mud up to our socks and by now the packs were starting to drag on our backs. The line of men were becoming congested and many halts were had but on the move; one couldn't sit down but had to stand. The fuzzy wuzzies were again proving their worth too as they were carrying our main stores. Overhead, the planes were bombing and strafing their targets ahead of us . . . Pushing on we finally reached our first halt for the night.
>
> I just realised that today was mother's day and the Padre was holding a service so I joined in. It was held in the jungle with the

boys all sitting around. He preached a very nice service on mother's love and just made me realise how much we owe to you. Had a good tea of hot bully stew and some fresh pumpkin we found . . .

[Next morning] We pushed on about 10 o'clock through dense jungle and teeming rain. The track was a quagmire and the going hard; we made good time until we struck a swamp, consisting of sac sac and vines. What a picnic this was. Up to our waist in slimey mush and still with a grin up. Never was I so fed up with the so-called mopping up campaign. We certainly needed an outsize in mops to dry this up. After about an hour's marching we again struck more swamp and finally reached our objective and what a spot. But making the best of a bad job we again pitched camp. It was pouring rain as per usual. Dead beat we tried to sleep but it was impossible. All night trigger happy chaps kept firing away at shadows and noises which kept us all awake. From here our operations commenced. Companies were pushed out probing the Jap's defence.

Sergeant William's description is more vitriolic:

"To the laden and labouring humanity such an order became an ordeal . . ." He described the swamp as "so deep and dangerous we had to detour from the ordered route. The bastards that issue these movement orders should take the head of the column — they might learn something."

He refers to Charlie's own campsite, on the night they got through the swamp, very unsympathetically: "Battalion HQ were compelled to stay in their own bog as the nearest decent ground was disputed for occupancy by the Jap."

A few lines further on, to my surprise, Sergeant Williams, who obviously does not like Generals and other commanders who send men through swamps, and who enjoys seeing Battalion HQ in a bog, makes a point of admitting: "The new CO is now a confirmed and popular member of the Battalion." — Coming from Sergeant Williams, that is a compliment.

It was at 1700 hours on May 10 that Neil Wilkinson and Charlie, with the aid of the compass and, I believe, an artillery registration, got the troops through the swamp to the Big Road and settled the men down for the night. But not in a way that Charlie would have recommended, according to his report on jungle fighting. Congestion of troops put them at risk from mortars. That night there was, luckily, only a probing Japanese patrol which was beaten off. One Japanese was killed. The next morning, an inexperienced, curious young soldier moved out of the perimeter to have a look at the body. *Crack*. He was shot dead by a sniper. That is how death came in the jungle: quickly, suddenly, from an unseen enemy.

There are no maps available to illustrate the battle for Wirui. The information in the official war diaries is very sketchy, so this piecing together is inevitably inaccurate. It is rather a record of the experience as told by the men.

Moving along the Big Road north towards Wirui, they encountered their enemy, already identified as Kato force. The Japanese had a T-shaped block across the road, taking in most of the razorback ridge that commanded the Wirui Mission, their objective. To win Wirui, three features: 620, 710 and 770 had to be cleared, as well as a spur called Klewalin. From May 11 to 27, the 2/11 fought bitterly to move the Japanese out of these fiercely defended positions. The night of May 15 was the crisis point of the battle for Wiriu that no 2/11 man will ever forget.

The terrain: formidable razorbacks and spurs shrouded in mist; slushy, vine-entangled ravines; tracks, sometimes overgrown, thrusting through dark, dripping, dense jungle. The razorbacks were narrow, sometimes only feet wide, so the tracks were *very* narrow. That is why they were forced to move in lines and the man in front knew he was the one most likely to be picked off. That's why so many fine young subalterns died. If a man wasn't patrolling, every minute alert to the possibility of an ambush or a sniper, he was required to charge up a spur, in a frontal attack, under machine-gun fire.

The jungle was enemy enough. Insects and disease, mud and rain, poisonous vines and leeches. "In that tangled sodden hell two or three hundred yards is half a day's walk." Nights were the testing time when, as Woop commented, the boys got trigger-happy, shooting at shadows and strange noises.

The companies got their orders, each having to play an

individual role until the last day of the battle. C.H., as Commander, had to direct each company and co-ordinate the whole action. As Woop says, "He was the hub of the wheel".

On May 11, A Company, led by Captain G.J. Greenway, went forward first to take care of feature 770 but hit 620 by mistake. An understandable error, as maps were poor and the features identical. On 620 there was stiff opposition from a well dug-in force armed with light machine-guns. It took two days of "gory" fighting to oust the Japanese from their bunkers, finally with flame throwers. Private Maitland and one other were killed. Incidents like this occurred on 620 until May 22, when the last pockets of Japanese resistance were cleared. On May 16 a patrol from 620, out scouting, was ambushed. Private McCarren was killed and so were two others. This was a typical ambush. One man was wounded, his thigh fractured. His mates did not leave him. One carried him on his back to get him out. Another of the patrol was ordered to run for help. He detoured to avoid Japanese, got lost and didn't find his way back until the next day.

B Company, led by Captain G.E. Royce, had to probe along the Big Road before moving up to a spur linking 620 with 770. In the first few days of the battle those patrols lost three killed. Scattered along the track were native settlements or huts. Sergeant Williams tells how one night, two Japanese sneaked into huts in an area held by B Company to get out of the rain and to sleep. They were too noisy. Afterwards, one man said: "Well, they're sleeping now, the silly baskets."

On May 15 (the day of the unforgettable battle for 710) B Company was operating on the spur opposite 770. Lieutenant Vern Chidgzey took a patrol out on the spur on May 15. He was killed. As Ted Byers said, C.H. was very upset about his death. On the same spur Lieutenant Anderson also died on May 23. The brave men who headed the line up those spurs and along those tracks walked a tightrope to death. And they called it "mopping up". B Company completed its job on the last day of the battle, when they moved quickly to the support of D Company in a dramatic finale.

I have a picture of C.H. during the battle, a scene to be

enacted again in Korea, for that was his style. At night he sat in his tent, crouched over maps and reports, dimly lit by a hurricane lamp. Alone, he would have to make those decisions that every man depended on. Afterwards he would meet his officers, or, if they were out in the field, transmit his orders. As one man gratefully said: "He would listen if you said you couldn't do it." During the day he would go out to the companies giving them that personal contact that Sergeant Williams deemed so important. "How are you?" he'd simply say. As Bruce Ferguson, Charlie's second-in-command in Korea (later CO) said: "It's the loneliest job in the world." To that job, Charlie gave his all.

Battalion HQ during operations is of necessity clear of the front line. The CO is the head and heart of the battalion. Apparently the native carriers realised this. (And C.H., according to the War Diary, had firm ideas that they should not go forward until it was safe. "Then they were called forward under a guard.")

Ted Byers related a touching incident concerning the carriers that must have come as a complete surprise to Charlie. In the middle of the jungle, in the middle of a battle, he found himself the recipient of a gift.

"Come and have a look at this," Charlie called to Ted.

Headed along the track towards Charlie, Ted recalled, was a very young, completely naked native boy. He was carrying — you'll never believe it — a jam tart to give to "the boss". It was still warm. Charlie, visibly touched, could think of nothing except some cigarettes he had on him to give to the boy, and handed them to the smiling young fellow.

Ted explained it was unusual for the natives of the "Boong Train", the carriers, to have children accompanying them. And, he added, the flour and the jam must have been stolen from their own stores.

C Company, led by Captain Stoneham, was given the job of cutting a track to the mission, and had a completely unorthodox experience, different from the other companies. It is not clear who threw the book away, but C.H. certainly wrote about the irregular methods used by C Company in his report on the action at Wirui. In effect C Company beat the Japs at their own game. They outflanked the Japanese, surprising them so that they panicked and retreated. This manoeuvre was made possible by a native police boy who planned the attack sprung on the Japanese and insisted that he himself should lead the men into the planned position — for, he complained, the Australians were "too noisy".

I have located another article by Sergeant Williams, who fought in C Company. He called his article "Three Grim Days — A story of C Company."

> The company received its orders to push into the vastness of the Wewak Mountains. For many miles the road runs round the side of the mountain and goes by the high-sounding name of the East West Road, but is really a track cut in the dense growth of the jungle bordering on the Southern slopes of the Torricelli Mountains.
>
> The main approach march began early in the afternoon. There were many obstacles which had to be cleared. Native Police Boys had already made a reconnaissance of one of the Japanese positions and believed it was held by about 16 and set in a vegetable clearing on the hillside. They had the usual weapons comprising automatics firing at a rate of 1,000 rounds per minute, rifles and grenades. It was a nasty looking job. Lieutenant Arthur (Butch) Ingraham of Fremantle, my Section Leader, Hardiman and a small relieving unit with attached Police Boys made their way stealthily up a valley bed. Strict silence was maintained as we progressed over the many natural obstacles, the Police Boys at times gnawing through small vines. They were magnificent bushmen.
>
> Our forces arrived at the perimeter: they could see without being seen, and were within fifty yards of the unsuspecting enemy, whose numbers were many and whose sentries sat. Slowly and carefully under cover of the jungle, the Native Boys took our men into position, from whence a terrible toll of the Japanese would be taken when the attack opened. It was not long to wait: the signal was to be a rifle shot. The preparation was so complete that one of the men was able to rest the barrel of his rifle through a vine which had been bitten through by a Native Boy. A terrible and devastating fire was tossed into the enemy position, but not a shot was fired in return. One Japanese officer was eating rice in a nearby hut — he was killed instantly and so

were 15 of his men, a complete enemy force, which, had they not been surprised, could have inflicted serious casualties on our boys, but all was not over, for the enemy was counter-patrolling ...

Though it was a problem for the company commander who had to relinquish his authority to the native, "It's the results that count," as C.H. argued. C Company lost only one killed, Private Dale, when the Japanese launched on C Company a fierce retaliatory attack on May 24, which was successfully repelled. On May 26 C Company completed their objective with the cutting of the mission track.

It was D Company, with Hill 710 as their objective, that ran into trouble. D Company was commanded by Captain Clive Baylis nicknamed "Hotspur". Because 710 was very steep, a suicidal, uphill, frontal attack was inevitable if the feature were to be captured. According to the Duke of Wellington, frontal attack should be avoided at all costs. In New Guinea there was no alternative.

The Padre made his customary visit to the men of D Company on May 14, the eve of the attack on 710. And the soldiers wrote their letters. The next morning, following an artillery concentration, Captain Baylis roared the order "Advance!" and they charged, clawing their way up the razorback. But the attack failed, in the face of at least six machine guns and a Juki.

Later that day, at 4.30 pm, Captain Baylis decided to renew his attack, a decision some may question, as it was getting dark. Again his men charged up the spur, this time getting to the summit. Then the Japanese counter-attacked with a blood-curdling Banzai charge. Leading the charge, screaming, was a Japanese officer wielding a sword and a shot-gun. The Australians resisted with fury. The hand-to-hand fighting between men equally matched in courage and determination was "bloody and vicious". The Japanese were beaten off, retreating to a nearby spur from which they harrassed the exhausted diggers for days, sniping from trees they strapped themselves into.

It was eerily quiet after the battle ceased. Black night fell and it began to rain on Hill 710 where twenty-one men lay wounded, bleeding, quietly moaning — needing attention, quickly. They had to be got out. But how?

One senses in the records Charlie Green's quick expedient thinking that in no time had a hundred men springing into action to evacuate the wounded. A relay of men, lying on their backs, passed the wounded down the razorback to a track; from there they were carried by stretcher bearers, in the steepest part by Fuzzy Wuzzies. Waiting at the Big Road were jeep ambulances. There was even a tractor which hurried to the scene to pull the jeep ambulances out of the mud when they got stuck. Despite the risk, torches were used to aid the stretcher bearers and the jeeps were given orders to use their lights.

Sergeant Williams put it succinctly, and almost reverentially. He said: "Mateship defied the jungle."

When Ted Byers, back at HQ, heard what was going on "up there" he felt he had to go out and help. He didn't ask for permission; he dropped everything and set out to join in the rescue. Along the track he encountered one wounded man staggering along using a tree branch as a stick. With a shock Ted saw by the torchlight that he was dragging a bandaged, bloody stump. To Ted's protestations, he replied: "I'm OK, mate. There are some blokes who are really sick, up there." C.H. never commented, said Ted, on his leaving his post that night. He turned a blind eye. Nor did Ted confess to Charlie that he'd had trouble out on the track. He didn't know the password. When challenged he could only reply. "It's me, Byers, you silly bastard!"

Woop wrote his version of what happened on 710 from a distance, from hearsay — the hearsay that grows into legend:

> Well we are still here Mum and have had a decent clash with the Japs. We suffered heavy casualties but held our ground. No doubt the animal is full of fight yet . . .
>
> Once again the Fuzzy Wuzzies show their worth in evacuating wounded. The track was torturous and greasy and some very stiff pinches. It was pitch black and how in the name of God they made their way and kept their feet I don't know. They carried the boys through. One can't realise what a job they do unless one is there.

> Surely we are indebted to these men.
> 
> I see, in the paper where the good old 6 Division made headlines again. It's about time we were given a go. We may make home yet, who knows . . .
> 
> The Jap is stronger than estimated and will take shifting from the ridges. He is full of fight and fights to a finish.

As the battle drew to an end, A and C Companies had completed their part. D Company were on 710, but only tenuously. B Company had to deal with a redoubt on 770. B Company, which had been moving along the spur towards 770 (the spur on which Lieutenants Chidgzey and Anderson were killed) knew, through the brilliant silent reconnoitring of native police boys, that there was a redoubt, a defence system, on 770. After an accurate pounding by the artillery, they had to take the redoubt "with painstaking infantry work", meaning they had to clear the enemy out by hand on foot. On May 24, having won 770, there was only 710 to secure and the 2/11 would have completed its allotted objective.

That wasn't so easy. In order to use artillery support, D Company, on 710, had to dig-in and prepare, with Australian diggers' genius for improvisation, adequate overhead protection. C.H. decided that an all-out effort was to be made to complete the Battalion's task. The artillery softening up was spectacular. Early on May 27, 3000 shells were concentrated on the Japanese positions following an RAAF Beaufort bombing. Then, according to Sergeant Williams, D Company took the brunt of the attack, supported by B Company, which moved down a spur to link up with them. After forty minutes of mayhem, "shooting, stabbing and bombing", the Australians were victorious. Not without loss. Lieutenant Bill Abbott's daring leadership cost him his life, Private Penglase was also killed and six were wounded.

Woop had the excitement of being close to the last concerted push that won the battle of Wirui. He wrote:

> Over the last few days Mum, things have been happening. I went out with the boss to one of our companies who were putting on an attack. The artillery fired 2000 shells in 20 minutes on the Jap positions. How in the name of hell anyone lived through it beats

me. But as soon as the barrage lifted and the boys attacked he was full of fight. It is amazing how he survives and just shows what we have to fight. The boys are pretty tired and have all had it. Living in the mountains on hard rations and never seeing the sun is no picnic. They are always on the alert and never know when a Jap is taking a pot shot. It is really a war of nerves.

Woop is not one to give praise, but he saw reason to acknowledge Charlie's achievement:

The boss has done a great job and made a vast difference in the Battalion since he took over command. The boys admire him and have every confidence in his ability. I am his back-stay and hanger-on. I am well-contented with my job and with him.

The gallantry of 2/11, especially on Hill 710, brought a visit from 6 Division commander, Major General Stevens, and the announcement of awards. Captain Baylis "Hotspur", won an MC and three others won Military Medals: Sergeant W.A. Summer, Corporal G.W. Bell and Sergeant F.G. Hicks. Bernard O'Dowd was awarded a commission in the field. Charles Green won a DSO for "leadership of a high order".

After the capture of 710, the men, as Woop said, had "had it". They were relieved by the 2/8 Battalion and sent to the beach to rest for a week. The battle over, the test passed, C.H. noticeably relaxed. As Alec Matheson said in the Fremantle pub, "the atmosphere changed; breakfasts became hilarious". They discovered their grim CO, Chuckles, could laugh after all.

On June 8 the 2/11 moved back on the job, this time to the less demanding role of defending the Boran 'drome and the right flank of the 2/4 Battalion. This task was no less nerve-wracking; it entailed constant, vigorous patrolling to prevent Japanese infiltration and to repel suicide attacks the Japanese would spring at any time, anywhere.

Ambushes were the hazard now. On July 1 a patrol led by Lieutenant Ryan struggled for hours to get through dense jungle in order to scout a track. After crossing a creek, they had to move up onto a ledge; below them was a sheer cliff-face drop. Here they were ambushed. Private Birmingham was wounded and Private Bingham was seriously wounded in the back. The patrol fought its way out, some men engaging the enemy while the others struggled out with the wounded. Private Bingham suffered greatly being carried by his comrades for two hours through hellish jungle to get back. He died.

Not all stories about patrols are horrific. This story, that Woop tells, shows how men could lighten their hellish tasks.

> Woop to C.H.: "I want to go out and visit my mate, on patrol at X post."
> C.H.: "You'd better take one of the bottles with you." (Charlie always kept two bottles of whisky on hand.)
> With delight Woop went with the whisky and a thermos of tea. At the post he said to his mate, "I've brought you some tea."
> "You beaut!" Instead of pouring tea, Woop poured a mugful of neat whisky. The fellow seized the mug and gulped.
> Woop: "You should have seen his eyes glow in the dark."

What of the enemy, the hated Japanese? It's hard to keep perspective remembering their vicious use of the bayonet and the sword, their fanaticism, their barbaric torture. Yet we know they have an aesthetic, spiritual side as well. In retrospect, Australians could respect their bravery and reverence for a warrior's death.

Probably the story of Hiroyuki and Fumiko is more representative of the ordinary Japanese than the beserk leader of the Banzai attack on Hill 710. Hiroyuki would be the ordinary powerless, simple soldier who carries the gun and gets killed. On his body were letters written to his wife, Fumiko. The Red Cross and the Intelligence, between them, put their story together. I kept some lines from Kiroyuki's beautiful letters to his beloved Fumiko, who was expecting a baby. Their content seemed familiar; they could have been Charlie's letters to me — recollecting past shared moments, dreaming extravagant dreams, expressing deep love. Hiroyuki repeated the entreaty, "send a photo of our son as soon as he is born".

Hiroyuki had some thoughts about his enemy, too. He told Fumiko that the enemy (the Australians) didn't have the spiritual strength of the Japanese and for that reason they couldn't win the war. But in another later letter, he had second thoughts about the Australians: "We are wrong about the Australians. They are very aggressive and physically very strong. They are much taller than we; they wear funny big hats and their faces are red."

The Red Cross discovered that Fumiko could not receive the letters: she died in childbirth one month before Hiroyuki was killed.

On July 20, the 2/11 needed resting again. Malaria, which the men were not supposed to get, was affecting twenty-five per cent of all troops. Officers had been threatened with court martial for allowing malaria to occur. The implication was that either the men were deliberately not taking their atebrin or the officers weren't supervising the prophylactic programme. The men of the 6 Division "developed a bit of a complex" over being doubted. The casualties, too, were beginning to worry the soldiers. They were starting to ask: "For what?" They were aware that fine men, subalterns in particular, were being sacrificed unnecessarily.

Somewhat jaded, Ted Byers, once again at the rest camp at the beach, drew up pages and pages of movement plans for the 2/11's next mission. The order was changed: the Battalion was to be moved to the Sepik River. That meant a plane lift and even more complicated plans, involving the calculation of weight of every article to be moved. Then a whisper came that something big was to happen. "A furphy," thought Ted disbelieving.

On August 14, a signal came through: "WAREND".

Ted ripped up all the sheets of plans and figures and whooped with joy.

That night, so Neil and Alec told me, Chuckles got tipsy.

They said the A Bomb was used to shorten the war and save lives. I can't help thinking about that, especially now that I know how many lives were dribbled away, fighting for inches of ground with an enemy who would never give in, who fought, likewise, for honour, "the empty bubble", and a piece of rotting jungle.

The war ended and peace broke out. No longer soldiers, men would go home to try to find themselves. A lonely, difficult task. Few would experience again the fellowship of the Army or the soaring of the human spirit to the heights it did that night the men were rescued from Hill 710.

Sergeant Williams, in his tribute to men's ability to endure privation and to fight in the true Anzac tradition, exclaimed triumphantly how "mateship, doggedness, unquenchable sense of humour, illimitable confidence in our own superiority were the ingredients that held the battalion together with an incredible esprit de corps".

Lance-Corporal Ben O'Dowd (L) and Charlie Robinson (R), (2 /11 Battalion), Cairo, 1940.

# 16
# 2/11 Bn, Wewak —
# "To shine in use"

> I am a part of all that I have met;
> Yet all experience is an arch wherethro'
> Gleams that untravelled world, whose margin fades
> For ever and for ever when I move.
> How dull it is to pause, to make an end,
> To rust unburnished, not to shine in use!
>
> *Ulysses* by Alfred, Lord Tennyson

In a surprising way Charlie Green's talent for leadership sprouted anew when the fighting was over, like new growth in a fire-scorched bush. At the war's sudden end his camp did not sink into a monotonous, trivial routine, waiting for the Army machine to lumber into demobilisation. He made a lightning transition. He transformed his military camp into a hive of industry, more like a polity. With excitement and unusual energy and his familiar sure touch, he experimented in fathering a little society that could have been a model to aspire to once they all got home. Home. That was the object now. That is what they had fought for. The longer their separation from home, the more they would have idealised it, making them very vulnerable.

C.H. wanted the boys prepared for their return as thoroughly as they had been prepared for battle. Anticipation was one of his leadership skills. Had he instinctively anticipated how vulnerable his men could be in the transition from the Army to civilian life? Was he aware of the big gap there would always be between the combat soldier and society? The soldier had been through experiences that only his comrades could ever understand. He'd been hardened to live by do-or-die principles that were clearly understood within bounds that you crossed only at the risk of death. Going home could well be like going without a compass into the featureless desert, where a man might easily get lost. As Charlie did. Charlie, of all men.

Meanwhile, his capacity for leadership seemed limitless. Temporarily it was. What is surprising is that it took off in the most unexpected direction. Charlie, who had always avoided study, who had shown no leaning towards intellectual pursuits, became metamorphosed. Caring for men, shepherd-like, was now appearing in his style of leadership. Yet he, himself, was only twenty-five. His qualities were to merge, impressively, in Korea.

The observations of Tom Mawhinney come to mind. (Tom, by the way, wrote two accounts of C.H.: one for me and one for General David Butler. General Butler, while serving under C.H. in Korea, was so impressed by the young commanding officer, he did some private research into his development. Both accounts say much the same thing.) Of Charlie the youth, Tom said, "he was in no way unusual, not keen on study, a good eater, with a wonderful capacity to handle horses."

To General Butler, at a later date, he said much the same thing:

> "He was an ordinary boy, not keen on study, a good eater, liked, was good at cricket, had a real flair for handling horses, a quiet unassuming man, intensely loyal and really humble, a man who worked hard and a man who could apply the principles of war when in the field as well as in theory."

Tom knew C.H. all his life. He served with him in 41 Battalion before the war and in 2/2 Battalion during the war. He was also stating the community perception of Charlie.

"Not keen on study": that makes me wonder. Very intelligent people are usually intellectually curious. Charlie didn't seem to be; but he seemed to absorb knowledge through his pores. There was nothing in C.H.'s background to stimulate intellectual development or curiosity. On the contrary, he'd been taught to belittle learning. Herc boasted of himself as a self-made man. Herc, who couldn't write, who never opened a book, was living proof that it was the man who succeeds. He owned his own farm, he had the best herd of stud dairy cows in the district, the biggest cream cheque, won prizes at the Agricultural Show. When other farmers' animals were sick they consulted him. How often did he cure a cow or a horse when a vet couldn't? At first his stories, comically related, amused me. I was impressed, until I suspected some tyranny behind the dramatics.

Take Herc's relationship with Blue. Poor old Blue, the cattle dog that lived off vegetable peelings and scraps. Herc's slave. Herc, sitting on the veranda puffing his pipe and whistling Blue all over the paddocks, herding and driving the dairy cows home to the bails. Savage Blue having his fangs pulled out with pliers so that he couldn't injure the cows.

Men observed that Charlie came from a hard background, that his father was a "hard man". Steve Scott, the batman, went further when he said Herc was "a rotten old bastard". Looking back, I wonder if Herc's whistle didn't reach Charlie's conscience. Was he, too, under remote control being pulled back to Herc's dream? Would he, in another environment, have explored his intelligence? Would he have wanted to? Possibly he was by nature the true man of action. Happy in the doing, not in the contemplating.

It comes as a baffling surprise that C.H. just once put so much value on education. When I lived with him he showed no interest in books, learning or the arts — to my disappointment. Yet I was to discover that in New Guinea he introduced a program of education for the soldiers with an enthusiasm that electrified the project. Its success surprised everyone. Men still remember it as something inspiring. What prompted him? It is something of a riddle. Effendi would say: "That was his infallibility." He could always foresee the problems and come up with the solutions. There were big adjustments ahead. The men's. His own. Even so, I am more inclined to think he seized the opportunity to explore himself, for as well as talent he had vision. Romantic though he was, his vision was not unrealistic. It was aspiring, but it was steady and clear. He had an opportunity. There was the time — about three months — and the resources: his and his men's. He added a new dimension to the role of commanding officer.

When the war ended on August 14, the Battalion was at Wirui beach, resting, waiting for their next movement. They were intended for the malaria-ridden Sepik River to do some more "mopping up". The jungle and the fighting had marked the men. They were yellow, thin, hollow-eyed, hollow-cheeked. To get them fit, C.H. had ordered a before-breakfast sprint along the beach, a dip and a good breakfast. That is, when strikes in Australia didn't cause shortages. After breakfast there was sport. Within days of the war's end, the fitness program was extended to the remarkable education program. There was nothing quite like it in any other battalion.

The 2/11th War Diary reports: "the CO orders all possible facilities required for education training to be provided." Everyone who had some skill or expertise was pressed into service. Then, when the response of fifty percent ensured it was "a goer" as Ted called it, C.H. ordered the erection of huts for the lecture rooms and study areas. The building materials were confiscated from ex-Japanese supplies or scrounged. Electricity was installed and then, as the final touch, gardens were planted.

It might have been while all this activity was going on — leaving no room for boredom or a slack discipline — that this scene occurred. C.H. and Ted were watching all the activity somewhere near Battalion Headquarters. C.H., his weather eye open as usual, must have been making a mental note of how many jeeps were moving around. Suddenly he said: "Ted, I've seen twenty-three Jeeps." He would have checked the number and the boomerang and kangaroo insignias, and observed that the establishment of nine, contrary to orders had been exceeded. "Find out what gives with bloody Transport."

Ted said he knew what the answer would be. It was no

trouble to exchange a few slouch hats or samurai swords for jeeps with the Americans. The problem was accounting for the fuel.

When Ted looked into it he was told "Don't ask bloody silly questions. We've had them since Aitape." Like most of these stories, this one has no ending. You just imagine.

Some War Diaries, depending on the bent of mind of the Intelligence Officer who compiles them, are very thorough. The 2/11's, the work of Neil Wilkinson, is full of details. For instance, he records that Gracie Fields visited the area at about this time and sang to a packed, cheering audience. No doubt she would have given them "Wish me luck", her signature song.

According to the War Diary, as the education unit developed a staff was appointed to run the courses which ranged from basics like Maths, English, Physics to Bookkeeping, Mechanics and Farming. C.H. himself lectured on Farming, giving four units: Maize, Potatoes, Mixed Farming, Dairy Farming. Ted said C.H. attended a course on Accountancy as a student, "so he could manage the farm when he went home". That startled me. He had talked more freely to Ted, it seems, than to anyone else. Ted's memory for details, forty years after, is remarkable. He said it's because the project impressed him so much. Also, as Adjutant, he did the paper work.

Talking about the troops, C.H. used to say: "We have to get them thinking about what they are going to do when they are discharged."

C.H. himself allotted tasks to the dentist, Captain "Sparrow" Farrow ; the RMO, Captain Stuckey, and the Padre, Reverend Watts. The dentist was to lecture on mouth care and "to go through them all and get their teeth fixed up before they go home". The RMO's task was to lecture on sex. Ted clearly remembered C.H.'s words: "You know, Ted, the girls are not necessarily going to feel the same as the boys, when they get home." The Padre's job was to lecture on Psychology and Human Relations.

The success of the whole scheme lay in the simple, profound principles that informed it. The troops were not obliged to attend. Their interest was stimulated and the courses met their needs. Those not engaged in courses were attracted to lectures on all sorts of things. As well as Health, Hygiene, Sex and Psychology, there were subjects like Politics and Citizenship. One, for example, was "Portrayal of the Japanese". So comprehensive was the program, detailed in a long report in the War Diary, that it extended to counselling men who had personal problems. The most common problems was that their wife or girlfriend had run off with another man, probably a Yank or a "Choco".

All that I had discovered made me very curious. I began to wonder if C.H. wished he had been educated.

"Ted, do you think the education scheme was prompted by his own background?" I asked.

"What do you mean?"

"Well, he left school at thirteen himself."

"What? You're joking. — Well, I'll be blowed." Ted was disbelieving.

Charlie's last remaining letter of that war, one to survive my purging fire, was written on September 18, three days before my twenty-second birthday. He is involved and excited about his work — a clue, I believe, to his need to fulfil his very real talents.

> ... after tea I am going to attend a debate we are running — competition between companies. The subject is "That there should be a bachelor tax". Should bring forth some heated argument. We are doing a lot of this sort of thing now and the chaps like it too. They come along in hundreds to hear these debates ...
> 
> Here I am again but the debate had to be cancelled because one of the team could not attend at the last minute. The padre is down there at the moment running an impromptu discussion.
> 
> We had a lovely meal of fish this morning. Yesterday four of my officers had a fishing trip similar to the one I had but they had more success. In all, they collected 60 fish, all with grenades which have proved the most successful bait by far. I am trying to organise another fishing party just as soon as I can — you know how I like fish!
> 
> ... It seems definite enough that we shall be home towards the

latter end of next month. I am counting days darling... Yes, it was hard to see these chaps going off in threes and fours. Needless to say I felt very envious.

In Ulmarra on September 21, I received what was the largest box of flowers I'd ever seen. They remain in my mind. Still, wherever I see flowers on their way to someone, my heart leaps and I hope it's a happy-ending story.

During this period, C.H. had an opportunity to exercise power and authority in a way he would never be able to again. In the war he had won a DSO for outstanding leadership. In transforming what could have been a mob of impatient discontents into a community of disciplined enthusiasts, he demonstrated how much he had to offer his country in peacetime. Nobody noticed, it would seem — except the men who benefited and who remember.

I would place what Ted repeatedly called "Charlie's Final Speech" as the climactic act of his AIF service. What he said and the way he delivered it was inspiring. This was the speech Bernard O'Dowd has always remembered. C.H. reminded everyone that they "should stick together at home, the way you did in the war". What impressed Ted was the tribute he paid the men, and the way he thanked them on behalf of his country and personally for their magnificent performance. So far as Ted knew, no one else above his rank had done that. What a lot it meant to men to be thanked, to be appreciated. One soldier, talking about his war experience, said: "A thank-you meant more than anything, more than a medal."

The speech was given not long after the war ended. C.H. called Ted to his tent one day and told him he wanted a parade organised. "I want to speak to them as a whole before too many drift off, now that the early discharge scheme is about to start."

"The parade took place in a small clearing amongst tall palm trees and bordered by mangrove swamps," Ted recollected. Later, he wrote down all he recalled of that day, about five close pages, a document with a place in history, setting out the background of the Battalion's situation and the important points C.H. made. Here is a summary:

He commenced by expressing his own, and he believed the whole country's, thanks for the fine job done by the Battalion as a whole.

Whilst acknowledging that most of them were angry because of the shortage of rations, he exhorted them to return home with the attitude of doing their best for the country as a whole. He stressed that the ordeal they had come through successfully and the fact that they had served overseas ought to fit them to adopt a broader outlook which he wanted them to keep and apply when they got home. He said he felt that if they did not, then much of their suffering isolation and difficulties would be proved not worthwhile. He put it to them frankly to go back and be good citizens in every respect.

He then referred to his own decoration, the DSO, and stated that he regarded this not as a personal decoration but as an award to the Battalion as a whole and every member was to be congratulated and he hoped they would be as proud of it as he was.

He talked to them about preparing themselves for return to civilian life and encouraged them to take full part in all the special classes which he was instrumental in starting; e.g.: motor mechanics, book-keeping and many others.

I can certainly remember the mood of the troops on receiving his address and their reaction. It was just tremendous. The troops as a whole, gave him three hearty cheers.

After describing the speech, Ted Byers went on to make what he headed: "Personal comments from me":

From the date of his arrival in the Battalion he was constantly moving amongst all the troops and in particular amongst those involved in personal contact with the enemy.

He certainly had his finger on the pulse of the troops and knew their feelings and problems.

I felt his speech was a tribute to his own appreciation of his unit and in fact in a way a tribute to himself.

The irony of it. There were all those dreams of his. There were his foresight and his aspiration. And for him, when he got home, there was the anti-climax. How much of an anti-climax, I was not aware then. Learning what men experienced and endured gives one perspective. How blind or insensitive they must have thought us, the civilians.

Reflecting on all this, I thought that perhaps Woop, who

for so long lived close to Charlie, might know more than most about what Charlie was considering for his own future. On one of my visits I asked: "Woop, did Charlie discuss his plans for the future at all?"

Woop thought for a while. "Only once that I can recall. After the war ended, the army began seeking volunteers for the Occupation Force in Japan. I said to him 'What do you think about this Japan business, boss?'

'Why?'

'If you go, I'll go with you?'

'I am interested, but can't go just now. I've not been married long. I want to go home.' "

Which reminded Woop, who chuckled over the incident, that Charlie made sure he went home with promotion. He got him one stripe so that he was discharged as Lance Corporal. "However", Woop went on, "I insisted that I got discharged from the old mob, the 2/2." And he reflected sadly that he never saw C.H. again after they shook hands in New Guinea. He still has the pipe Charlie gave him as a present.

There was one more big parade for 6 Division soldiers to mark the end of the war. On September 13, the day the Japanese officially surrendered, the Division as a whole were on parade taking the salute from General Horace Robertson, or "Red Robbie" as he was known. Red Robbie, who took over from General Stevens on August 1, 1945, revelled in organising "a big show". With his fondness for ritual, he organised, so Ted told me, the creation of some interesting insignias to commemorate the day the Japanese General Adachi, who had so skilfully led the Japanese XVIII army in New Guinea, had to suffer the humiliation of handing over his samurai sword to his victors — as did many of his officers. Once again Ted Byer's crystal-clear memory focuses on the highlights. He can still see Charlie receiving the samurai sword of Major Kato, the Japanese commander that 2/11 Battalion defeated. "Charlie Green stood over everyone else. That I see as clear as if it were yesterday."

Interesting. Tall though Charlie was, he is remembered so often to be "over everyone", when in fact his six feet were not exceedingly tall. As the late Sir John Dunlop said, "He stood tall . . ."

Somewhat gleefully Ted added an unhistorical anecdote. All the precious insignias bearing kangaroos and boomerangs that had been made for the occasion "were swiped". Several signals went out to 6 Division ordering "the insignias be returned — or else." "He never got them," laughed Ted.

History has on record what General Adachi wrote before he committed Hari Kari, some time after his humiliating surrender:

> During the past three years of operations more than 100,000 youthful officers and men were lost and most of them died from malnutrition. When I think of this, I know not what apologies to make to his Majesty the Emperor and I feel that I myself am overwhelmed with shame . . . My men and officers all followed my orders in silence without grumbling and, when exhausted, they succumbed to death just like flowers falling in the wind. God knows how I felt when I saw them dying, my bosom being filled with pity for them, though it was solely to their country that they dedicated their lives. At that time I made up my mind not to set foot on my country's soil again but to remain a clod of earth in the South Seas with the 100,000 officers and men, even if a time should come when I should be able to return to my country in triumph.

"Like flowers falling in the wind." Apt words to sum up warfare. Helpless youth and beauty wasted. Like the boys on Hill 710 and on all other battlefields all over the world.

When the movement order came on November 5 for the troops to embark for home and civilian life, the War Diary says it was received "with mixed feelings". They had hope for the future and regret that they were leaving behind the dead, their mates and the biggest experiences of their life.

I was in Brisbane to meet C.H. when he arrived. Full of expectation, nervousness, excitement, I expected my handsome hero. I wasn't prepared for the shock. In the distance I could recognise him by his tallness, as he came down the platform. (Or was it the wharf?) He was carrying, wrapped up like a mummy, Major Kato's samurai sword. "Is it really him?" I panicked. He looked terrible. He was yellow, thin, hollow-eyed; his cheekbones protruded and his face looked shrunken. What must he have looked like during the battle, months before?

Later, I remember urging him to wear his dress uniform rather than jungle greens. Perhaps then he would look more like the old Charlie. I seemed to forget he was about to become a civilian and to put away the uniform to which I felt he belonged, looking every inch a commander of men.

Rehabilitation, had I realised it, had begun.

During the discharge procedure, he was given an aptitude test should he want to avail himself of the soldiers' retraining scheme. "They told me I could do anything I wanted," Charlie reported to me. It did not enter our heads to regard that as a tangible possibility. No. We had to get on with "a normal life".

Out of the blanks of my memory emerges something else that happened in Brisbane. When I think about it, I realise how lucky we were that it happened then; in fact we were lucky it happened at all because I was still very naive, and constrained. To me it was like an invitation into the mystery of the world. We'd come together as husband and wife. Unexpectedly it seemed as though a great wave swept over us drawing us somewhere up, out of life. Where it was bright, quiet, holy. Then the knowing. This is marriage. This is what the words mean: "whom God hath joined together let no man put asunder." Our souls had intertwined. And no matter what happened, we would always be indivisible.

Charlie and Ted said goodbye on the steps of the Brisbane Town Hall. Whereas Ted can remember the very spot, I have but a dim recollection of the incident. Ted's face, though, was familiar when I sought him out nearly forty years later.

We didn't go to Western Australia as C.H. had hoped. Instead, we went back to Ulmarra.

That should have been the end of the story: the walking off arm-in-arm into the happy-ever-after. That's what we'd expected, dreamed about. Little did we realise that in our luggage we carried time bombs.

# 17
# What happened to the dreams?

> Had I the heavens' embroidered cloths,
> Enwrought with golden and silver light,
> The blue and the dim and the dark cloths
> Of night and light and the half-light,
> I would spread the cloths under your feet:
> But I, being poor, have only my dreams;
> I have spread my dreams under your feet;
> Tread softly because you tread on my dreams.
>
> *He wishes for the Cloths of Heaven* by W.B. Yeats

If you learn too late to make amends, you are left with an aching "if only" stuck in your soul. Like a fishhook.

I have come to the dreaded point where I must account for what happened when C.H. came home from the war. And how his dreams dissolved. In life, as in literature, there's the turning point. Blindly, you chase a dream to dizzy heights. If you take a wrong step you hurtle helplessly headlong down. It's more comfortable to believe you had no choice, that someone charted the course the day you were born. But I prefer to believe we are able to tear off our blinkers and learn to read our maps.

Charlie was home from the war and his troubles began. He was in uncharted country. An all too common experience for veterans. For the soldiers coming home from the war in 1945 — and those in 1918 — there was no map. Nor any expectation that one would be needed. The war was over; they were coming home, back to the familiar, where they belonged. There they would pick up where they left off.

But what they were in effect doing was leaving "home". Leaving their brothers, their family, and the special Army occupation each had mastered. They became confused. Instead of the soldier being happy, he was grieving for his loss. He could not seem to find his home, that place he had yearned for during those long nights in the desert sangars or the jungle pit. Everything was different. There was no comfortable niche waiting to slide back into. He didn't fit. He was not an innocent lad any more; he was a man who had learned terrible — and wonderful — things that nobody else knew. It wasn't comfortable finding himself untrained and unprepared for civilian action; his apprenticeship on rifles and bayonets proved inappropriate for peace.

Out of the army! Demobilized! Were they so free after all? There was no more saluting. But there was nobody to draw up the plans, allot the tasks, give the orders. No bugle blew to tell them when to get moving. There was no mate to depend on, laugh with, or cry with. They were terribly alone. The old world had disappeared; you had to watch out or someone might pull the ladder from under you. Some didn't make it back. And some needed a lot of beers to ease their confusion. Sooner or later they settled down. After all, hadn't they been trained to adapt and survive? But they never forgot that they had brothers once, caring enough to give their lives for their mates. So why are they surprised now, years after, when suddenly, for no reason, they remember . . . and the eyes become moist.

Who would have thought Charlie Green would have had difficulties. For six years he had been honing skills that were, surely, as necessary for peace as for war: anticipating, resolving, organising, managing men. But who, except a few in the New Guinea jungle, knew of his vision and his potential? Many should have.

He came back full of confidence from his army achievement. He wanted to be a success at home too. He expected it. To share his future, he had, he believed, the wife who was more than he had ever dreamed of. He had been making plans before the war ended. He'd admitted in a letter that if he could own a big farm and a nice house, he'd be the happiest man alive.

It's what happened to his dreams that I have to live with. That's why, whenever I drive through the country, I can't forget, and can't heal. I see Charlie's dream, a continuous frieze: there are white-faced fat cattle ambling over green pastures; corn peeping up through ploughed ground; wide, high, clear blue skies; misty mornings; soft evenings, when trees throw long shadows . . . there's the track leading to the farmhouse, a horse waiting in the home paddock; indoors the fire is glowing and someone is filling the kettle for him. The happiest man alive.

He didn't get the farm; or the success. And as he never broke his silence, no one can be sure how else his dream failed.

It seems incredible that we did not talk, did not attempt to ascertain what each of us wanted or how differences might be reconciled. It is understandable, however, if you realise we were intent on protecting our special love that we had created word by word, dream by dream. If we talked we might have had to admit our disappointment; if we remained silent it might work out.

I think we had a sense of guilt, too. A soldier's kind of survivor guilt. Charlie had survived; many hadn't. Being together should have been enough. But all this is retrospective. What did happen in the end could not have been further from our anticipation.

After our blissful, promising reunion in Brisbane, we went back to Ulmarra. Not forward, back. After that my memory blanks out, except for those incidents that are scored in my brain. Like the marks of a branding iron.

An early shock for returning soldiers was the housing shortage. The first days of our life together were spent renting a room in someone else's house, without any hope of finding a vacant one for ourselves.

Next, I remember the job Charlie took. Hastily, I have always thought. Surely he could have found something more satisfactory. The alternative — I am sure it was an alternative — was never discussed. Here always wanted Charlie back at

Swan Creek to realise *his* dream: the biggest, best farm on the Clarence River. There's no knowing whether C.H. wanted to comply or to escape from him. And there was, too, that marriage condition of mine, that I never wanted to live on a farm. Herc's younger son, the one who wanted to be an engineer, complied. He remained on the farm and married the farm girl next door.

Most likely, Charlie wanted his own place, to create and build the way he had developed his Battalion. That required what he couldn't muster: capital and an enthusiastic, hard-working partner.

Not one of us really thought of C.H. Six years of his life had been robbed by war, six vital years in which he would have established himself. He had, understandably, a sense of urgency. That's how he came to take the job with the Producers' Distributing Society in Grafton. The job was not very different from the one I'd had in Ulmarra, dealing with farmers and farm produce. It was then a nationwide organisation, when small farms were viable. I am sure C.H. thought that with his farm experience and his army record, PDS could find a place for his talents. Another good reason for going to PDS was that C.H. immediately assessed he would be able to work for the manager, Harry Bancroft. Harry, formerly a farmer himself, was an exceptional human being. He was intelligent, refined, wise, compassionate, loving, genial, idealistic. Above all he was passionately concerned. He and Charlie grew very close, like brothers, like father and son. With me, Harry shared similar close feelings, especially a love of literature.

Charlie's first pay packet was a little brown envelope containing six or seven pounds, little more than I'd earned at the factory in Ulmarra, and about half his pay as a Colonel. With an apologetic little grin, he handed the still-sealed envelope to me, saying, "Can I have a couple of bob for cigarettes?"

C.H. wasn't going to tolerate being in a rented room for long. "I've spent too many years in a tent," he said, when he asserted his rights as a returned soldier and served a notice on the owner of a row of houses for one cottage about to become vacant. It was not far from Bancrofts. I called it the D.H. Lawrence house. Once those little wooden boxes of houses were all over Australia, usually built in rows for miners, or railway workers. The front bedroom steals one end of the front veranda just as a laundry does from the back veranda. Outside, as though hatched, sat its tiny wooden replica, the little house — that quaint, now legendary feature of the Australian landscape. The gas bath-heater that left an eternal green stain down the end of the bath and the gas copper were our only luxuries. Up the back steps, elevating the house above flood reach, I had to carry lumps of split wood that Charlie kept in a pile, to feed the hungry, cantankerous, sooty, fuel stove. I liked the bare simplicity of that little house.

Once we had moved into Bacon Street, Charlie immediately went to work creating a vegetable garden. I remember Woop saying, "God, he could walk". Whereas I often think how he could *work*. I would not have disappointed him in my own willingness to work. In that I am no slouch. We were compatible in most things. He marked out the big block of land. The small front garden was to be my concern. Charlie said, "I'll dig it for you. That's all." Most often, he'd get up at sunrise, don his beloved slouch hat and set to work. He'd do a couple of hours digging or planting before he cycled round to PDS. Then after work, and his cup of tea, he'd go back to the garden. Echoing his old farm rhythm, or his army routine. Or was it his frustration?

One morning, not long after we moved, Charlie came in from the garden with his first offering. In his slouch hat, which he held out to me, was a big, plump lettuce. We both knew what that meant. He said, with a little teasing smile, "There you are," as though to say: "You see. I've kept my promise."

I must have shown my pleasure for that was the beginning of what became a ritual that I loved. He'd come in bearing in his slouch hat his latest offering from the garden, and alert me to the magnificence of its size or colour. He grew all sorts of things: huge, red, tender tomatoes; giant cabbages; potatoes. But especially I remember the strawberries. With the strawberries, I complemented his efforts by learning to make quite spectacular glazed strawberry tarts, on the biggest pie plate I could obtain.

It's the lettuce I remember, though. Lettuce remains in my mind an emblem of Charlie. A fitting emblem. I see the soil still clinging. Like him. Basic and simple.

With others we deal in symbols all the time, sometimes without awareness; often because we are not good at words. Charlie ritualistically grew lettuce, as he'd promised the day he proposed. Until this moment it did not occur to me that any unconscious motive could have been at work. He could have been saying: I need to work in the soil. Please understand me. But perhaps it simply meant what I always took it to mean: I love you.

Before long, our world had shrunk to Bacon Street. Grafton the town did not have an identity in my mind. It wasn't like Ulmarra, small, familiar, idiosyncratic. Grafton is obscured by trees. At least, that is all I remember apart from the clock in the main street. The people never seemed to emerge. I especially remember the jacarandas, splotches of purple subduing all else in view, fringing a blue sky or lying underfoot, a thick purple carpet. And everywhere there was the strange mating of the jacaranda and the flame tree, purple and crimson side by side. Jacarandas dominated the eyes and the nose. People used to suffer from a complaint known locally as "jacaranda fever".

Soon our dreams were shrinking and losing direction. Charlie's confident desire for success in whatever he did could not be realised in his inconsequential job. And I have to admit that I lamented the loss of my hero.

There was solace. Harry Bancroft lovingly fathered Charlie, who, for a while, gave himself up to this novel experience. Harry Bancroft, his wife Tot and their four children lived in Alice Street, on the corner of the next cross street to us. Their corner block showed off their large wooden house and its eye-catching garden. Their marriage was what we would all suppose it should be: sweet and warm. They had suffered the loss of a child. The Bancrofts became more than friends. They

Above: A civilian again, Charlie and Olwyn at a ball in Grafton, 1946
Below: Charlie and Anthea at 'Woodlands', 1949.

*The name's still Charlie* 219

Above: Elvie Smith and her son saying goodbye as the Greens leave Grafton, 1949.
Below: Charlie playing with Anthea, Queenscliff, 1950.

were part of us. On summer evenings we sat on their wide, cool veranda. Winter evenings would find us round the kitchen stove, drinking tea, talking. Later, Elvie and Harry, another entwined couple, came to live a few doors from Bancrofts and joined our circle.

Countrytown life began to envelop us. You feel the roots going down deep, so deep they are hard to dig up. Belonging is cosy. We were so involved in others' lives, we knew their every detail: when Tot pruned her roses; when Elvie made jam; when the fellow round the corner got drunk. It is easy to sink so far into that cosiness that you cannot remove yourself.

For all the cosiness, Charlie was impatient, as Harry recognised, anxiously. I can best explain Charlie's unrest in his own words. He was always saying "racehorses will gallop". How could he passively continue in an unachieving role? He was compelled to act, sooner or later.

His hopes were raised once. I remember him poring over maps, showing me land in Western Australia that was to be divided into soldier-settlement blocks and balloted. He applied, full of hope. Because the land was in Western Australia, he was the more interested. I sensed he was keen on the thought of settling near his "boys". His bond with the 2/2 was different: it was not so much with the Battalion as an entity as with individuals. I was hopeful too; I liked the thought of tackling an undeveloped block, like pioneers. But nothing came of it.

My not getting pregnant was another disappointment. Charlie assumed it was because of the atebrin and the malaria. He joked about it sometimes, using army metaphors, funny but unrepeatable, to describe his imagined infertility. Unproductiveness was agitating him more than I realised. There was a gain though. We had a year, alone, to unlace and explore my sexuality that had been awakened that day in Brisbane.

In 1946, I had my first experience of seeing into the future. It could not be called a premonition. Rather a foreseeing. It was a hot, Saturday afternoon in November. Charlie had come in from the garden. The air was heavy with the smell of jacarandas. I could feel the cool linoleum against my damp back. Transported out of time, beyond ecstacy, there was only light, a flame of brilliant light, then darkness, then nothing. Conscious again, I whispered to him: "I am pregnant, I know." He said nothing. I added, knowing: "This child will be special. It will have special power. I hope it knows how to use it."

I believed that I would be different when I was pregnant. I would not be sick, according to the code of martyrdom I had learned book, chapter and verse. ("If you stretch up to the clothes line while you are pregnant you will strangle the baby.") How else get a rest from pregnancies, from the washing? Easier to suffer honourably than to admit, "I hate being pregnant" or "I don't like doing the washing". To be fair, the pill made it easier for the next generation of women to tell the truth. It also made pedestals redundant. All set for a graceful pregnancy in pretty smocks, I found myself as sick as a dog, dishevelled and unready.

In January 1947, Charlie was given holidays. We did not go to Yamba, the place he used to talk so much about to Ted in New Guinea. Was the choice different because we were about to become parents or because C.H.'s inner voice was nagging him? We went on a camping holiday, and Herc and Bertha came along too. The purpose was to tour around "looking at properties", and, I think, to look up old army mates. We got to Mudgee, where I remember being delighted by the change to the pastoralist scene that looked to me more attractive than the drudgery I attached to cow yards. But there wasn't delight enough to lessen my nausea, or rather my day-long "morning" sickness I had vowed not to have. In the Memorial Park at either Parkes or Orange I crouched, heaving, into a flower-bed. Finally I said to C.H.: "I want to go home by train. You can all finish the trip in peace."

Early in 1947 Charlie got excited again. He'd seen a house he wanted to buy in Alice Street where the Bancrofts lived. It's the big white house I still dream about uneasily. Sometimes I am agonising because I mistakenly left it to go to the city — or conversely, I am isolated in the country having left the city. There is another dream of the beautiful big house with wonderful potential. In this dream, I am agonising because it is terribly in need of repair and I haven't the means to do it. Its enchanting possibility as a family house was one of its attractions. In the meantime it was divided into two flats, the income from one helping to pay it off. The main kitchen, on the side of the house we moved into, was itself about the size of a city flatette. In the front garden were large date palms. By our bedroom was a frangipanni which on summer evenings flooded the room with perfume to remind us of our wedding. The house stood on a double block of land, providing enough ground at the back of our flat for a vegetable garden and a fowlyard. But the real thrill for Charlie lay beyond that again. Attached to the property was a large block of vacant land unsuitable for building.

Charlie had ground to farm on! No sooner were we settled in Alice Street than he got the use of horses and a plough. He ploughed and then planted potatoes. I should have been alerted, and touched, by a man trying to farm in a suburban backyard. Probably I was too preoccupied with my own important task, preparing for motherhood. Following the code after all.

While the potatoes were growing, C.H. transformed the big kitchen into a housewife's delight. He put in cupboards, a sink and windows to let in air and light and enable me to look out on to the huge, laden mango tree. We worked on the remodelling together. He enjoyed my fetching and carrying for him and the companionable "smokos". He liked to turn work into play.

Strange how in his letters words poured out; face to face he was a man of few words. More than often, he'd communicate in gestures, or symbols. He had a habit, for instance, of catching my eye at the window. Slouch hatted, he'd lean on the spade and say, "Is the jug broken?" Meaning, he'd like a cup of tea. That was when we were closest. I remember most poignantly not what he would say but what he would do. Some things he did were as suggestive as poetry, as spare as haiku.

It was near my confinement that Elvie fortuitously moved into a house opposite us. She and her Harry's closeness was more ethereal: both were saintly, naturally and undemonstrably. All the gloomy lessons I'd learned were challenged by Elvie's radiance. To her, life, babies, marriage, womanhood were a sacrament. By chance she, too, was pregnant and "due", as they say, within days of me. One day, in her illuminating way, Elvie cured my dread of childbirth. She said: "You know, Olwyn, coming into the world is very difficult for the baby. Imagine it. We have to help the little thing all we can." That was Elvie.

Meanwhile, C.H. found something else to do. (I felt we were already too busy.) He began an accountancy course — to boost his chances of advancement at PDS, I suppose. Wrapped up in numerous tasks in that big house and garden and in the baby's coming, I observed only that Charlie didn't enjoy studying. And accountancy was the last thing in the world likely to convert him.

There were some false starts, panics and a few cups of castor oil before the labour began. Our baby had a natural, easy, quick passage into life on August 1, Wattle Day, 1947. I heard the Doctor say: "It's a girl." "It's Anthea," I said, with a sudden strange sense of relief. This was another instance of premonition: relief it was a girl, for I felt I could not face, alone, the responsibility of rearing a male. I was inadequate. Males had to do what I couldn't: they had to cope with fighting and violence. That flash was, eerily, very accurate — as my premonitions tended to be.

Charlie came through the ward door carrying a bunch of flowers. His eyes looked large, soft and unusually shiny as he bent down to kiss me and whisper, "Thanks for the beautiful little girl." It was pre-arranged that I would name a girl and he a boy. I'd wanted, since I was fourteen, to have a daughter I could call Anthea, a name I discovered in a poem by Herrick. A Greek name, meaning "flower", so Charlie liked it.

It was when I got home from the hospital that the trouble started. I wonder if I had post-partum depression. When the milk didn't "come in" I got anxious, setting up a vicious circle. The baby, moved from breast to bottles and back, and forced into the clinic-ordained strict four-hourly regime, screamed and screamed. Perfectionist that I am, I felt hopelessly inadequate and became quite demented. In retrospect, I call it one of my ratty periods. Charlie summed it all up some time later. He said laconically: "I don't want to go through that again." With hindsight, I'd throw away the books and the bottles and nurse the baby till it was satisfied. That might have avoided a terrible period that left its scar. I felt cheated of the full pleasure of my experience of early motherhood.

It wasn't plain sailing for Elvie either. Her baby was born six weeks prematurely. She and Harry retreated into an all-sterile house to ensure their "premmy" didn't get an infection it might not be able to survive.

It was just after the baby was born that my father died, further bewildering and confusing me. Had he lived, he would have lent Charlie an ear, if not a hand. C.H. was one of the few men my stern father looked up to. Even he recognised the commander in him.

Another year turned round. It was January, 1948. This time we went to Yamba, camping, as befitted our slender means. My sister, Wilma, and her husband, Lindsay, joined us. There were cards in the evening, supper made on a primus, a lot of fun. They were there to witness a funny, unforgettable incident that sticks in all our memories. Charlie had come back from the campsite toilet one morning, laughing, eager to report. He mimicked the voice and actions of the source of his mirth. He'd met the sanitary man, a hair-lipped wit who, as he put in the empty can and heaved the overflowing one to his shoulder uttered this plaint, snuffily: "All a man gets out of this job is a fallen womb, a floating kidney and a hat full of shit."

In times of exasperation thereafter, you'd hear C.H. muttering about his fallen womb or his hat full of shit. We all understood and laughed.

Another incident occurred at Yamba that seems to have had some deep, strange significance. C.H. and Lindsay had been fooling around mocking the youths who paraded on the beach, admiring the girls and seeking attention. In a burst of high spirits they raced into the surf. Within minutes I saw

Charlie come out again. "Strange," I thought. Stranger still, he hurried not towards me but across the beach towards the tent. Then he thought better of it and came to me. "God," I thought, "what's happened?" His face looked old and shrunken. In his hand he had his teeth, broken in two. He'd been dumped by a wave, lost his teeth and had to dive after them. That night he made a joke of actually sticking them up with Tarzan's Grip so he could put them in for appearance' sake. What bothered him, I remember, was that our bank balance was too low to immediately replace them. It might have been coincidental, but after that he seemed restless.

It was probably at this time C.H. began agitating. He wrote to Head Office of PDS asking what his immediate prospects were. There were other feelers put out, too, about jobs and prospects. Around April 1948, he had a temporary boost to his spirits. He was appointed CO of 41 Battalion, to be reformed to train citizen soldiers. That pleased him: to command the militia Battalion where he began his army career as a boy in the mid-1930s. Enthusiastically, he set about getting the 41st affiliated with a British Regiment, the Argyll and Sutherland Highlanders, little knowing he would be serving beside them again in just a short time. He gave a radio talk on the re-establishment of the 41 Battalion. It was a good speech. I hope I told him so. When I questioned an expression he used, I wanted him to realise the need, in his position, to watch his grammar. Sometimes it could lapse into the "I-done-its" that I didn't think suited his position or his presence. It annoyed me, too, that it did not seem to matter to him. We didn't sort out whether it was correct or not. He replied: "You take away my confidence." What was at issue wasn't recognised or resolved. That left a scar. How amazing that couples can be so bodily attuned and yet, at times, so far apart.

Our daughter's first birthday was captured in a photo. We were all there, including Herc, Bertha, Wilma, Lindsay. My sister gave Anthea a pup, also in the snap — a wire-haired fox terrier that grew into a singularly neurotic, exasperating but amusing animal that tagged after her as she toddled around. Herc took one look at it and said in his theatrical voice, "it looks like old Sandy McPhee". So it was called Sandy.

What I recall next came like a bolt out of the blue, I couldn't believe it. One evening, home from work, Charlie announced: "I have to go to Melbourne."

"Why?"

"I have to be interviewed for an appointment to the Regular Army at my old rank of Lieutenant Colonel."

"Are you going to think about it?"

"No. I have made up my mind. I have already applied."

I wish I had asked him to explain. Perhaps I was afraid of what he might say. That he anticipated resistance. That he was unhappy. He assured me that he would not leave me alone, ever, unless his duty required it.

That was one of the biggest shocks of my life. Leave my home? the Bancrofts? the Smiths? For Charlie there was no other apparent solution. At least he was in command again, giving truth to his own oft-muttered "racehorses will gallop".

# 18
# Cloudless days

Cloudless day,
Night, and a cloudless day;
Yet the huge storm will burst upon our heads
  one day
From a bitter sky.

>  *Counting the Beats* by Robert Graves

For the second time Charlie uprooted himself and left the Clarence River. This decision was to lead swiftly, inexorably to his end. Like a Greek tragedy. Ordained or precipitated? I am not sure. At first, it seemed as though he'd made a good decision. For a while our new life was like a balloon ride on a clear, blue-skyed day in crisp champagne air.

Between C.H.'s bombshell that he'd joined the army and our leaving Grafton there is a blank. Shock leaves what feels like shell holes in my mind. According to Army Records, he joined the Regular Army on January 6, 1949. His first posting was not until April 29, when he was appointed Instructor at the School of Tactics and Administration, Seymour, Victoria. So for a few weeks Anthea and I must have been alone in Grafton, waiting to join him.

There is a photograph of our departure from Grafton. C.H. had come back to drive Anthea and me, and the dog, to Seymour. Elvie and her son, who'd become, as we had hoped, a playmate of Anthea's, were there to wave us goodbye and shed, with me, a few tears. In the photo we all look a bit stunned, as though we are thinking: *This can't be happening.*

There was an incident en route that I've not forgotten, not

merely because it was amusing. Sandy, the dog, was suffered by Charlie. A bewhiskered antic of an animal that would tremble when stressed or excited was not his idea of a dog. He was used to blue cattle dogs, or red kelpies that worked on the farm, did as they were told and lived outside. Nevertheless, he made a cage on the running board of the car to carry the animal. Two days from Grafton — we stayed in Sydney overnight — we stopped by the roadside, somewhere out of Goulburn, to have a break. The dog, out of its cage, sniffed the air, smelt the new, exciting smell of sheep or rabbit and took off. It disappeared over a ridge; we heard it racing backwards and forwards yapping hysterically. It was chasing sheep. Whistles and calls brought no response. After some time C.H., exasperated, said: "We're leaving. No self-respecting man would own a dog like this."

Afraid he would, I said, "You leave him, you leave me."

I told myself I was amused that C.H. the great tactician was left posted by the roadside helplessly awaiting the inclination of a dog. But something else was going on, I suppose. A testing. Our different backgrounds would often leap at us like this. Later, in Victoria, the scene was played again over a different incident. Charlie appeared with a rifle, ready to shoot the dog. I pleaded and I think I cried. He lowered the rifle. The dog lived on to some extraordinary age, years after C.H. himself.

At Seymour, when we eventually arrived, I was in for another shock, for which C.H. would have prepared me, I am confident. Our quarters were a mess hut, in what had been an Italian prisoner-of-war camp in an isolated bush setting. I can dimly visualise now the camp itself and the typical bush road that led to it. Because of housing shortage, the army allowed personnel of any rank to occupy huts in the camp at a nominal rate, and left them to make their hut as habitable as they desired. Ours, though previously occupied, was the least habitable. Water, sewerage and electricity were laid on (except that the electricity voltage didn't allow us to use many appliances, and certainly not too many at a time).

Keeping house there was more like camping; the bare

essentials were all that were necessary. Cooking was a different matter. The stove had two fireboxes and two ovens, both of which I kept going all day in the winter, which was about to set in when we arrived. If C.H.'s pile of wood got low, I would delight in splitting more. With each blow, I aimed to split the block cleanly. A great feeling. It's like hitting a bull's eye in target practice. Otherwise, the axe jams and there's the struggle of extracting the sharp axe head. C.H.'s axes were always sharp. I wasn't prepared for cooking in sheep country. Meat, let alone cabbage, seemed to bring every blowfly in the universe. In the windows, over which a former occupant had organised some wire screens, dead blowflies mounted up in piles. Cleaning them out became a regular chore.

The real adventure of living in that hut started when it got really cold. I'd sit by the stove, reading and knitting if C.H. were late. At bedtime we would don coats to go to our bedroom. The problem was the roof. Looking up you could see the daylight or the moonlight through an aperture. The iron roof, unlined, did not join at the peak. A hood covered the aperture to keep out the rain and someone had wired the space to keep out birds and insects. There was nothing to keep out the cold. C.H. presented me with all kinds of arguments why I should go to bed early, before him, so that the bed would be warm. He would look at Anthea to make sure she was covered and comfortable, then he'd get in beside me and curl his body around mine in the usual enveloping, protective way he had adopted.

Things bare and simple appeal to me. I loved the hut and the life there in that first year of our new life. Even washing was an event. After all, who else could enjoy the risks of hanging washing on a line flapping in the wind, surrounded by meandering sheep or, sometimes, cattle. One day I looked out the window to see a big fat steer approach the clothesline and snatch off, selectively, first a pair of pants and then a bra — then swallow them.

I am sure my memory has happily extended the length of the hut. At the far end, in the unused part partitioned off from our "bedroom", which I turned into a play area for Anthea, I set up my sewing machine, so that while she played, I could make curtains to civilise the hut. In its mess-hut days, the trucks would have backed into this end of the construction to unload through the barn-like doors, reminding me of the factory store in Ulmarra. On warm days I would fling open the heavy doors. That was like unveiling a mural. A blue mountain would almost tumble in. Joyously I'd look to see what the mood was that day. The sky was usually a radiant, cloudless, clear, pure blue and gum trees would shimmer in the bright light. On softer days, when a stray cloud would pass over, the farthest trees became dark and mysterious looking. In the foreground some white cockatoos would sit in a bare tree or fly off screeching after the one on the topmost branch signalled a warning.

I think it was here that I began to understand Charlie's love of the earth and sky. This, though was the landscape of our Australian consciousness: dun-coloured ground, khaki scrub and blue, blue skies. Muddy cowbails and paspalum paddocks don't often spark the artist's brush or pen; nor did they ever stir me.

It wasn't long before C.H. appeared one day with a spade in hand, wearing the old familiar slouch hat, ready to re-institute the ritual. He'd found, obscured by grass, its protective wire netting broken down, a plot that the Italians had worked once. Sometimes one could almost feel their presence in the vegetable plot, untouched since they left until Charlie re-dug the soil and re-erected the fence.

When he brought in the first crop of lettuce, he explained that in the different climate he had to sow a different type of plant. The strawberries he eventually produced there were bigger and sweeter than any he had grown before. My strawberry tarts would centre the table when he brought young officers home to tea at the weekend. Sometimes, on Sundays, the kitchen was filled with hungry young chaps, eyeing off what was coming out of the ovens — probably a roast and an apple-pie at the same time.

The snag in life for me was the narrow environment of the Regular Army, particularly the officers' mess, the centre of it all. It seemed as though time had slipped — back to pre-war days, to tradition and protocol. This has all changed now, especially after Vietnam, the great leveller. How different were the AIF messes I went to with Charlie at Southport and Beenleigh. Then the atmosphere was comradely and electric as it is when men during an interlude between battlefronts live as though there are no tomorrows.

The war over, the army had temporarily lost its direction. It was all regalia and no fire; like a dramatist with all the costumes but no plot. If Charlie found it awkward not being a Duntroon graduate, or painful because it was so different, he never said. There was always the spade and the Italians' garden where he could go and dig. Charlie never lost touch with himself.

For me there was an uncomfortable gap. Between the bags of blood and bone at the Ulmarra store and the fine-china tea parties (required officers' ladies activity) and, worse still, the cocktail parties, where people seemed to speak a different language, and where I kept my eyes glued on epaulettes to get it right. Getting it right was the problem: which knife, which glass, which dress, which word? I can still hear my voice clanging amidst the so round vowels. I took solace in fantasies that one day, somehow, I would use language so well, I'd never have to worry about wrongness again.

Charlie's dream of a farm had not been abandoned altogether, I learned. Shortly after he arrived in Victoria he made a friend, and it is significant that this new friend lived on a property that would make just about anyone want to abandon whatever they were doing to farm that ideal place. It was a dream in actuality. C.H. would say: "If I owned this I wouldn't call the King my uncle."

One day, on manoeuvres in the countryside, C.H. and another officer decided they needed to traverse this attractive property. They went to the owner to get permission. And that's how C.H. met Mrs Elsie Gidney, the owner of Woodlands, at Kerrisdale, in the Goulburn Valley. Mrs Gidney told me later she took an immediate liking to C.H.; she said he had an honesty and sincerity she found refreshing. He told her he was soon to be joined by his wife and child, and that he would like to introduce us to her. Mrs Gidney, a widow, lived with her adopted daughter, who helped her to manage her 600-acre property, more as a hobby than a serious commercial venture.

I remember the day C.H. drove us out to Woodlands, excitedly pointing out its inimitable qualities. A gravel drive wound around a huge rose garden to the entrance of a sprawling homestead. Living rooms welcomed us with glowing fires, bowls of roses and trays laden with tea, cakes and sandwiches. After tea, we went to see the property. At the back, beyond a covered pergola was a lagoon, big enough for the use of the boat lying on the reflection-filled water. On the glassy water floated white geese that set my imagination alight. Mrs Gidney's lagoon and Yeats' poem are inseparable in my mind:

*Unwearied still, lover by lover,*
*They paddle in the cold*
*Companionable streams or climb the air;*
*Their hearts have not grown old;*
*Passion or conquest, wander where they will*
*Attend upon them still.*

Beyond the house were the river bank pastures, the centre of C.H.'s more practical attention, top-dressed to a brilliant green. Fields shaded by gum trees bordered the river. Grazing there languidly were brick-red, white-faced Herefords and round, white balls of wool that had, if you looked closely, little legs buried in the grass.

And there were stables too. One of the highlights of Charlie's year was the breaking-in of a new horse for Mrs Gidney. I remember seeing him working slowly, patiently with rope and bridle to tame the nervous horse. One day he saddled it; it reared a few times then settled down as he proudly rode off down along the river bank. He would have been exultant had it been his farm, his horse — his dream come true.

I told C.H. that if Woodlands was what farming might be,

I'd move to a farm immediately. It was, of course, far beyond our means.

Towards the end of 1949, C.H. learned he had been accepted as a student for the 1950 session of the Staff College in Queenscliff, Victoria. "Another move," I grizzled. He explained that if he were to have a career in the army, he needed to get the qualification "p.s.c." (Passed Staff College). Acceptance was in itself an honour, as students were selected on the grounds of suitability and potential.

At Queenscliff, with his old style of finding the best solution, he rented an enchanting house called The Hermitage in Bethune Street at the high, bay end of the street. As I remember it, time exaggerates the charm of the house, a fairy-tale place filled with nooks and crannies, a lot like Mrs Gidney's. Outside, in the big bushy garden, Anthea and the dog loved hiding in the bushes and behind trees, which, until the dog arrived, sheltered a few rabbits.

The owner, Mrs Lakeland, became a close friend who also grew to love C.H., whom she affectionately called "Charles". For me she had gentle words of advice and gems of wisdom. She would say, for instance: "Look in the mirror before you leave home. Then you see yourself at your best. Don't look again, but believe you still look the same as you did when you set out." I tend to do that still. Mrs Lakeland, of Scottish ancestry, was both canny and exceedingly generous in the way that is least easy — that is, in her acceptance of people and the time and attention she would give to her friends. To me she was a mother whom I did not want to leave when the time came.

Winter arrived once more. We were comfortable in that house of open fires and window seats, where we could sit and gaze at a vast stretch of water that would sparkle and expand in the sun or dim and diminish in the fog and rain. C.H., for the first time since I had lived with him, was obliged to study regularly. There was no avoiding it. I do not remember now whether he gardened so frequently. The vegetable plot at

Queenscliff must have been small. All I can see is a row or two of mignonette lettuce. His routine was rather to play some sport after lectures finished, come home, have his tea and begin to study. I would knit and read, not happy, he would say, unless I was doing at least two things at once.

It is strange what incidents stick. One day, as we were going out of The Hermitage gate on our way to some army function, C.H. looked me over and said: "You can do better than that." I went back and changed. Off to a function now, at the gate I pause — and remember.

I could feel my love for him growing deeper. When I thought about it my body would warm and tingle. One night I sat and watched him, his fine head bent over a book. Some impulse made me put my knitting down, go over behind him, put my arms around him, hug him and whisper in his ear: "I love you very much." He turned around, coming back to earth with a look that melted my heart. His eyes took on that soft, shiny look that spoke of his essence, and he smiled his little smile. When I went back to my chair, I noticed his knee bobbing, another little habit of his that registered emotion.

Mutually, simultaneously we decided it was time to have another child. His confidence must have returned. No longer was he saying: "I'll never go through that again."

Despite my general impression of army life being empty, we enjoyed some fine army friendships at Queenscliff and at Seymour. At Queenscliff the couple we were closest to were Canadians, Mary and George Hale. George fought beside the British at Normandy on D-Day. I recall stories he told about "Monty", General Montgomery, and the fun we all had when Charlie and he would return late in the evenings for hearty suppers around the fire with us wives. Charlie was very taken with Mary, to the extent I once felt a painful twinge of jealousy and exploded in tears. You know when another has qualities you yourself lack.

The gods get jealous, too, they say. I remember the day I had the premonition. I was walking around the house, tingling with contentment as I brushed out fireplaces and filled bowls with flowers. Reflecting on how happy we were, I suddenly had a strange surge of fear. *"We are too happy!"* Then came the shock realisation — *"Something terrible is going to happen."* My knees went to jelly, and I stood leaning against the table in the room that looked out over the bay. Seeing the water brought me back from that strange sphere beyond time that some special sense takes me to, but I realised my heart was heavy. I did not mention this to C.H.

I am not sure any more whether it was hours or days later, but when he walked through the door, in the afternoon, long before he ordinarily got home, and I saw his face, I knew. He looked white, and heavy-hearted too.

"What's happened?"

"I'm being sent to Korea. I have a week before I leave."

We fell into each other's arms and clung together, saying no more. I was sure he had had a premonition too; both of us were too stricken to talk, to say all that we feared, how unprepared we were for the world suddenly to turn upside-down.

"The things we do for King and country," I remember he added, trying to sound jovial. He could have said, proudly, even triumphantly: "I have been selected to lead the Australian contingent to the Korean War."

Shock had set in as far as I was concerned, with the result that I have no clear memory of events. Here and there a few images survive; what I do recall are only those incidents that penetrated my cloud of horror. Telegrams poured in, to my incredulity. Why, I wondered, do people congratulate a man being sent to war? Why is he suddenly the Army's centre of attention? What irony. It was this man, who did not really belong in the Regular Army, that the chiefs of staff selected at a time when they were obliged to consider one thing and one thing only: who could best do the job? A difficult decision. Every expectation was that it would be a Regular Army appointment. All eyes -- the eyes of the country, the eyes of the world — would be on that little band of Anzacs, the best fighting men in the world. There was the tradition to uphold. Their leader needed to be a man who could be relied on to do credit to Australia and its tradition.

Recently it was suggested to me by a senior AIF officer of World War 2 that had C.H. survived, no matter how brilliantly he had performed, no matter how great his potential, the system would have held him back. He was not Staff Corps. Be that as it may, his lack of formal education was a genuine limitation.

It's time to think again about what happened. So great has my preoccupation always been about the "why's" of the tragedy, I have not seen the situation whole. I've overlooked the pride Charlie must have felt, even the excitement at the thought of accepting a huge challenge. He was being recognised again.

Before we left for Grafton, where C.H. had decided to take me, there were farewell parties at Queenscliff. It is the one the army wives gave for me that I remember. Word must have got around that Mrs Green was distressed — or perhaps it was very apparent. The Mrs Brigadier or Mrs General, I do not remember the woman, only the voice, gave a speech during which she lectured me on the proper conduct of an officer's wife. She decreed: "An officer's wife had an obligation (I don't remember the exact words) to bear up cheerfully and not to burden her husband with her evident distress." She was right. She might have taken me aside, though, and pointed all this out helpfully, the way Elvie did when she told me about babies. If I'd been a different person, instead of being terrified, I would have been gloating; for wasn't my husband suddenly one of the most important men in the Army?

Soon we were driving on the long road home to Grafton. We drove all through the night, maintaining a heavy silence most of the way, not knowing what to say. At Grafton, C.H. did everything he could to settle us in by organising to have furniture moved and other things done, important to our comfort. He wrote lists of what to do in various circumstances; they looked painfully like a precaution should he not come home.

We went to Swan Creek for C.H. to say goodbye. That afternoon he did a strange, unexpected thing. He leapt on a horse and rode off, bareback, towards the river bank. Seeing his tall form in the distance nostalgically farewelling his birthplace made me bleed; the act suggested, I feared, that he did feel the foreboding that he would never return.

The fragile minutes sped till we faced his last night at home, possibly "The end of lying down together". How do you talk to a man you believe you will never see again? I always think of those lines a soldier, Alun Lewis, wrote, for no words of mine could convey the chill I felt when I touched his warm skin, and shivered: "Would I ever feel him again?"

*Your kisses close my eyes and yet you stare*
*As though God struck a child with nameless fears;*
*Perhaps the water glitters and discloses*
*Time's chalice and its limpid useless tears.*

It was not a night for passion, just for holding each other, whispering. He said, "Look after Bubby for me."

He knew the child had sensed something was wrong. When Charlie cut his finger and I bandaged it, she kept fretting over "Daddy's sore finger" believing it to be the source of all the anxiety. When he didn't come home she still kept asking about "Daddy's sore finger" — concluding, eventually, that was the cause of his disappearance and death. She was too young to understand her loss. Ultimately she felt it deeply.

I went to the Grafton railway station to see him off late that September afternoon. We seemed to be the only people on the platform. How unreal it seemed. "Here is a man going to war and nobody is aware," I thought. He was in uniform already. Magnificent — yet no longer did this thrill me as it once did. Instead, I saw shells and danger. Death. I could hear the train approaching and then it jerked to a halt. Already he was remote. His face was gone, because I could not bear to look and think: "The last time." There were no words. Nor did he embrace. He did something he had never done before. Knightly, he picked up my hand and kissed it. Then disappeared on to the train.

He was gone.

# 19
# The cow

> When the world went up in fire,
> And the soul that was mine deserted
> And left me, a thing in the mire,
> With a madden'd and dim remembrance
> Of a time when my life was whole.
> Carry me into the darkness, sir,
> And let me find my soul.
>
> *Despair* by Olive E. Lindsay

He was gone.

Returning to the empty house and the empty bed, I wondered if I could survive if he never came home. There's no blurring in my mind of those black days. Nightmarishly they live on. So does the cow incident that now seems pathetically theatrical. But it happened. Its bizarreness a measure of my distress.

With Charlie gone, I fell victim to my premonition. I became possessed by the idea that Charlie would die and that would be my fit punishment. All that he wanted was a normal life with the woman of his dreams, and a nice farm. He'd be the happiest man alive. His dreams didn't come true. Because I was snobbish and fastidious I hadn't wanted Charlie in a flannel shirt and Wellington boots, squelching around in the cow yard, tied to cows day in, day out, for ever. I'd wanted tall, handsome Charlie the commander in an elegant home leading a sophisticated life. Only some convincing sign that I repented could assuage an angry God or restore Charlie's belief that I was the wife he'd dreamed about, the wife who loved him.

I seized on the idea of the cow, though I have no recollection of how it came about. I'd show God and Charlie. I'd learn to milk. Before Charlie left we must have planned the cow and talked about the farm we'd get this time when he came home. It must have been Charlie who organised the cow with Herc. It arrived after Charlie left. Herc sent it in a truck. It was a little, cream, gentle-eyed thing with a pedigree, whose nickname I can't recall. Herc, with his sharp eye and razor perception, named cows after people. He'd say, "That's Mary," and you'd know there would be some uncanny resemblance to its namesake. One cow was named after me, someone let fall one day.

The cow went into Charlie's paddock, the one at the back of the house where he'd once planted potatoes. Probably it was Charlie who threw up an improvised bail, before he left. Or it might have been Harry Smith. Harry and Elvie were brought into the scheme. They could have seen through the drama and joined in to help, out of love for Charlie. By this time Harry and Elvie had two more babies, twins, to provide for. They kept fowls and grew vegetables, and after the cow had to be taken away, they got two goats. One goat would have been lonely. It astounded me to see those butting creatures with their strange, yellow, slit eyes overwhelming their backyard. Until I learned to milk, Harry and Elvie would come night and morning with a milk bucket, going through my place to reach the paddock.

From Korea Charlie was to write, curious and amused, wishing he were a fly on the wall. With a little smile he would have mused on Harry and Elvie sterilising everything. God knows how he pictured me! "Your farm," as he called it, didn't go to plan. I didn't learn to milk. After Charlie left, I was desolate. I could not function. It was as though all the blood and all my life had been drained out of me. Try as I might, I couldn't drag myself around. If I'd cried, it might have been easier. It was the end; it was too late, said my burdensome pessimism. I did not learn to milk. I couldn't.

Then it started to rain, as though nature itself was disturbed. It rained and rained. Confined in the paddock that became a quagmire, the little cow had to be hand-fed and milked, night and morning. In dripping oilskins and gum boots Harry and Elvie would struggle past as I looked on dumbly.

Recalling all this, I had one of my typical nightmares last night:

> Charlie and I went to Finland, apparently on a holiday. There, we set out to find a particular house. When we found it we realised it was different from all those around it, and we were pleased. It was old and basic, and appealing, compared with the other modern ones. Expectantly we set out across the street to enter the house. That's when Charlie slipped in the mud. At first he gestured amusedly how deep the mud was. But then he started sinking; he kept on sinking till he was up to his neck. Then he indicated he was trapped and was going under! As he sank out of sight he called, "I can't see." I tried to scream for help but no sound would come — this was the frightening part of the dream. Then I panicked and wildly sought help, desperately trying to make a sound. I noted though that instead of going to his aid, I ran around frantically. Someone appeared and said, "That's very bad (or evil) mud."

That's all I recall. After such a dream, I remain haunted for hours. Since I've been told that "dreams are a message from you to you", I endeavour to untangle them. In this dream there was the recurring theme — losing Charlie.

Fear of losing him was the reason for invoking the cow. An impotent talisman it turned out to be.

Some healing of the soul has given me clearer, fuller vision. These days I wonder: "Had I been able to combat the premonition and embrace Charlie's appointment confidently, as an opportunity for him, how different it might have been. He might have come home!"

And he might not.

# 20
# Korea, 1950 —Getting the feel of the Battalion

> If I should go away,
> Beloved do not say
> "He has forgotten me."
> For you abide,
> A singing rib within my dreaming side;' "
>
> *Postscript: for Gweno* by Alun Lewis

When Charlie left to take up his command on September 10, 1950, he had only six weeks left. Six weeks to live. In that time, he moulded another Battalion for another war. In the space of a week he saw his Battalion blooded in the first of three major battles. Then he faced death; a death that came on him unexpectedly. The day he died, the tide of battle turned.

In those six weeks his ability and bravery were so evident, he was decorated with a Silver Star, for "gallantry in action" and "superb leadership" — by the Americans.

He had earned a hero's death; but his was a disturbing end that left questions, not answers. "Kismet," said Bernard O'Dowd, who served with C.H. in both 2/11 Bn, and in 3RAR.

I dreaded the upset of bringing it all back, especially of opening up his last letters from Korea that I had always kept apart. I didn't anticipate that past and present would become indistinguishable. Charlie came near and alive. I could see him, hear him, feel him. It seems he is still there behind some barrier. Perhaps time is only an illusion that can momentarily dissolve. Suddenly I discovered my rage. Like a pipe bursting, the rage erupted in me, out of me. I'd never before reached my anger, buried under the hurt and the guilt. After that came the long denied tears — the real tears.

I was the more ready then to look again, coolly, at the strange course to his end. Kismet it may be, but it is a chilling design.

On June 25 1950, when the Korean war broke out, no one took much notice. Few people knew where Korea was. If we'd known it sat like a wart on the coast of China, had Japan as a neighbour over the water, and Russia at its back door, we'd have realised it was important. Korea's political division at the 38th Parallel, a heritage of the winding-up of World War 2, separating Communist from non-Communist, was crossed when Kim Il Sung's army invaded South Korea to unify the nation under Communism. The Communists thought that Synghman Rhee's Presidency had brought the South to the point of revolution. The United Nations subsequently decided to field an army to defend South Korea. General MacArthur, who had overseen the recovery of Japan, who had saved the Pacific, seemed the right man to command the UN Army.

It took MacArthur's brilliance to turn back the aggressors but not before the defenders were pushed into a last-stand position at Pusan, in the south-east corner of Korea. Then MacArthur struck. His one brilliant stroke, the landing at Inchon, coinciding with a counter-offensive out of the Pusan Perimeter, saved the day. With the Communists on the run, he prepared to chase them out of South Korea and out of North Korea, too. However, he provoked what the Americans and the British didn't want: Chinese intervention. It was the day the Chinese mass-infantry assault began that Charlie died.

Australia, acting independently and contrary to Britain's wishes, announced on July 26 that it would send ground forces to Korea. The obvious unit to be committed was a newly founded Regular Army battalion, the Third Battalion of the

Royal Australian Regiment stationed in Japan. But 3 RAR was only at half-strength; to reinforce it, on August 8 there was a call for volunteers, to be called "K Force". Unbelievably, recruiting officers were flooded with applicants. The Army selected 500 men on the basis of their experience in World War 2, and their general suitability. The recruits were flown to Japan on September 3 to join 3 RAR and ready themselves quickly for Korea. Political pressure demanded their immediate deployment. In particular, the Americans said, it would boost the morale of the American people. And, at the time, ANZUS was on the drawing-board.

Tradition was being broken. This was an expeditionary force with a difference, unlike the AIF. Volunteers and regulars traditionally antagonistic (especially the officers) were to be blended under the colours of a permanent Army regiment to be sent overseas.

The government required the best man possible to lead the Australian force for Korea. There must be no risk of incurring unacceptably high casualties. A spotlight would be on the Australians. They had the Anzac reputation at stake. The decision of the Military Board surprised many, especially in Army circles. It selected Charles Hercules Green, a soldier with an AIF rather than a Regular Army background. The choice meant pulling him out of Staff College. He was granted the coveted p.s.c. halfway through his course. This was unprecedented. There could be no greater indication of the trust that was placed in him.

So anxious was I that I did not realise, or recognise, what an honour C.H.'s appointment was. It wasn't important to me. His life was my life, and that was being threatened. Had I seen it dispassionately, I could have thrilled to the fact that C.H. had been given the opportunity of his life. He had only to acquit himself well and his sense of achievement and his career were ensured. I remember him saying it was an honour. What else he felt I don't know. Now, having followed him a long way and talked to many people, I know a lot of Charlie remains unread. I keep thinking of what Effendi said about the C.H. he sensed but never found. The reason is probably very simple. Charlie was naturally reserved and dignified. If someone had asked him, he would have told them. Sir Fred Chilton is probably the most accurate. He said: "He was simple, in the best sense of the word."

C.H.'s emotions at the time were very mixed and deep-felt, but he had his habitual equanimity to stabilise him, that wonderful ability that was like Bertha's: "he did not let anything lean on him", to use the Mrs Want's words. It was what the soldiers call "taking things as they come". I was the storm: he was the calm. Down the years I can feel his calm now, touching, soothing. I've sensed this quality all through his story. I can even feel it rubbing off — at last.

Charlie fell at the height of his capabilities: a cherry blossom death. Now, with more perspective I can see that his life took an inevitable course, though not the one he would have preferred — so far as I know. Once again he experienced achievement and self-affirmation, as he needed to, by proving that his country chose well. Under his leadership, the Australian force had enough dash to win admiration and battles. And enough individuality to earn itself an affectionate nickname: "Old Faithful". Above all, it exhibited a standard of performance that impressed everyone: the British, the Americans, the Koreans.

The men who tell the end of Charlie's story are mainly those who worked close to him in 3 RAR: his HQ staff and officers of the Battalion's companies. I wasn't able to find an "everyman", like Woop, mainly because of the nature of the unit with its ever-changing members, and because I wasn't able to track down Bill Redmonds, the batman, who keeps cropping up beside C.H. in the writings about Korea.

The Charlie Green they describe is essentially the same man who commanded 2/11 Battalion: a bit older, a bit wiser, a lot more confident. Charlie the leader they can readily describe; Charlie the man remains, to some, a bit of an enigma but a man to be respected. He is remembered for his exceptional leadership and for his untimely death, the shock of which has reverberated down the years.

When I was in Perth quite recently I had a telephone call

one day from a man who introduced himself as Colin Ellis. He said:

> I heard some people talking and I felt I wanted to get in touch with you. My brother, Desmond, served under your husband — "Greenie", as he called him.
>
> My brother was killed in an accident soon after he got home from Korea. I was only fourteen at the time but I remember him and his mate Harry Taylor, who was also in Korea, talking about the war and about their CO, Greenie. He must have been very popular. Sometimes they would talk about the way he was hit. It bothered them. They said they would have felt better if he'd got it when he was up in the front with them and not when he wasn't looking.
>
> I used to think about it a lot. I thought, "Great people should go on for ever".


September 10 was a proud day for C.H.'s old Battalion the 2/2: one of them was to command the Australian force for Korea. They wrote in their journal *Nulli Secundus*: "Colonel Green takes with him to Korea, in addition to a Field Marshal's baton in his haversack, the kind and sincere regards of his comrades of all ranks who served with him during the war."

Charlie's new Battalion 3 RAR (the fourth battalion he was attached to) was stationed at Hiro, in the Hiroshima area of Japan. It was the first unit of the new Australian Regular Army. The Battalion was founded in November 1948 by redesignating 67 Battalion, raised for the Occupation Force in Japan. In 1950, 3 RAR was under-manned and under-equipped; when the Korean War broke out it was winding up in Japan ready to go home to Australia. It hadn't trained as a unit for years; now, in one swoop, it was reinforced by about 400 men, mostly World War 2 veterans. The old hands weren't sure whether they swallowed the reos or the reos swallowed them. It was an identity crisis. What C.H. found was, in their own words, "a rabble" that did not impress him.

"Rabble" is not how Charlie described them in a letter. He

Above: Charlie Green on exercise with 3RAR in Japan, 1950.

Below: Teabreak during the exercise with L-R: Charlie Green, unknown, Captain L. Watts and Captain E. Ayrton, Japan.

Above: Charlie accepts a gift of flowers as 3RAR arrives at Pusan, Korea.
Below: L-R: Charlie, unknown soldier, Lieutenant Alf Argent, Korea.

had just two weeks to transform the unprecedented mix into a fighting unit for an even more difficult mix, also unprecedented. He was to operate in a British brigade, in an American commanded United Nations army. He set aside his personal emotions and gave his all.

The Intelligence Officer of 3 RAR, Alf Argent (later Lieutenant Colonel) wrote in *Australian Infantry*, 1972:

> Lieutenant Colonel C.H. Green, DSO assumed command of 3 RAR on September 12, 1950, the day after the last draft marched in from Australia. Although he was to command for only six weeks he was to leave a mark that 21 years have not diminished.
>
> Although he didn't say anything, the new CO could not have been much impressed with what he first saw in his new command. The basic material was there all right — and events were to prove that it was good material — but there was a distinct lack of cohesion and the standard of sub-unit and unit training was poor. The parts did not fit well together, which of course was only to be expected.
>
> The CO remained surprisingly calm and seemingly above all the turmoil. I only saw him angry twice, when there must have been many times when it would have been easy to get upset. Once was about an overloaded jeep of the anti-tank platoon during training and the other time was in Korea when a platoon area was a mess of ration boxes, papers and tins. The platoon commander on the first occasion suffered a severe tongue lashing. So did the second one.
>
> Lieutenant Colonel Green was a tall, dark, sinewy man with the bearing, and unhurried deliberateness one usually associated with men of the land. Pressure never seemed to bother him. He had a fine touch and the presence of a natural leader. His command in Korea was always firm and sure. The somewhat pell-mell advance on North Korea usually meant an "O" group at night and orders over the radio by day. He always gave good, clear, concise orders. He kept well forward, in fact immediately behind the leading company group. Like the second-in-command, who was to command later, he had an eye for country and was an extraordinarily good map reader — all the more remarkable considering the poor maps of those early days. After six weeks he had moulded the battalion into a solid fighting unit.

3 RAR was to see a lot of active service, after C.H.'s period:

four years in Korea, four years in Malaysia, two years in Vietnam. It has suffered a lot of casualties: 200 killed and more than 1000 wounded. The Battalion won the US Presidential citation in the famous Battle of Kapyong, Korea, in 1951. Many of its members have been decorated. Recently, Old Faithful has added to its title the suffix "Para", becoming 3 RAR (Para). One of the recent COs, Lieutenant Colonel Gallagher, says: "It is still an infantry Battalion. Parachuting is just one of its special skills."

For his second in command in Korea C.H. had a man he had known for a long time — Bruce Ferguson. It was a comfort to have an old, valued comrade like Bruce, also a thirty-niner and, by a remarkable coincidence, a 2/2 Battalion man. Bruce was an experienced, brave officer. He won an MC on the Owen Stanley track. When C.H. was killed, after a brief interim Bruce succeeded him as CO of 3 RAR. He was CO when 3 RAR won its Presidential citation at Kapyong.

Bruce, who had been stationed in Japan with the occupation forces when the Korean war broke out, held a dinner party so that C.H. could meet Captain John Callander, the Adjutant of 3 RAR, and one of C.H.'s key men in Korea. There must have been an almost immediate rapport. Later, when I met Cal, he said about C.H.: "I liked working with him."

Bernard O'Dowd of 2/11 Battalion became Officer in Command of HQ company, 3 RAR. Bernie explained that Korea was a different war: a professional's war. "We didn't want any laughing boys. We were glad of this serious young man." I picked up from Bernie that he "sometimes got the feeling he (C.H.) wasn't ready for what was thrust on him." He went on to say how very professional C.H. was and that no one ever doubted his ability. It seemed to trouble Bernie that Charlie remained "a bit of a mystery". "Who," he queried, "ever got close to him?"

These fragments, like pieces of a jig-saw, came together to produce a clear, consistent picture. Several times I heard the same phrases, especially this one: "He was the right man, in the right place, at the right time." Perhaps some of it is already legend. After all, he was the father of the unit; it was under C.H. that 3 RAR was blooded.

He is universally remembered as being cool, calm, quiet, reserved and honest; for leading from just behind the front yet not interfering with the Company Commander's decisions; just being there in case he was needed. "For this," Cal said, "the troops idolised him."

C.H.'s quietness is legendary. Recently Brigadier Jim Shelton, a lieutenant in 3 RAR in 1951, after Charlie's death and later CO of 3 RAR in Vietnam, said he had been asked by a reporter, to describe 3 Battalion. Jim replied: "It's a very quiet Battalion." To me he said: "I believe that was a stamp Colonel Green put on the Battalion."

Another story kept cropping up. One night a company surrounded by the enemy was under extreme pressure. The company commander "lost his cool" and wanted to retreat. It was a critical period in the battle. C.H. (also known for not refusing requests) said: "You'll just have to hold on." And he did.

Though strict, C.H. cared about his troops. As Bruce Ferguson said, "He had the welfare of every man in the Battalion at heart." According to Cal, "The last thing he did of an evening was to settle the Battalion down. Then he'd have his tea before he got to work. Always he insisted on having his tea before he made plans for the next day."

However, from the number of times I hear such comments as "he didn't show emotions" or, as Alf Argent said, "He never unmasked himself," I get the impression they would have liked to have found out what made him tick, personally. This privacy of his had nothing to do with dishonesty. As Alf Argent astutely concluded: "His honesty was always a feature of his style of leadership. He always presented the truth about situations. There were no dramatics. He did it his way — the honest way. There's no point in not being honest. Soldiers wouldn't fall for dishonesty. And if you go outside your character, it doesn't work." Caesar is said to have treated his soldiers as men who were "entitled to demand and were able to endure the truth".

Not long ago Bruce Ferguson, whom I saw a couple of times over the years, was at 3 RAR's Kapyong Day Ceremony, at Holsworthy. We were sitting in the mess of 3 Battalion, looking at the sculpture of C.H. the young officers had commissioned. "That's his little smile," said Bruce. He reminisced for a while. Then out of the blue he said, "I am sure Charlie thought he was going to die. He made certain I was familiar with everything. We used to go for little walks talking about things. He liked to draw me out. When I was in a tight spot [after Bruce became CO] I'd say to myself, 'Now what would he have done?' " Then, after a pause: "It's the loneliest job in the world."

C.H. immediately set about getting to know his new officers. He called a meeting in the mess. "I remember," says David Butler (later Major General), then a young lieutenant commanding a platoon, "he came in confident and cool. He addressed us. What he said, if you analysed it, was trite, yet he had some ineffable power, a mysterious something that had a tremendous, dramatic effect. He had us. I and a group of young lieutenants were terribly impressed. And the interest in him has not waned over the years." He continued: "In his speech to the officers that day, the Colonel talked about the mystique of a Battalion, saying, 'It's like a planet'."

C.H. was attributing to it its own life, as Jo Gullett did when he said a battalion has achieved a "state of grace" when it is ready to fight. 3 RAR went on to develop its own character, epitomised in its affix, "Old Faithful", for its reputation of always being there when it is needed, for often going to the rescue. For being solid, reliable, expert, faithful, lovable. The stamp of C.H. Green, perhaps.

To assess the unit, a four-day exercise, "Bolero", was held at Haramura. It was tough. To make it harder, a typhoon raged throughout. The new CO was seen standing knee-deep in mud, coolly giving orders and quickly detecting weaknesses. His verdict: "It's not working."

Some of the measures he took "left junior officers agape". Incompetents, two company commanders for instance, "were skidded right out". Another, "who messed up supplies, leaving the troops without food, was demoted on the spot".

COs get tested too. The General, none other than Red Robbie, Lieutenant General Sir Horace Robertson, who had commanded 6 Division in Wewak at the end of 1945, said to C.H. at the end of the exercise in the typhoon: "Right. Now can you get them back to camp at Hiro by midnight?" C.H. said he could.

Getting the whole Battalion back meant efficient organisation, fit and keen troops. They had to march twenty miles. They made it, as they proudly boast.

It was on this exercise that Archer Denness, OC of C Company, caught C.H.'s eye. He said: "You can always rely on Arch." Arch, unaware of this, told me: "He trusted me, though he didn't know me from a pocket full of beetles." Denness' moist eye revealed the deep feeling he had for the man who honoured him with his trust. And with the honour of commanding the company that launched the attack the day the Battalion was blooded. "How he could manage men! He created a massive impression. Not often in a lifetime do you find a man like him," said Arch emotionally.

While the Australians were fighting their mock battle in Japan to ensure their readiness for the real thing, the Americans were landing at Inchon. William Manchester, MacArthur's biographer, says the daring gamble on a two-hour tide, was "one of the greatest feats in military history". At the same time the American 8th Army and unspecified ROK (Republic of Korea) units were forging west to link with the Inchon force to recapture Seoul. This was achieved on September 28 and victory snatched from Kim Il Sung. Everyone thought the war was over.

Nevertheless, the Australians hurriedly patched up the Battalion's apparent defects in the ten days they had after "Bolero", before leaving to strengthen the British two-battalion strong force, already in Korea, into a brigade.

Just before embarking for Korea, Cal reported, the CO called for a full Battalion parade — one of those memorable occasions. He wanted to address the troops. They stood on the big gravel parade ground, in full battle gear. Their Colonel's words haven't been recorded. But it is remembered how "he stood out, over the others". The troops liked to be able to identify him: "That's Greenie" — who, as one of them said, "Was like God to us. He held our fate in his hands."

In Grafton, no longer home without Charlie, once again I waited for letters. There were nine. (These are the ones I kept bundled up, afraid to re-read until I started this book.) My instinct was right; they did disturb me, but not in the way I expected. The closer he got to battle the more unrelated his writing was to grim actualities. The only explanation is that he was protecting me. I hadn't yet had the kind of experience (as soldiers say of battle) that would rid me of all the bullshit. I was on the brink of it. I wish I had been mature enough to give Charlie the opportunity to unburden. Instead Charlie was repeatedly reassuring me with avowals of his love, and bearing his ordeal alone.

The nine letters fall into two groups: four ebullient ones from Japan and five from Korea that grow leaner, as foreboding creeps in.

These excerpts from the Japan letters have been selected so that repetition can be avoided and Charlie's own voice be heard:

12 September, 1950

I cabled my arrival which should have reached you long before this. The trip was long and tiring and by the time we touched down in Japan I was ready for a good sleep.

Since arriving I have been in such a whirl that I scarcely know who I am. There's a lot to be done and not much time to do it in. I have only seen parts of the Battalion to date but they are very impressive and officers are a great bunch. It will be the best unit ever and everyone is enthusiastic and morale is high.

There is such a lot I would like to write about but time is pressing. At first light tomorrow we leave for a four-day exercise so I shall write again when we return . . .

The barracks and quarters here are really lovely . . . I have a house, a lovely little place with two bedrooms, lounge, etc, central heating and a house girl to keep it and my gear in order and from first experiences she is very good at it. Unfortunately I will not have much time to enjoy these luxuries.

This trouble is not as bad as you would believe; in fact it's rather more like civil war and with our unit we will have little to worry about. I am going over to see the whole thing for a couple of days and get first-hand information but it will be a little time before we move.

16 September, 1950

... we began a pretty tough four-day exercise during which a typhoon passed over us. Have never seen such wind and rain ... Despite all this I enjoyed the exercise for it gave me an opportunity to get the "feel" of the unit. Some weaknesses were revealed but the unit is generally in good shape.

You would remember Captain Watts darling at Seymour? He helped us shift our furniture. He is my signal officer and is doing well. Ken Mackenzie's brother is a Lieutenant and second-in-command of the sig platoon. He is very much like Ken — voice is identical.

Tomorrow, Sunday, night I am dining with Bruce Ferguson and his wife at their house. He married a Canadian girl, so I will hear that Yankee drawl again ...

It seems as if the Korean war will soon be over. Big things are happening right now and the feeling here is that it will not take long ...

20 September 1950

Darling tomorrow is your birthday and I did intend to send you a tele from here today but in the hustle and bustle of getting this unit equipped and trained I have forgotten it. In fact I have been out some twenty miles from here where some of the companies are on exercises and only returned about six o'clock. I will send a cable first thing tomorrow. Before leaving Grafton I did think of your birthday. I do hope you like it ...

The unit is shaking down well and they are a very happy bunch. They will do well when the time comes and we have lashings of equipment. I may be taking a short trip over there next week, but this has not been confirmed yet ...

24 September 1950

Had a lovely long letter from you dated September 13 a few days ago . . . I will write whatever I can and from now on my letters may become a bit infrequent but I can assure you darling that whenever possible I will be penning you a line. In fact we will be seeing kilts in a few days, no doubt before you receive this. Should there be large gaps between letters sweetheart, don't worry. In fact we haven't much to worry about in this campaign and the battalion will be on top from the word go . . .

Have you seen anything of my people darling? I haven't had time to write. Could you tell them I am well and that I will write when I can but somehow I feel that they will have to get most of their information from you because whenever I have any time to write one letter that letter will be to you of course . . .

I shall be well looked after during this campaign. I have a first-class batman and driver; in fact better than I have ever had which makes such a difference in a time like this.

On September 21, my twenty-seventh birthday, the flowers arrived. He hadn't forgotten, though there was every reason why he could have. As usual, they were wine-red roses. They were like our life together. Beautiful and transient.

I shivered. His departure was like an amputation. After five years of having his body close it seemed as though we had merged into one. My body ached and pined for the missing half. And like an amputee, I've never been without the sensation of the part that has been severed.

His absence was felt in other ways. Soon the big house and business matters overwhelmed me: the lawns never seemed to stop growing, nor the weeds, especially in his vegetable garden. And down in the paddock the cow demanded the attention I had promised it, but never gave. Instead, I watched Harry and Elvie go to it, night and morning. Disabled, I could do nothing. I wonder if I admitted the truth to C.H. when I wrote. I doubt it.

However, with Herc's help I must have begun immediately to look for a farm — finding a suitable place could take months. Herc was quick to come up with a proposition that presumably I sent off to C.H. in Korea. His reply came by cable later — the timing of which added to my grief. In his letters, Charlie makes no reference to a farm, though he does to the cow. So I have no idea what he really thought about it all. His letters from Korea don't talk much about the future.

C.H. flew to Korea on September 27. The next day he and General Robertson were at the wharf at Pusan to meet the troops. Pusan, the gateway to Korea in the east, is wedged between the murky, dirty harbour and high surrounding mountains.

It was some welcome, as C.H. reported to me. The Koreans are partial to ceremonies. Bands, an American Negro, a Korean and 3 RAR's own all played. A Korean girls' choir sang while other girls presented bouquets. The rest of the crowd waved an array of flags, finding, eventually, the Australian one. They had, the troops learned, a flag for every conquering army. Yet for all the Koreans' apparent willingness to accomodate occupiers, they maintain, as they have done for centuries, their individuality. They remain Koreans, different from other Asians: less formal, more open, more direct, inquisitive. They still cling to their national dress, the *hambok*, a garment dating back to the influence of the Mongols. The vivid, flowing dress keeps history alive on the Korean landscape.

All that, and reception committees too, were a bit much for the Australian diggers as they marched ashore. With more than a touch of banter, suggesting that once again the Australians' reputation preceded them, a British journalist described their arrival:

> The voices were strident with a broad twang and sharpened vowel sound; they were voices immediately, and, in some quarters, apprehensively identifiable as Australian.
> The men streaming down the gangways of the American ship *Aiken Victory* seemed to be bigger and tougher looking than the men of 27 Brigade; their faces were square, leathery and tanned, and on every one was a broad grin. They were certainly older, and on a large number of left breasts could be seen ribbons, outward and visible signs of war service in North Africa and the Pacific. They wore slouch hats at rakish angles.

It was to be the same, everywhere, even in North Korea: "Welkum" signs and flag-waving.

From Pusan, the Australian troops were transported by train to Taegu and thence by foot to a dry river bed five miles north-west. They camped in the open that first night in Korea. Their supplies hadn't caught up with them: a problem that was to plague them all the way to the Manchurian Border.

At Taegu they joined the two British Battalions: 1 Battalion Middlesex ("Diehards") and 1 Battalion Argyll and Sutherland Highlanders (the kilted "Rories"). It was with the Argylls that Charlie had got 41 Byron Scottish Regiment affiliated. There was now a brigade, immediately renamed the 27 British Commonwealth Brigade. The leader was Brigadier Aubrey Coad. As C.H. said in a letter, he was "older" and a fine man. Cal said he was "a gem". The British had already seen fierce, indeed tragic, action. On September 21 they had fought the battle of Hill 282; dreadful casualties occurred when the British were accidentally battered and napalmed by the Americans.

That incident suffices to point up the Brigade's difficulties in Korea. They had to depend on the Americans for support — air strikes, artillery, tanks — and for transport and supplies. That's how they got the nickname "the Cinderella Brigade".

Brigadier Coad had been fed tales about the Australians. The God-help-you type. Though he was apprehensive, he didn't have a closed mind. He went on record later as saying the Australians "were the finest fighting battalion he had ever seen". But they did take some getting used to. He was very surprised to learn that they wouldn't salute, only wave. In the end, said Cal, smiling, "he waved back". One night — no one said where — some Australian stretcher bearers went to a local village and got on the hootch. Coming home, they fired their Bren guns over the Brigadier's command caravan. Another story minus an ending.

Charlie won the Englishman's respect and affection. In a letter dated December 1, 1971 to Major-General Butler, Brigadier Coad wrote:

254                    *The name's still Charlie*

L-R: Charlie Green with British officers, Lieutenant-General Sir John
Harding and Air-Vice Marshal C. Bouchier RAF, Korea, 1950.

Brigadier Aubrey Coad with Charlie Green, 1950.

I still have a picture of Charles and me walking together to see what was going on in one of the battalion's battles. This picture is in my dressing room and has been since I retired. This shows how much I respected and liked him.

The Brigadier spoke of C.H.'s leadership. He noted that Charlie never stood any nonsense and he observed with interest during his "O" groups (when he issued orders) that "he never heard him call any of his officers by their Christian names. I often wondered if this were part of his technique of command, as it was a bit unlike the British approach — anyway it was most successful and I think he laid the foundations for Bruce Ferguson, who followed".

The Brigade remained at Taegu until October 5 to perform their task of "mopping up" pockets of enemy left behind the advance, an enemy turned guerilla. These North Koreans discarded their green uniform to dress as refugees or to don the white or hessian pyjama-type garment of the peasants. (Because of the white pyjamas, sometimes the Koreans are called the "white people"). In this way they could harrass very effectively.

On October 5, 27 Brigade was flown by DC4s and C119s to Kimpo, the airfield near Seoul, the ancient South Korean capital set between mountains.

# 21
# Korea — "This cold and lonely feeling"

> And your bright promise, withered long and sped,
> Is touched, stirs, rises, opens and grows sweet
> And blossoms and is you, when you are dead.
>
> *from an unnamed sonnet* by Charles Sorley

3 RAR saw little action at first because the North Koreans did not put up much resistance. This was read as a sign they had retreated; they were in fact stalling for time.

In this period, the diggers got a taste of mountainous Korea and the nature of the war on wheels they were committed to fighting — and the chaos. The first thing that struck the Australians were the roads, that were jammed with vehicles trying to move, breaking down, having accidents. There were trucks, carriers, tanks, guns, jeeps all moving over roads built for oxen. These narrow dirt tracks, often edged with deep ditches, ran through sewage-manured paddy fields in the valleys and zig-zagged from ridge to ridge and over jagged mountain peaks. Korea is all mountains and valleys. In the valleys rivers had to be forded when the rains came. And in the rains the dust turned into a sea of mud. That was about mid-October. As the diggers went north, the temperatures plummeted; lack of maintenance and freezing conditions meant break-downs, frozen engine blocks that cracked, frozen radiators. Add to that poor organisation and poor communications and you have what Brigadier Coad called "a bloody shambles". Up north, 3 RAR was often short of food, and the hungry troops resorted to scrounging in the countryside.

If Woop had been there, he could have reminded us that

one of the reasons soldiers don't talk is that the reality is so bloody unglamorous.

At this stage, one Aussie soldier, referring to the US troops, commented: "They weren't our idea of an army." It was not hearsay that often a column of Americans in tanks and trucks would be brought to a halt by a handful of guerillas from a strategic rocky outcrop. The Americans' answer was to blast away with everything they had. When there was no alternative, reluctantly they climbed out of their vehicles to deal with the enemy on foot, restricted by necessity to the use of a minimum of ammunition, instead of their futile preference for wasteful, indiscriminate firing. Already, a lesson of war was in evidence: firepower is not always conclusive.

John Callander spoke of the incredulity of some American observers who, after watching Green brief his men, and see them do the job using infanteers with little support, could only exclaim: "Boy, you guys sure know what you are doing."

Another cause of confusion at this stage of the war was that one American regiment was vying with another for the honour of being the first across the 38th Parallel. It was a race. I suppose that is why in one instance a bewildered corps of ROK troops found themselves converging on the Australians, somewhere in the hills, both headed for the same target.

In addition, it is said that MacArthur planned the tactics for the Korean War from his HQ in Tokyo, 1000 miles away. Too far to be in tune with its progress or, most importantly, the enemy's logistics. Hence the "mismanagement" the historians refer to.

Before the Australians could move off, they had to wait for their vehicles. They got impatient. Two soldiers, Privates Rex Wilson and Ernest Stone, keen "to have a go", to get into the race and beat the Americans across the 38th Parallel, "took off", to use Wilson's own words. They headed for the noise of the firing, got a ride on an American tank and joined an American assault team at the Parallel — where they were found in a weapon pit by MPs, who had flown from Tokyo to go and get them. They had committed a serious offence.

One reporter wrote that C.H. saw them being brought in,

one wounded. He leapt out of a truck and blasted them: "*Where the hell have you been?*" In all, eight men absconded. As the war historian R.J. O'Neill says, the CO, who could have thrown the book at them, showed leniency. "He simply ordered them back to their platoons without further ado." The reporter claims "he had a twinkle in his eye".

Before long Wilson and Stone and everyone else got all the fighting they wanted. At Kimpo, during the only pause they were to have in four weeks, the Battalion was able to operate fairly normally — and formally. C.H. ran a tight ship. Reporters observed the thoroughness of their lines: well dug in; well camouflaged; clean and orderly. All precautions were taken except that diggers would not wear their steel helmets, preferring their slouch hats.

To retain some formality, officers gathered for the evening dinner in a mess tent, where the following little one-act drama was partly played out. A lull in activity gives soldiers an opportunity for some mischief.

The main character is Porky, the Battalion's Hygiene Sergeant, traditionally known as "Sergeant O'Blowfly". Sergeant O'Blowfly, who comes under the control of the Regimental Medical Officer, has the job of looking after the CO's latrine. When on the move, he has to dig him a slit trench. Porky was a most unsoldierly looking fellow who had come up with K Force. He was overweight, not very clean and preferred playing with mortar bombs to doing his assigned job.

The evening after they made camp at Kimpo, the MO, Captain Bryan Gandevia (later Professor) went to dinner at the mess tent, to be greeted with a blast from the CO.

CO: "Doc, that bloody hygiene sergeant is about to become a corporal. He's put my latrine right plumb in the middle of Battalion HQ where everyone can see me use it. Get him to put a screen around it, would you?"
 When he was able to find Porky, the MO lined him up.
MO: "Sergeant, the CO's not happy about his slit trench. He wants a screen around it. Understand?"
Porky: "Yes, Sir."
 His face was a study.
 The MO checked the next day. Sure enough there was a hessian

screen around the CO's slit trench. Satisfied everything was OK, he confidently went to the mess the next night.

The CO was waiting for him with another blast.

CO: "Doc, that bloody hygiene sergeant is a disaster. Do you know what he's done now? He's put a screen round my latrine all right, but he's left no opening. I had to crawl underneath it."

The MO said: "When I tackled Porky I was met with a completely dead-pan face. That was Porky."

End of story.

In a serious vein, the MO told another story about C.H. Bryan Gandevia was new to the army and new to war; consequently the job was, at first, difficult. He "didn't know the ropes". Not long after the unit got going on the road a difficult situation developed. Action was imminent. Captain Gandevia received orders during the day to leave his 3-ton truck behind. It contained all his equipment. That evening, he got a message to provide a mobile RAP at dawn next morning. With his truck miles behind, this was impossible. He was furious for being so badly informed. He went in a rage to the CO's tent and sounded off in no uncertain terms about the lack of care and consideration. Though the doctor did not explain how C.H. handled him, he came away satisfied. "The CO gained my utmost respect. I never again had any trouble," he said.

On October 7, C.H. went to Seoul for a briefing at I Corps. A guess would be that he was looking for maps — map reading being his forte — as well as battle plans. His Battalion was on its way.

For the first part of the war, from Kimpo to Yongju, the British brigade came under Major General Hobart Gay's US 1st Cavalry Regiment. General Hobart Gay comes through as a breezy "MASH" kind of figure until you look closely and find he was a thoughtful, good leader. To keep the record straight, he had good reason to have a grouch. His 1st Cavalry, which took the brunt of fighting at the defence of Pusan, had so many casualties that they should have been rested. The British Commonwealth Brigade was to have come to their aid. It didn't. The reason given for the delay in fielding the Australians is senior staff rivalry between the British and the

Australians. Over appointments, for one thing, and because a Britisher, apparently appointed over an Australian, was very derogatory about Australian soldiers. The same old complaint as in the Middle East!

Gay, to his credit, held no resentment. He got to know C.H. quite well, and when he died Gay praised him unstintingly. This made headlines in the newspapers at the time: "He was, in my opinion, the best Battalion Commander in Korea," he said. According to a British reporter he was so genuinely upset that no one doubted his sincerity.

Once on the Korean roads, the Australians discovered the "Land of Morning Calm", as Korea is called in its literature. In a letter C.H. commented on the peacefulness and also the autumnal beauty of the hills ablaze with crimson, amber and gold. The din, smoke, and dust of war were to detract from the beauty of misty mountains and tranquil valleys. Apart from the scenery, C.H. found nothing attractive about Korea. Tossed out of a jeep, he had bruised ribs that gave him some pain. Someone noted, without bothering to find out why: "he was taking a lot of aspros."

It is a wonder that C.H., with his countryman's eye, did not comment on the primitive Korean agriculture: buffalo pulling wooden ploughs; peasants crouching in the fields using sickles; squat, thatched mud huts that huddled in hamlets or close to the road. Nor did he mention features of the Korean landscape. Their town architecture, for example, reflected their history and culture. The more substantial houses have a distinctive ribbed, curving blue-tiled roof. Clusters of huge urns stand by doorways to house their staple kimchi, a fiery hot pickled vegetable to see them through the bitter winter. On the hillsides are curious earth mounds under which they bury the dead. C.H. does note how the poor Korean peasants are prepared to switch flags and bow and wave to whichever army passes through, caring only that their home or farm escapes the flying shells. Many didn't. One million South Koreans became casualties in the Korean War.

As the American regiments were racing each other to the 38th Parallel, MacArthur was meeting President Truman on

Wake Island. Truman wanted to warn MacArthur, whom he called a "brass hat prima donna", not to antagonise the Chinese and not to advance to the border. MacArthur reassured Truman there was nothing to worry about. All the while, the smoke drifting skyward in Korea was not only the smoke of war. In the far north there were unprecedented forest fires burning. Under that smoke-screen, undetected, unsuspected, thousands of Chinese troops were sneaking across the border to prepare for an assault.

Sariwon, fifty miles north of Kumchon, is a name to conjure up the image of a "bloody shambles". When it was captured, the troops in the van found that what wasn't reduced to rubble from air strikes was alight. North Koreans were still withdrawing through the town, not knowing it had fallen to the British Argylls or that the Australians had skirted it, to set up a road block five miles north.

In the main street the marching Argylls were astonished to find a column of the green uniformed North Koreans converging on them from a side street. The North Koreans were excited at what they thought was the belated arrival of some welcome allies. They broke ranks to welcome them, calling: "Russki! Russki!" The Argylls, one step ahead, got their weapons ready for when the mistake was discovered, stalling for time by uttering the only Russian words they knew. They got the upper hand of the inevitable skirmish fairly quickly. And took a lot of prisoners.

The Australians experienced a similar incident. On October 16, they made camp by the road in an apple orchard. (Apple orchards are as typical in Korea as orange orchards in Palestine.) That night, in the dark, Bruce Ferguson, Major Thirwell and some guards sat in jeeps by the roadside near the camp waiting for their rations to arrive by truck. Late as usual. Bruce heard marching feet. That didn't sound right. He flashed on his lights. Green uniforms! The man at the head of the column, seeing the strange Australian uniforms, called out: "Russki!" It so happened that Bruce had an interpreter with him. Like the Argylls they stalled for time. Bruce called up C.H. on radio and asked for reinforcements quickly. Then he thought of a ruse, the daring of which deserved to succeed. They fired some shots, started the jeep moving along the column of North Koreans, announcing through the interpreter: "You are surrounded. You have two minutes to surrender."

"Those were the longest two minutes of my life," said Bruce. Their haul of prisoners was 1982. Courageous and dashing: the stuff of Anzacs.

Between Kimpo and Yongju, Charlie wrote twice.

October 8 1950

My Darling,
Once again I have time to write just a short note during a lull in the turmoil of movement which we have experienced in the last few weeks . . .

I am feeling very well now — my cold has cleared and my rib is just about better. Did I tell you that I was thrown out of a jeep on a bumpy road and hurt a rib; it wasn't broken but apparently badly bruised and for a few days it was a bit sore.

Have you taken delivery of the cow darling? I can see a lot of fun in store for you and Elvie — I would love to take a peep over the fence when the milking was to take place. Mum told me she was very quiet and they were able to milk her without putting her in the bail.

This country is not very pleasant — at least under these conditions. The dust on the roads is terrible. Even after just a short trip one is coated with dust and I feel that I am forever dirty. Very soon of course it will be cold; I believe that during November-December it reaches 10 below zero so I hope the whole thing is over before we experience this. The landscape in places is quite attractive. The roads are lined with poplar trees and there are many running streams . . .

October 17 1950

. . . As you have no doubt already heard, we are well north of the 38 parallel now; however one would never know the difference as the country and the people are exactly alike on either side of this imaginary line. The civilians up here still wave South Korean flags at us and I have no doubt that when we ultimately enter the capital of North Korea we will still be seeing South Korean flags. I suppose a few months ago they were all waving North Korean flags.

The landscape is quite pretty now. I doubt if I have ever seen a better example of autumn colours as one can see on the hills around us. This is the one and only aspect of it that is any way attractive though.

By now you would have established your farm. I'll be anxiously awaiting a report on the cow. I'll bet there was quite a ceremony on the day of her arrival. Elvie and Harry would be more thrilled over all this than you darling, I suppose.

On the road again the Australians were in the lead. The next objective was Pyongyang, the capital of North Korea. Any defence of that city was expected at the mountain pass leading to the city: the North Koreans were anxious to spare Pyongyang the destruction Seoul had suffered. Pyongyang, like Seoul, sits in a cradle between wooded mountains and contains ancient treasures.

At Hwangju, the Australians, to their surprise, got orders to detour. The Americans wanted to be first into Pyongyang. By this time it was raining heavily, but this didn't prevent General Paik, a South Korean mounted on a horse, from leading his South Korean regiment, marching on foot, first into the capital. In the censored press, the Americans received the honour.

MacArthur himself was there to meet the victorious troops and intimate to the world the war was virtually "all washed up". The Australians, who should have been first in, were halted just south-west of the city, after a sweep through the valley on the flank of some Americans.

Charlie writes of this:

October 18 1950

Tonight with things very quiet, I thought of nothing better than dropping you a line sweetheart.

We have had a couple of interesting days. First we led the advance up the main road in the direction of the capital and on that night took some 2000 prisoners.

Yesterday we did an independent job on our own and made an advance of some thirty miles in the day, capturing quite a few enemy and much equipment. The speed of our advance impressed everyone so I hear. General Robertson was over today and although I didn't see him he sent a message of congratulations. At the time he arrived we were having a bit of a fight with some tanks and he very rightly didn't bother me whilst I was so engaged. We had a good day today also — destroyed all the tanks without a casualty.

I am hoping that more mail will come in tonight or tomorrow. We haven't had any for some days but I guess that with the speed of our movement the mail has been unable to catch up. Tomorrow, however, we hand over the leading role to another unit so perhaps mail will catch us.

Today we heard that the capital of NK had fallen or at least was entered. Surely the NK's will "pack up" now. I really think that their leaders have left for Russia and there is no one to officially organise a surrender. Despite this the fighting is over. Certainly nothing of an organised nature left now.

Darling, I have been thinking of you such a lot . . . I am very proud of my battalion. They have done well in the past day or so. Incidentally you will be pleased to know that I now have a first-class batman; for example tonight he is cooking NK chicken for supper. During a lull in proceedings today he dished me up some tinned bacon and NK eggs which was very nice. He keeps his eyes open and a little loot makes the menu more attractive. Not that one can complain for it has been the best war I have experienced so far as food is concerned . . .

I feel that with this thing closing down up here that I may be home much sooner than we imagined. These are only my thoughts mind you, and if I stay on in the army I will for certain, I feel, be posted to Queenscliff. Let all this wait. We will just concentrate on getting home first.

While Charlie was writing this letter, MacArthur was countermanding his previous orders. Now he wanted a dash "all the way to the Yalu" before winter closed in, so they could all be home for Christmas. At Christmas that year, with the US chased back to the 38th Parallel and the Communists about to launch an all-out offensive, an American soldier who was asked what he wanted for Christmas said: "Gimme tomorrow."

MacArthur ordered a large-scale parachute drop of men and arms on October 20 to an area in the vicinity of Yongju, to cut off, as he thought, the remaining NK army. It would be wedged between the airdrop and the push to the Yalu and easily crushed.

The 187 Airborne Regimental Combat Team, nicknamed "MacArthur's Own", under MacArthur's personal direction, set out from Kimpo airfield to put paid to the NKs once and for all in the areas of Sukchon and Sunchon, north of Pyongyang. Each man was "a walking arsenal" armed with a .45 pistol, carbine or rifle, and a lethal dagger. Before they were dropped, aircraft rocketed and strafed the ground. Then 1470 men dropped, followed later by another 4000, as well as howitzers, jeeps, guns, trucks, trailers, ammunition and other supplies. It is hard to believe such an armada could get into trouble. It did, because the main body of North Koreans were already north of the drop, on the northern side of the Chongchon River. Between the airborne team and the British Brigade there were North Koreans pinning down the paratroopers.

That is how 3 Battalion RAR got its first real battle of the Korean War. They were sent to rescue the beleaguered Americans. The war historian R.J. O'Neill said: "they were to face the test as the Australians did in 1914 and in 1941, in the first battles of WWI and WWII."

3 RAR was blooded in an apple orchard. Fruit of sorrow. The apples thudded to the ground as rifles cracked, guns pounded and men shouted their urgent rallying cries. Intimating man's unending suffering — all for an apple.

It was October 21 when they received their baptism of fire. Or blooding, as they call it — though that day, miraculously, no Battalion blood was spilt fatally. About half of the men had already been blooded in World War 2; they understood the significance for the Battalion, and for Australia, of how they measured up that day in the battle of the Apple Orchard.

No one could have been more aware than Charles Green,

the CO. One journalist described him in the battle. The tall, slouch-hatted figure was seen ranging through the apple orchard, coolly directing the fierce battle, with a walkie-talkie to his mouth. "Annoyingly casual" wrote one observer. Only C.H. himself knew how he felt in the apple orchard that day as the moment of truth pounded away. Quick decisions. Knowing that if his Battalion was baptised with victory, it had a good start — to become a winner. His boys did it in the way of the Anzacs: with rifles and bayonets, nothing more. No aircraft, artillery or mortars to make it easy.

But for the Australian media in Korea, reporting the war, it is more than likely their action would have been swallowed by the American Army and gone unnoticed. For they were now attached to the US 24 Infantry Division under Major General John Church, a no-nonsense man, keen on results.

This is how they fought the battle. After 3 RAR passed through Yongju the night of October 20, they could hear the noise of battle ahead. The paratroopers, trying to strike south, ran into a 2500-strong regiment dug in on high ground just north of Yongju, the most advantageous of positions.

At 7 am, 3 RAR, "unbathed, unrested, and hungry too" because they had been ordered to push on along the Sinanju Road, struck the enemy that had the paras pinned down a mile farther on. Contact occurred at the bend in the Sinanju road, about a mile north of Yongju, where the road turns north east to skirt around the high ground in the broad valley. Well dug in with artillery and mortars, and well camouflaged, the NKs were waiting, ready to rain down fire on the open position below. At the foot of the hills was the apple orchard, giving little cover. Koreans, like the Japanese, drastically prune their trees. On the left (western) side of the road was a paddy field, dotted with wigwam-shaped rice stooks, looking for all the world like the tents of an ancient army.

The NKs held fire until the body of the Battalion had passed. Then they opened up. C.H. gave the signal that they had made contact, but Brigadier Coad said no support could

Above: Brigadier Aubrey Coad visits 3RAR in
Korea – Charlie Green on his left.
Below: Coad shakes hands with Padre Alan Laing.

*The name's still Charlie*

Above: Brigadier Coad (sitting nearest camera) instructing Charlie Green and Captain John Callander on the situation.

Below: American and 3RAR officers discussing the recent Battle of the Apple Orchard near Yongju – Charlie in slouch hat.

be given as they could not locate the encircled Americans' position.

The tactics for this battle were devised on the spot. In the lead was C Company, led by Major Archer Denness, riding on Sherman tanks. Behind them was the CO with his Tactical HQ. With his instinct for ground and the right decision, C.H. deployed his Battalion quickly.

C Company clipped on their bayonets, leapt to the ground and went straight into the apple orchard, in the foothills of the ridge held by the NKs. Lieutenant Colin Townsend's 8 Platoon moved under the protection of a spur; Lieutenant Robin Morison's Platoon attacked frontally, from the road; Lieutenant David Butler's remained on the road, to deal with any enemy that might break out of the orchard. Two companies went to higher ground to the right of C Company and the remaining company came up on the left near Lieutenant Butler's position on the road. Colonel Green with his HQ staff went into the orchard, behind C Company, which had cleared the first line of defences and was going on to the next line, over a small knoll.

No sooner did Battalion HQ enter the orchard than it was directly attacked by a large band of NKs. A lot has been written about this incident. Brigadier Coad himself wrote that the CO's batman was killed beside him. This surely can't be true: no fatalities were reported that day. Coad could be confusing this battle with the one at Chongju, where HQ was again under attack. To beat off the attack the HQ group, including the CO, fought back-to-back, with the CO proving a "deadly marksman". This was not in the war diary. Bruce Ferguson's account is recorded in R.J. O'Neill's official history. Bruce said: "The personal courage of Lt Colonel Green was amply shown on that day as despite the intense battle swirling around him at Tactical HQ, he was still master of the battlefield and completely unworried by the cheeky efforts of the North Koreans." Bernie O'Dowd remembers C.H. saying to him, "Clean this lot up, will you?"

By midday the battle was virtually over. The Australians who had gone forward had met up with the paratroopers.

Back at the road, however, quite a few NKs driven from the hills had got down into the paddy field to hide among the stooks and in the ditches, where they were sniping and "making an infernal nuisance of themselves". Brigadier Coad's description of what he saw in the paddy field is quite famous. He wrote: "I saw a magnificent sight. An Australian platoon lined up in a paddy field and walked through it as though they were driving snipe. The soldiers, when they saw a pile of straw, kicked it and out would bolt a NK."

That's the same image that Banjo Paterson used to describe a mopping-up operation at Bloemfontein in 1900: Australians going through the long grass flushing out Boers, as though they were driving snipe.

Among the North Korean dead, they found the body of a tank Colonel wearing a strange uniform with red stars on it. His papers were hastened to Intelligence for translation and analysis. The red stars were an ominous sign, as they were to learn.

There was more excitement for D Company later that day. Fanned out across the paddy field with some troops flanking the road, they were astonished to see a NK truck approaching. The driver waved and they waved back. Then they stopped him, a few well placed bullets kicking up the dust. When the driver got out at bayonet point, he is supposed to have cast worried looks over his shoulder at his truck as he was led away. The troops discovered why. It was a payroll truck containing, D Company claim, two and a half million bank notes. "We're millionaires!" they joked, but could find no other use for the money than to light their cigarettes.

The dash to the Yalu went on unabated, headed for "the biggest military ambush in military history".

October 22 found the Brigade twenty-five miles farther north, halted at Sinanju on the Chongchon River. Temperatures had plummeted and they were beginning to taste the bitterness of a Korean winter. Vehicles began reneging. The war that was supposed to have been over before they got to Korea was really just starting.

At Sinanju, the bridge had already been blown and there

was a wide fast-flowing river, banked by waist-high mud flats, to get men and vehicles across. Peasants lined up to welcome them, shouting "Manzai, Manzai", bowing, waving flags (South Korean of course) and tossing amber-coloured apples at the soldiers. When the Middlesex Battalion got into trouble trying to cross the river in assault boats, the locals pitched in and helped. That was risky, for no one knew who the enemy was. Witnessing the trouble the Middlesex had, 3 RAR went farther upstream to cross the river at Anju, where some engineers were able to repair a damaged bridge.

At Anju, the Australians received an issue of winter dress from the Americans. They welcomed the padded jackets, but they would not wear the caps, at least not yet. It is reported that Driver Charles Symes vowed, "They can have my strides, but they're not getting my hat." Diggers would repeatedly refuse twenty American dollars for their slouch hat. That surely is a measure of their pride and their morale.

At about this time, somewhere south of Pakchon, 3 RAR adopted a North Korean boy and took him along with them. I heard of this from Bill Hamilton, a Korean veteran who works at the Canberra War Memorial. Then I learned that the Korean, Yung Choi, lived in Sydney. I traced him and got his story. Some of it I produce from memory and some I have verbatim. Yung told how he soon felt so at home in the Battalion he did not want to leave, as he could have done, to go to Seoul to his father. Being with the Battalion "made me feel like a man," he explained. (He has since received an Australian medal.) The grisly things he saw during the time he spent in the RAP did not put him off. He told, for instance, how the Black Corporals who go round in a truck after a battle to pick up the dead would, when approaching the RAP post, hold up so many fingers to announce the number of the dead; how the bodies were washed, tied up, wrapped up and stored till they could be buried. And how their belongings were parcelled up to be sent home. As I listened I realised, chokingly, that Charlie, the CO, and the ordinary soldier lost their differences on the back of the Black Corporals' truck. And I shuddered.

Yung Choi had a long story to tell. Here's the core of it:

> While I was staying with my mother at my grandparents' home in North Korea, the war broke out. I was sixteen years of age. When the Communists arrived in my village, my mother told me to escape to Seoul where my father was living. I set out to walk. I went over mountains and through valleys. Before long I lost my way. Then I got very hungry. I stumbled on to a battlefield where there were a lot of dead bodies lying around. Because I was so hungry, I started looking for food on the bodies. While I was searching, I heard a call. I looked up on the ridge and saw some men with funny hats on. I thought they were Russians. They called out in English which I could understand because I could speak it a little. They told me to come up to them with my hands up. They took me back to the Battalion and handed me over to Father Philip and he took me to Dr Gandevia, the medical officer. I stayed with the Battalion for two years and nine months. The first thing they taught me was to make my bed, out of blankets, underneath the RAP truck. Then I began to learn to do things to help Dr Gandevia. I made coffee for the wounded; I made beds; I learned to bandage. And when there were wounded North Koreans, I could interpret for them.

Musing why he elected to stay so long, when he could have gone to his father, Yung explained: "There's no comradeship like that in the army." Indeed, the bond was so strong he hastened to become an Australian after the war.

He remembered the CO, though it would have been only a matter of days after Yung was picked up that C.H. died. But he could not have imagined this accurate image:

> "Oh, I often saw him moving round from hill to hill. You'd know him anywhere. He was like a God. I knew all our lives depended on him. In all the confusion, he was the only one who knew the way. He had the map. He was the one we depended on to look after us. He hardly ever slept. He was always moving around checking up on things. He was a real commanding officer."

Wondering about the irregularity of it, I asked Yung Choi if the CO knew he was there. "He must have. Everyone knew I was in the RAP. He probably closed his eyes." Much later,

Yung Choi was able to get on the payroll when the army was allowed to employ Koreans. They were called KATCOMS.

Late in October, I read in the newspaper that the Australians were engaged in some stiff fighting. That frightened me. Something did not add up. The war was supposed to be all but over, yet the fighting was obviously getting worse. Charlie's letters took on a different note. The chill you will detect is not, I believe, merely from the physical cold.

And in the paddock, the cow took sick. Each day it grew worse so that we were forced to phone Herc and ask him to take it away. I was not in a hurry to tell Charlie, so he never heard of the very short life of my "farm" as he called it.

His letter of October 25 would have been written after they crossed the Chongchon but before they reached the next river, the Taeryong, where they had to fight another battle, a harder one.

October 25 1950

> A lovely big mail arrived yesterday and contained two letters from you. It has been nearly a week since mail arrived and it was very much appreciated, particularly yours my sweet; I am always looking for them . . .
> My goodness it is cold here now darling. Water freezes and although the days are sunny the breezes are biting cold. We were informed that it would turn to cold conditions suddenly and this has happened within the past three days. My bed is now cold as well as being terribly lonely and the only answer to the two problems would be to have you with me, my sweet . . .
> Our task will soon be over up here darling — a little further to go and that will finish it except for garrison duties and heaven forbid that we will be kept for that. I will be making some approaches regarding my personal employment.
> Must away now darling as we are again on the move. I miss you such a lot dearest and hope and pray that we will be together soon.

As the Battalion goes towards the waiting jaws of a well trained army, poised like a giant trap, you have to wonder about war. How many campaigns should never have been fought? How many are caused by one man's mania? Taking Charlie's experience, Greece was madness; Wewak was more so. And in Korea he was caught up in another action that wasted life — not the war itself so much as the obsession to push to the Yalu.

Considering the waste and the suffering, it is inexplicable that there has not been an end of war, or that men will continue to fight when the situation is futile, as we have seen our men do at Tempe Gorge, at Wewak and were to do in Vietnam. Plato wrote: "Only the dead have seen the end of war."

In the past, the brunt of war has been borne by the infanteer, at the end of a long chain of command, in some distant place, like a jungle razorback. He is at the mercy of his leaders' decisions; dependent on his own and his comrades' courage. That requires a lot of trust. As one soldier said of Charlie, "he had our fate in his hands". Yung Choi expressed how godlike they thought the man was who "had the map". I've never felt I could ask a soldier about his experience at the edge. When it is all reduced to "him or me", pulling the trigger, the dead faces, the ghosts. There would not be words enough. He would not be able to explain that pain he has felt ever since, that won't go away. He probably has difficulty with pride because it sits so uneasily with death.

The pity of it. As Wilfred Owen said of war, "the poetry's in the pity". The pity is that it is at improbable killing fields where the human spirit flowers. A sandy desert, a mythic mountain pass, an eerie jungle, a cold oriental hill. On these fields we lose our best blood and seed, that might have bred more of its kind.

What is the future of the digger, so important to our national identity? He entered our consciousness at Gallipoli distinctive for his nonchalant bravery and his slouch hat; he reappeared on a different stage in World War 2, to affirm the legend. It might not have been noticed that he was in Korea (where he was unwilling — symbolically — to take off his slouch hat). There's unease about the poor fellow conscripted for Vietnam. He found himself overtaken by change. In an American-type uniform with giggle hat. And unesteemed in a dirty war. What did not change in Korea or Vietnam was men's readiness to honour the legend. This was recognised by the American Presidential citation for bravery awarded to 3 Battalion RAR at Kapyong, Korea, and to D Company, 6 Battalion RAR at Long Tan, Vietnam.

Will technology and changing attitudes so alter men and the face of war that the slouch-hatted legend will pass into history? War, it seems, is inevitable. But it may change so much that certain conditions will disappear. Those necessary ones that transmute men's spirit; those familiar colours, that distinctive uniform, the unit that inspires men to fight like tigers, and the trusted mates, to die for.

I cannot determine Charlie's personal view of war. He had a job to do; he wanted to do it well. And doing it well meant keeping that balance between courageous and cautious decisions that got results, but not at the unnecessary cost of life. He had little time, as a commander, to think about himself.

At the next battle 3 RAR suffered its first fatalities. The men themselves dubbed it "The Battle of the Broken Bridge at Picnic Corner". It was no picnic. It took place on October 25. 3 Battalion was in the lead again. When they reached Kujin, one mile south of Pakchon, where the road to Manchuria turns west across the river, they found a high steel and concrete bridge had been wrecked, a typical delaying strategy. All that remained of one span were the steel girders and jagged concrete. Twenty feet below, the icy water of the Taeryong ran swiftly. An arctic cold NK evening was about to close in, with a piercing wind blowing straight from Manchuria. Later that evening a large pale moon rose; its sickly light betrayed the men who struggled across the bridge to fight, or, later, struggled back wounded. With cold as severe as that, "a man couldn't hold his Bren". The frozen steel burned the hands.

They reached the bridge at 4 pm. Because 3 RAR was in

the van, it was their role to establish a bridgehead on the other side of the river, so that the advance could continue.

C.H. put Lieutenant Morison in charge of a party that went across the bridge "to have a look". They crossed by climbing the broken span, "swinging from girder to girder". The road on the other side ran through a fifty-foot cutting into a ravine. The reconnaissance party, to their surprise, found fifty North Koreans in their green uniforms suddenly emerging from their camouflaged holes with their hands up. They came down the road towards the Australians, presumably surrendering. When they got close, a rain of fire came down on the North Koreans from higher up. No one is sure whether they were fired on for surrendering or whether they were being used as a decoy. Watching from the other bank with his field glasses, C.H. ordered Morison back. He returned with ten prisoners.

At about this time, a spotter aircraft chanced overhead. C.H. radioed it and received the news that two companies of NKs were dug in on the bank overlooking the bridge. At that, C.H. remarked: "We have an obstacle." Quickly appraising the situation, he called for an air-strike and tank-support, only to learn he could have neither. It was too late for the air-strike and the tanks could not get across the river until they repaired the damaged ford, some distance away at Pakchon itself. The tank commander said it would take all night. He could provide tanks in the morning.

C.H. decided to surprise the enemy by getting a bridgehead across the river under cover of darkness, before the North Koreans could bring up reinforcements to harrass them. At 7 pm, A Company, under Major "Speed" Gordon, and B Company under Major Max Thirwell crossed the river. It's not clear whether they all got over by climbing the bridge, using two quickly constructed long ladders, or whether they waded: in the official accounts there is mention of the icy water. Once across on the west bank, A Company went to the left of the road and B Company to the right to dig in near a power pylon. The digging in, in the frozen, concrete-hard ground was, they quipped, for once a welcome task to warm frozen soldiers, and a way of alleviating tension.

Back at the east bank, artillery and mortars were ordered to plaster the enemy position on the other side of the river, to divert attention from A and B Companies' crossing. D Company, which had the job of going into Pakchon to clear the town, found a noisy band playing and a body of North Koreans turning their uniforms inside out, showing the white side to indicate they wanted to surrender. (The white side of their uniforms was for camouflage in the snow.) Arch Denness' C Company was placed to the east of the position and Battalion HQ was to the south. During the night a platoon of D Company, with the job of guarding the engineers as they repaired the Pakchon ford, had a very lively time, as their casualties showed.

Suddenly the War Diarist became very time-conscious. He recorded: On the west bank at 7.30 pm North Koreans suddenly appeared before B Company, trying to form up to attack them, but mortars prevented that. The diary continued:

> 8 pm. On the other side (the east) of the bank, C Company and Battalion HQ came under shellfire, but for some reason the shells didn't go off.
> 10.30. B Company were attacked again, losing two men.
> 11 pm. The C.O. sent 8 Platoon of C Company across to reinforce A Company.
> 11 pm. Once again the NKs appeared in strength before A and B Companies. At this critical stage of the battle, Colonel Green laid down artillery and mortar fire that quickly repulsed the NKs.

Casualties mounted, creating the problem of evacuating the wounded. It was an evacuation nearly as dramatic as the one C.H. experienced in 1945, on Hill 710 in New Guinea.

In the moonlight, the bridge, the only means of getting the wounded out, came under fire as the stretcher bearers toiled back to the east bank. The stretcher cases presented the problem: they couldn't be moved down the ladders propped against the broken span. The solution was to lower the patient, strapped to the stretcher, from the bridge to an assault boat bobbing in the icy water twenty feet below. At the first attempt the boat sank, but after that all went satisfactorily until the last crossing was attempted. The swift rush of water swept the boat against a pylon, overturning it. The stretcher sergeant, Sergeant T.M. Murray, stripped and dived in the freezing water to recover the casualty and support him to safety.

Things settled down after midnight. In the deadly quiet, C.H. during his vigil looked at the Intelligence report that had just come in concerning the red-starred Tank Colonel killed in the Apple Orchard. The indications were that the Communists were ready to implement "COUNTERPLAN" which amounted to their switching from defence to attack.

C.H., given to drawing people out, asked one of his staff: "What do you think this means?"

"China," he was told.

"It could well be. In the meantime, we have to hold the bridgehead till dawn." (At dawn he could call down air strikes and get the tanks moving.)

October 26, 4 am. In their dug-outs on the west bank it was "too cold to sleep". An army public relations team heard from one soldier how they listened all night to a wounded NK moaning. They couldn't risk going to his aid for fear of a trap and of giving their positions away. Then they heard a strange noise and felt the ground trembling. "Tanks," they cursed. One soldier said: "Well, we've taken on tanks before without support. Remember Len Opie?" Len had acquired a reputation for being able to deal with tanks single-handed in the Australians' first skirmish in Korea.

Peeping through the camouflage covering their holes, they could see a great T34 coming down the road. 'As big as a block of flats," the fellow reported. "Coming after it are some fellows sitting up like Jacky in jeeps and after that a motor bike. A funny lot!" And from the way they were approaching, they seemed to have no idea the Australians were waiting for them.

Fingers on triggers, the diggers in the foxholes waited for the order. Soldiers' ability to hold fire is a measure of their courage, their discipline, and their leadership. There was not one panic shot. When the "funny bunch" got right between the two companies "they let them have it". The tank turned and hurried off. The fellows in the jeep and on the motor bike "weren't so lucky".

6 am. Some of the men waiting in the foxholes had drifted off to sleep, to be woken again by that unmistakable trembling in the ground that signalled more tanks. It was almost light; they could see another T34 clanking down the road, swinging its cannon backwards and forwards, firing in all directions, trying to draw fire, to locate the diggers' position.

The sun peeped through. Then they heard the welcome sound of jets. So did the tank, which "took off like a bat out of hell". Joyfully the diggers gave a cheer. "It's all washed up now." The picnic was over.

By 12 noon, 3 RAR had flushed the NKs out and cleared the way for the whole Brigade to cross the ford and once again take to the road. Headed for the Yalu, so they could finish off the Communists and be home for Christmas — as MacArthur decreed.

The Battle of the Broken Bridge cost the Australians a heavier toll than the Apple Orchard. Eight were killed, twenty-two wounded. Four of the casualties occurred not, as you would expect, establishing the bridgehead, but in D Company, whose task was to protect the engineers repairing the ford at Pakchon, over which the main force moved.

For his bravery attending the wounded Sergeant Murray was awarded a George Medal, second only to the V.C.

On the afternoon of October 26, at a Christian churchyard in Pakchon, the eight Australian soldiers were buried. They were the first deaths from battle. The Church of England padre, Alan Laing, who conducted the ceremony, said: "The Colonel, who went to the burial stood looking down at the graves of his men, obviously very deeply affected."

In that same place he himself was to lie beside those men, a few days later.

▼ ▼ ▼

At Pakchon, the troops noticed an unusual number of refugees on the move, an ominous sign they were learning not to ignore. Their orders, however, were to keep going to their next objective, Chongju. Charlie writes of this as the last twenty miles they had to do. Between the lines of his last letter, one can read some anxiety about the war in Korea. The chill he speaks of seems to have gripped not only his body but his heart.

Charlie's last letter:

October 27 1950

My darling Olwyn,

Once again we have a quiet night and a chance to get another short letter away. Have not had any mail since my last letter sweetheart, but since it comes only about once a week or thereabouts, I usually get a batch when it does come . . .

My goodness it is cold here now. Water freezes and keeping warm is quite a problem. The American winter clothing is now being issued and things should be better after that. We have some of it already and it is very good. I hope the thing will be over soon and that we are out of the place before it gets too cold and for other reasons too. I get very lonely for you darling and until we are together again there is no answer to this cold and lonely feeling.

Despite the cold the battalion is in excellent shape and is really a pleasure to command nowadays. They are a very fine lot and have done very well in two major actions to date.

How are you keeping my sweet and Bubby too of course. I do hope you are well and as happy as can be. We have only about another twenty miles to go to our final objective and after that the thing should be over. I hope that soon after that we shall be able to go home.

I suppose that dear little Bubby of ours is running around at home with bare tops on and is as brown as a berry. Does she like playing with Robert H now?

Must close and get to bed my pet; it is late and I am nearly frozen sitting here.

God bless you my darling and keep you well. I love you more than ever and hope that we are together again in a little while.

▼ ▼ ▼

I don't remember exactly when it happened. Time was no longer relevant to me. I was walking through the avenue of jacaranda trees, just around the corner from our house in Grafton. In late October the large old trees formed a canopy of purple. It was a walk Anthea always enjoyed. She would sit in her stroller, looking up at the purple-dappled sky, or down at the mass of fallen purple bells.

It was a relief to get out of the heat into the shade of the avenue that afternoon. The heavy sweetness of the jacarandas stung my nose, reminding me of sickness. There is always a lot of sickness in springtime. I wondered, why did the cow get sick? How will I manage on the farm, if we get it? I'll try. I'll do anything to get him back. There haven't been many letters lately. Will he like the idea of Bedford's place? — he should have my letter by now. The papers have been saying how hard the fighting has been lately . . .

There was a flash. Oh! I felt the shudder go through me as something seemed to hit my chest. I cried, "Charlie!" I am sure I knew. "Something terrible has happened." Knees gone to jelly, I dragged myself home, dread devouring me. And I waited . . .

There was no respite for 3 Battalion. Only three days after the Battle of the Broken Bridge, they were again in the lead preparing to take their last objective, Chongju, according to C.H.'s understanding. "The last twenty miles" as he said. At Chongju, the Battalion reached their farthest point north after a 400-mile advance in four weeks.

Nearing the Yalu, about 40 miles off, the nights had dropped to $28^0$ below zero. Some soldiers had at last given in. They were wearing caps. The determined ones wore balaclavas or scarves to keep their heads warm. But on top of their concession to the cold they jammed their slouch hats. "It was desperately cold. You could never explain to anyone how cold it was," I was told.

So confident was MacArthur's staff in Tokyo that the war was nearly over that they were planning victory celebrations. USA Intelligence completely missed the movement of the 300,000 Chinese troops over the Yalu.

Though it is not stated, it would appear that C.H. himself had obtained intelligence about the position the NKs had taken to defend Chongju. For instance, he ordered the use of American tanks and also a four-hour softening-up air strike on the enemy before he engaged them. He must have anticipated correctly. It was the stiffest battle for Coad's brigade since September 21 on Hill 282.

Four miles from Chongju on the road running west from Pakchon there is a pass through pine-covered mountains. Here a force of NKs, the anticipated opposition of at least a battalion strong, were dug in on both sides of the road. Even their tanks were dug in. Strategically, the advantage was decidedly with the North Koreans.

Arch Denness tells this story about the road to Chongju. I am not sure that Arch has the right spot, because I can't slot it into the battle, but it is important as it is an intimate glimpse of C.H. during a battle. C.H. was standing in a carrier, a few feet in front of a company strung out behind. It had been arranged that he himself was to signal the time to engage to the Company Commander behind him, who would then go into the attack. Later, he told Arch: "When I waved you on it was like riding on a charger. A thrill. It wouldn't happen again in a thousand years."


The Battle of Chongju took place on October 29. I have learned little to add to the account of the battle given in the War Diary:

*10 am*   The air-strike started. In four hours there were eight runs on the NKs' position.

*2.30 pm*  3 RAR attacked. D Company, under Major W.F. Brown led with one platoon of tanks. On a second tank, following, rode the men of 10 platoon, D Company, led by Lieutenant D.J. Mannett. It was this

Brigadier Coad (centre) with Charlie Green (right).

A portrait of Charlie Green painted by Alan Waite and held in the Command and Staff College, Canberra.

man who became the hero of the day.

D Company's objective was the ridgeline, on the south of the road — the left-hand side.

The tanks "made a right flanking assault along the road". The rest of D Company attacked frontally across paddy fields onto the ridge. There was very heavy resistance that accounted for one of the Australian tanks.

*4.30 pm* D Company's exemplary work won them the ridgeline.

At the minute D Company won its objective, A Company led by Captain W.J. Chitts ["Speed" Gordon had been injured] supported by two platoons of tanks, attacked the right of the road. To win their objective at 5.30 they too had to overcome stiff resistance.

*5.30 pm* With D Company on its objective, B moved forward to take up a position between A on the left and D on the right. Then HQ moved up behind A. After HQ came C Company, bringing up the rear, ready to deal with parties of escaping or marauding enemy.

All was quiet until 7 pm, just after dark.

The North Koreans, after bringing up reinforcements with more tanks and guns, launched a fierce attack to overcome the Australians.

D Company took the brunt of it. David Mannett, leading 10 Platoon, allowed the NKs to within a few yards of his platoon's position before he would allow his men to fire, then gave them everything they had. They accounted for 32 NKs killed. While 10 Platoon was keeping the enemy busy, 11 and 12 Platoons counter-attacked in support of 10 Platoon. Despite this, some NKs got through and began attacking Battalion HQ. Not before some bad moments, the enemy were beaten off.

The battle raged for two hours. During this time a rocket-launcher team destroyed one of the enemy's three T34s. One man, single-handed, got one of the tanks, though he says it was an accident. Private J.H. Stafford crept to within feet of a T34, took careful aim, and gave the tank's auxiliary petrol tank a burst from his Bren. The tank exploded.

*9.30 pm* This time A Company on the right of the road were furiously charged by NKs using T34s. The Battalion, using its own mortars and some supporting artillery, eventually broke that up at 11 pm.

After that the North Koreans gave up. Another battle was won. C.H. believed they had completed their task in North Korea. If MacArthur had been right it would have been all over for the Australians, who had finished their particular mission.

For his dashing and heroic leadership, Lieutenant D.J. Mannett won an MC and the man who dealt with the tank, Private Stafford, a Silver Star. The casualties were the Australians' heaviest to date: nine killed and thirty wounded.

(Now comes the irony. A couple of days later, the Brigade was ordered to retreat through the position they fought so fiercely to win. By December, with the Chinese on their heels, the UN forces were back south of Seoul. For this military disaster, and for bringing the world to the brink of war, MacArthur was sacked in April 1951.)

The Americans congratulated the Commonwealth Brigade for the blow dealt to the enemy by their "true fighting soldiers who had marched thirty-one miles in twelve hours" to win the battle of Chongju. With the congratulations came the announcement that they were to be rested.


3 RAR was sent to the Talchon river, just east of Chongju. C.H. was next seen talking to Bernie O'Dowd about the setting up of the camp at Talchon. The conversation is puzzling. I can only relate it as it was reported. Charlie said to Bernie, "Why did you put my tent here, Bernie, out in the sun. Why didn't you put it in the shade like that one over there?"

Bernie replied: "It's safest where it is. Mine's next to yours."

Arch Denness can't forget his last sight of Charlie at Talchon, and what he said: "Well, we've made it, Arch!"

There were many things for Charlie to do before he took the much needed rest his batman was urging. First there were all the reports to be done, including the dreaded casualty details. He made the effort, too, to send me a telegram, in response to the proposition that Herc had come up with, that he and Charlie should purchase Bedford's farm.

Desperately tired — he hadn't slept for three nights — he went to his tent. "Get your head down, skipper," said the batman. Charlie had no sooner lain down on his stretcher than he was asleep.

It was 6.10 pm, just on dark. Five enemy shells exploded on the other side of the hill from C.H.'s tent. The last shell, the last one the enemy fired that evening, cleared the hill, hit a tree and then found its target.

The batman was still at Charlie's side in the little tent, though his "skipper" was already asleep, fully clothed on his stretcher, too tired to undress. Incredulous, he saw the man beside him hit by a piece of shrapnel. It struck him in the stomach, leaving a terrible, gaping wound.

Shocked, the batman raced out of the little tent, calling out "The Boss has been hit!" The MO and the Adjutant came running.

John Callander said, "Don't be bloody ridiculous; it's impossible." Cal explained to me that what happened was a thousand-to-one chance. "An absolute freak." That one man only, and he the CO, in a safe position in the midst of a battalion of his men, should be killed by one stray shell fragment was so incredible it shocked everyone. Bernie O'Dowd said: "Kismet".

When Cal got to Charlie "He was still conscious. He said, 'Tell her I love her.' He then muttered something about his daughter as he became unconscious."

Captain Gandevia, the MO, said: "When I got to Charlie, he was very sick. Fortunately I had plenty of morphia, but not a great supply of dressings." The need for dressings was indicative of the nature of the wound.

There were no ambulances. In zero temperature, he was put on a jeep "without lights'", to be jolted over rough roads twenty miles back to Anju, whence they had come, to a Mobile American Surgical Hospital. He arrived at Anju with a blood pressure "of nil".

A reporter who had raced to the scene saw the CO being carried on the jeep, and heard him say faintly, "I could use another blanket."

A little after six o'clock on October 30, the Korean boy Yung Choi couldn't understand why everything suddenly became so terribly quiet:

> It was the night after the big battle. You could expect it to be more noisy than usual. The quiet was so unnatural I went to find out what was going on.
>
> I was told, "The boss has been hit. And there's no hope." Every man in the Battalion stopped that night; they just sat around and waited.

According to various journalists' accounts, the silent men mourned, and wondered at that selective stroke of fate. "*Why*," said one dismayed soldier, "when he was minding his own business? Why him? There were a thousand of us in the same area and he was the only one who got hit."

L-R: Charlie Green, Brigadier Coad and two unidentified soldiers,
29 October 1950. This is the last action picture of Charlie,
as he was killed the following evening.

Below: The burial of Charlie Green on 2 November 1950.

First buried at Anju, Charlie Green was re-interred in the United Nations Military Cemetery at Pusan, 18 October 1955.

# 22
# The last hours

> O the mind, mind has mountains; cliffs of fall
> Frightful, sheer, no-man-fathomed. Hold them cheap
> Many who ne'er hung there. Nor does long our small
> Durance deal with steep or deep . . .
>
> *Sonnet 42* by Gerard Manley Hopkins

A picture came into my head. I could see the telegram boy riding his bike round the corner of our street in Grafton, near Bancrofts' place. He was carrying a pink envelope.

I went to the front steps of our house that morning and waited for the boy on the bike. I sat on the step knowing he would come. As I sat there I remembered Charlie standing by the front path once with a spade in his hand, his slouch hat tilted back on his head, saying, "Is the jug broken?"

Just as I saw it in my mind, it happened. The telegram boy came round Bancrofts' corner riding his bike. He reached our place, got off his bike and came up the path with the pink envelope in his hand. I remained fixed to the step.

A thud hit my chest as I took the envelope. I opened it and read:

> Regret to inform you that your husband, 2/37504 Lieutenant Colonel Charles Hercules Green was wounded in Korea Stop Suffering from shrapnel wound Stop Further information received will be conveyed to you immediately Army HQ.

It was what I had dreaded; what I had foreseen. Wounded. There was still some hope. I began trying to reach God. I repented, prayed, begged, bargained, but could feel only black nothingness. I decided there was no God. That day passed and the next.

On the second evening, November 1, I went to bed early, not only because I was exhausted but because I wanted to be alone. Very late, about midnight, I heard a noise. Looking through the window I could see a couple of figures at the gate with torches. I went to the front door, opened it and put on the light. Harry Bancroft and our family doctor were coming up the path. I could read their faces, especially Harry's.

"He's dead."

"I am sorry," one of them said.

There are no words to describe what was like a mortal wound. Nor tears enough to heal.

The next day his telegram arrived, the one he sent before he lay down to rest on October 30. It read: "Suggest discuss with Dad re tender Befords Depends arrangements a lot don't think partnership good idea If some arrangements can be made and you like prospect I would be prepared to hundred pounds acre Charlie." According to the Grafton Post Office stamp, that telegram arrived on November 2. That was his reply to the proposition Herc had put forward. I was too deep in shock to notice the telegram or the irony. The impact came later.

I felt a great need to learn about Charlie's last minutes. I wanted to hear that he died peacefully, forgivingly, still loving me.

Letters and telegrams came from all over the world expressing shock and sorrow. Even from MacArthur himself. All the tributes meant nothing then. I wanted only to be close to him. I wanted to hear his words. Anything to hold on to him.

A letter came from Padre Laing, telling me some things I wanted to know. He wrote:

> "I know you will be anxious to know something of your good husband's last hours . . ." He explained how he went to the 8063 Mobile Army Surgical Hospital at Pakchon to see him. "He was not in any pain and was receiving blood transfusions as his blood pressure was nil. I talked to him for a while and he said, 'I know Padre I'm finished for soldiering'. He was very brave and he told me about you and his daughter. He then prayed with me and repeated the Lord's prayer and I gave him my blessing. He then slept for a few hours. At 2 pm he was taken to the surgery and to

the operating theatre. They did everything they could for him, and he left the theatre about 4.30 pm. The surgeons were amazed at his survival for so long. They knew at the outset his chances of recovery were nil. He was partially conscious next morning and was able to talk to me, saying he did not like the oxygen tube they had inserted in his nostril. He gradually became incoherent but the last words I heard him say were 'Write to my wife, Padre'. I stayed by his side as he gradually became unconscious and he died at 8 o'clock. His end was very peaceful — just a quiet slipping away. His vigorous will to live was gradually overcome by his weakness physically. Senior American officers everywhere I have met have expressed their sympathy as Colonel Green was so well-known to them... The men of the Battalion were profoundly affected by their CO's death...

"What amazed us all at the hospital was the Colonel's amazing will to live...

"May God bless and console you.
Yours sincerely,
Alan Laing"

I barely survived. I look back and say: "I was crazy for about three years." What saved me was Charlie. He inspired me to stand up and fight, to be worthy of him. There was, too, our child to care for.

I left Grafton to make a new life and to forget, neither of which I believed I could have done there. I made the new life. And because I could not forget, I felt compelled to take this long journey.

Harry Bancroft wrote to me in Sydney, telling of a ceremony at the Grafton High School a couple of months after Charlie died that he had officiated at. I did not go back for it. A fund had been raised to establish a memorial to Charles Green. I suggested that a fitting memorial would be an annual prize at the Grafton High School. This was celebrated by the unveiling of a portrait of Charlie, the occasion Harry is writing about:

> Well, darling, it is all over now; the shouting and the tumult dies, the deeds and glories of Charles Hercules Green are relegated to the page of history and the world goes on. Save for a passing thought, and an occasional glance at the scroll of fame, the

average person will soon forget such a one lived that merited so much exaltation. Merely a beautiful picture that hangs in a frame of gold is the last visible evidence of a once animate and beautiful soul endowed with all possible grace and charm . . .
Really darling, it was heartbreaking to see boys and girls with great tears streaming down their cheeks as evidence of their real sorrow at the untimely passing . I came home and had a good cry and have been down in spirit since. It brought back all to me; the days and weeks of sadness I endured came to me with a reality . . .
The newspaper gave an extremely poor report of the proceedings and is not worth reading."

No, it wasn't all over, Harry. Not by a long way. You and Tot are dead, and I am still here forty years later trying to make sense of it. What is surprising is that Charlie has not been forgotten. Recently, I learned that an ex-3 RAR man, Sam Beam, "and others" call in at the Swan Creek Memorial Gates, whenever they pass along the Pacific Highway, to pay their respects to the memory of Charlie.

Did I idealise him, as the counsellor once said? No, I don't think so. I hadn't really known Charlie. All those years I was the captive of a haunting, unshakable image: Charlie never growing old. Always strong, tall, handsome and heroic.

But dead.

It was a mystery the way soldiers appeared thirty years after Charlie's death to set me on this journey. And when I believed I had at last finished the story another mystery occurred — another soldier came forward. He was Charlie's driver, Claude Boshammer. It transpires he too was there with the batman Bill Redmonds (whom I was never able to trace) when Charlie was hit. Claude gave me an account of what happened that dusk, in the hills of Korea. Here it is, an uncannily apt postscript:

I went to Korea in September, 1950, as a Driver in the Machine Gun Platoon on the ship *Aiken Victory*. Shortly afterwards I was sent to Battalion Headquarters to take up a new posting as Driver to Lt/Col Green (Commanding Officer of 3 BN RAR).

We were constantly on the move, and the C.O. spent most of his time commanding the Bn by radio fitted to the jeep. I was very privileged in this respect to know "what was happening", "where the Companies were deployed", "what was expected from them", etc., as most troops would be ignorant of these things . . .

Often as we travelled the C.O. would point out certain features on the ground, and then show them to me on the map. This was great training for me also for later in my Army career. Sometimes the C.O. would have to report to Brigade Headquarters and also Divisional Headquarters, and I would have to act as bodyguard as well as driver. As his batman, Bill Redmonds, did not travel in his jeep, I would often have to prepare his meals, etc. also. Bill would generally have the tent pitched and evening meals prepared for the three of us each night. The tent would be 'blacked out' for tactical planning with his officers (if required). Bill and I would always be on guard duty on these occasions . . .

As we progressed northward, there would be daily skirmishes and actions, some more hostile than others. I recall how calm and collected Col. Green remained, as he handled all situations. He was never ruffled, but his firmness was a strong feature.

I recall one action which was a perfect example of this. We came under fairly heavy fire. The jeep's windscreen was splintered by one shot and another just missed the radio, making a big noise. I could not drive for cover as the road was too narow, so I started to dig beside the jeep. Col. Green was directing the action crouched beside the jeep radio. More bullets crashed around us and the C.O. grabbed the shovel from me, saying "Let someone dig who can dig!" I don't think he was angry with me, but he was carried away with the urgency of getting as low as possible . . .

It was getting colder and colder as we ventured farther north. Bill Redmonds and I had to report to the C.O. each night before he retired, to know what was required of us next day. I recall the C.O. sitting in his darkened tent, solemnly writing the names of the fallen and injured, and other events, in his book. He was a caring and concerned leader.

The C.O., like myself, had spent his youth on a farm. Occasionally we shared experiences from our different types of farm life. Also we shared the few photos we carried, and sometimes spoke about the contents of letters from home — especially things like the weather and crops and the like. Col. Green had a concerned interest for each member of the Bn. I remember that he often referred to us as "his men" or "his boys".

Toward the end of October our Bn. had been engaged in much heavy action and casualties were not light. However, by October

29 this action had been successfully brought to an end. I recall driving well up into a gully to where Bill Redmonds had the C.O.'s tent pitched and set up for the night. The C.O. was tired and lay on his stretcher to rest. Bill prepared the evening meal, while I serviced and camouflaged the jeep. When I returned to the tent, the three of us joked about who was going to eat the "Ham & Lima Beans" and/or the "Spaghetti and Meat Balls". We were getting sick of those foods and looked for other cans.

The C.O. told me to be ready just after "Stand To" in the morning as he wanted to go to Brigade Headquarters. He then reminded Bill and me that it was Sunday and, as we usually wrote letters home on Sundays, that we could use his table, as long as we were quiet as he wanted a good rest.

Very shortly afterwards — I had hardly left the tent — a number of artillery shells exploded around us. Unluckily one hit a tree near the tent. I was hit in the right shoulder and in the lower left leg... Both wounds were very minor and no treatment was really needed. However, Bill came running out of the tent shouting that the C.O. had been hit. I recall the loud noise of an explosion and the tent shuddering. I ran in and Bill ran for help.

I kneeled beside the C.O. and he wanted me to prop him up higher on the pillow. I tried to do this, but was experiencing great difficulty, as Col. Green was in great pain. I remember my hand and arm were covered with blood as I held him. He had been hit low in the abdomen. Shortly after (about 4 minutes) Captain Calendar [sic], Adjutant, and an R.A.P. orderly and some others arrived — I don't think the Doctor was there — and we secured the C.O. to his stretcher and carried him out to the ambulance, which had also arrived.

I remember very clearly that the C.O. was conscious and kept repeating things like "Cal, is the Bn. OK?" "Are the boys OK?" "Look after them, Cal, they are good men." "Look after them, Cal." He repeated this line of conversation whilst he was carried to the ambulance, and I heard him still speaking as the vehicle drove off.

Bill and I had a lonely meal that night. The time was about 6 pm — about dusk. Col. Green died one day later. I will never forget that dramatic evening — October 30, 1950. I will always feel honoured to have served under this leader.

Then 1/799 Pte C. BOSHAMMER

It is at Pusan, Korea, in the carefully tended UN War cemetery with its backdrop of wooded mountains that Charlie Green's body, after being moved twice, came to its final rest. Beneath a small bronze plaque that sits between rose bushes in a row of graves. Years after Charlie died, violets that sprang up under a tree in Swan Creek where he used to play as a boy were sent to Korea to be planted on his grave. The Koreans, not knowing what the plant was, put it in a bed at the end of the row — for fear "it might grow too tall".

# Epilogue

> Yet always when I look death in the face,
> When I clamber to the heights of sleep,
> Or when I grow excited with wine,
> Suddenly I meet your face.
>
> *A Deep-Sworn Vow* by W.B. Yeats

Sydney 1992

My dearest Charlie,
It's a long time since I've written to you. I didn't think you would get any messages. Now I am not so sure.
    You see, I've been going over the past. I went back over your life before you met me. I loved doing that. The picture of you as a lad reminds me so much of what Anthea was like as she grew up. I've been dwelling on the short but rich time we had together. The good times were wonderful, weren't they? It all seemed like yesterday and you were so vividly present. Then I had a dream about you. That's why I felt I should write.
    I think I have learned a lot, my darling. There's no point in questioning or regretting the past. It's gone. For years I worried about what happened to us. One thing doesn't frighten me any more. It is Time. Time doesn't exist. We make a big mistake in measuring it out in minutes or years, or in past or future. Our marriage was a lifetime. And the couple of frightening occasions when I saw into the future have made me realise that maybe, once in a while, we are permitted a glimpse of infinity. I think it is fear that prevents us from seeing into the future — or from seeing straight. It is forty odd years since I saw you, but they seem to have disappeared.

Lately, I've stopped having the bad dream that you were so far away and couldn't get in touch with me. I hated that dream I had over and over again. I could never understand it.

As I said, the other night I dreamt about you. It was a very different dream. You came close to me. Then a very strange, bright light shone down on the left side of your face, illuminating it so that I could see your eyes. The light showed me the tears in your eyes. That woke me up. I can't bear to think of you crying. Please don't cry. There must be no more tears — yours or mine. There is no need for us to cry. What we shared was too beautiful to cry about. And though we failed in a way, God knows, we tried.

I am not young any more, Charlie. I have wrinkles and grey hair. That youthful beauty you told me to preserve has gone. I still have a fair bit of energy, though. I've needed it when I have been minding those grandchildren of ours.

I feel a kind of mellowness now. And I don't have that physical ache for you that I used to suffer so strongly. In fact the way I feel keeps bringing a line from Keats to my head: "Season of mists and mellow fruitfulness." That is exactly how I feel. Remember how I love poetry. I can't stop it from running through my head. That's how we got Anthea's name.

I worked and saved to fill in the years. Now I can enjoy these autumnal days. I feel content, and, yes, I feel rich, even though I've never filled the gap you left. It wasn't an empty gap. I've always had your love to sustain me.

What I look forward to is seeing our two grandsons grow into manhood. They are beautiful boys. The younger one is the image of Anthea when she was little, in looks and in wilfulness. The only time you ever smacked her, I think, was for some very defiant wilfulness. She learned to control that and grew up to be an exceptional person — your daughter. The elder one is like me, some people say. There are others who say he looks like you.

In all those hundreds of letters I wrote to you, I always told you how much I loved you. I probably didn't tell you: You are the finest human being I have ever known.

Please be at peace and remember that I've always loved you.

> Your loving wife,
> Olwyn

# Epilogue to Second Edition

In this reprinted edition of *The Name's Still Charlie* the original 1993 text is kept intact. This postscript is written more than fifteen years after the original book was first published but in the interval I have learned much more about Charlie the soldier. I take this opportunity to add a broader understanding to my original work in some significant areas.

A wealth of information is contained in the anecdotes in this book and the reader can observe the legendary 'digger' fighting, enduring and joking through six years of active service in World War Two; and Charlie Green, the farm boy, learning the craft of leadership from his men and from the outstanding COs of 2/2 Battalion. After five years in the 2/2nd, Charlie was deemed ready to command 2/11 Battalion for the Wewak Campaign. Later, in Korea, his leadership was recognised as exemplary.

The following anecdote earlier in the book tells much about the 'digger culture' and also about Charlie's maturity at 25. 'Woop' Waters, an original identity in 2/2 Battalion, wished to accompany Charlie to 2/11 Battalion in 1945 as his batman – and he had reasons. In a letter home at the end of the war, he finished by writing about Charlie, "I am his back-stay and hanger-on. I am well content with my job; and with him". Very Australian! The batman is content with the CO. That suggests to me that Charlie had become one with the men he led and at the same time received their respect.

I believe that Woop's comment is a tribute. The Australian character seems to have remained an ingredient in the Anzac tradition and is an explanation, in part, of a recent observation made that the Australian army has its own distinctive style of soldiering.

It comes as no surprise to learn that battalions like 2/2nd and 2/11th remain alive years after the war ended. The 2/2nd was one example to illustrate that most AIF units had a similar story. In June 1945, even before the war had ended, some discharged 2/2 veterans who were keen to keep their beloved battalion alive, formed the 2/2nd Australian Infantry Battalion Association.

When the battalion was disbanded early in 1946, veterans returned home to an association that was already in place to receive them back into the fold. In their association, they continued to enjoy mateship, mutual support, and the sharing of 'warries' [war stories] at reunions.

They published their unit history, *Purple over Green* in 1977 and also issued a regular journal: *Nulli Secundus*. It assisted in keeping the men informed and the Association vital until 2001, when it was dissolved.

In the same year, another military association, 'The Friends of the 2nd Infantry Battalions' (formed in 1983 and based in Newcastle), took into its membership the few surviving 2/2nd men but, more importantly, took over custodianship of the memorabilia and insignia of both of the second battalions of the two AIFs raised in the same region.

To foster pride in the military, to proclaim unfading mateship, and to ensure continuity, The Friends, have also admitted into its association the citizen soldiers of the local Reserve Army unit, the 2/17th RNSWR.

The 2/17th is the local Reserve Army unit and is linked with 2 Battalion RNSWR, wearing original Purple Over Green colour patch of both AIF battalions

Today, on their colours, 2/17 RNSWR carries the Battle Honours of the first and second AIFs, demonstrating how in a community, AIF battalions and citizen battalions can keep their military heritage alive – and provide a source of inspiration to the community.

As I write this I suddenly realise the significance of Charlie's keeping by him a little notebook that held the home addresses of men who had been killed in New Guinea when he was commanding 2/11 Battalion. He would say that he hoped one day to visit the families. In those days I had no understanding of the bond he must have felt with all those men who fought so hard and died under his care.

The 2/2nd example allows an important distinction to be made between the experience of serving in AIF infantry battalions and regular army battalions. As mentioned earlier, the men metaphorically brought their battalion home with them and it has been the members' enduring source of pride, comradeship and support.

By comparison, 3 RAR members, coming from all over Australia, have their battalion, their war experience and a serial story. The 3 RAR veterans illustrate how their different battalion experience translates for them. They cannot bring their battalion home but it still remains a source of identity and pride.

Perhaps this explains why the Korean War veterans have not been successful in finding a unified voice to advocate for them or act as custodians of their history. It was not until 2000 that a Korean War memorial was erected in Canberra. The dead of the Korean War remain in distant graves in Korea and, sadly, there are still 44 unrecovered bodies of Korean War servicemen.

I have reviewed and reconsidered chapters of my book that cover Charlie's return to society after six years of WWII active service. It was a difficult adjustment period that thousands of veterans, experienced only in soldiering, faced at that particular time in Australia. Charlie's difficulty was aggravated by his proven competence as a commander which did not seem to translate into an appropriate niche for him in civilian life. His only qualifications were his farming and soldiering experience.

The earlier account of his brief period as a civilian was written over 30 years after his death. I was still in the grip of grief and guilt so my account was emotionally coloured. I ignored Charlie's only professed intention for his future – to return to farming. It was not until he announced in 1950 he was going to war that I was immediately struck with this realisation and an accompanying load of guilt. In those chapters I had admitted my guilt and with that admission I can in hindsight say my way to healing was opened.

When reconsidering Charlie's way of handling his post-war rehabilitation I realise it was typical of his character – I think he was acting pragmatically. He chose the best way possible for him in a difficult situation, a skill he displayed as a commander.

By 1948, when no civilian job prospects were apparent, the unforeseen occurred. The Australian army was reconstructed and a new regular army was founded. In the same year the CMF was re-raised and Charlie was available for service with his original 41 CMF battalion. He was selected to command it but then, a year later, he made the decision to join the regular army without consulting me. Perhaps he needed resolution so he made the lone decision to avoid more resistance.

Recently I forced myself to read again what I wrote so long ago and was stopped by the chapter, 'The cow'. My first response was some dismay at what seemed stylistically out of tune. Then I realised that the cow incident encapsulated my state of mind a few days before Charlie parted from me forever, to go to war. His death occurred as I believed it would, as I had foreseen it. The cow was a sort of talisman to ward off disaster. It was a symbolic gesture to Charlie indicating I would do anything to have him safe at home. I would go with him to a farm and in the meantime I would prepare myself by learning to milk cows. Charlie's complicity is hard to explain. Perhaps he appreciated the gesture; perhaps he was touched at my very late understanding and perhaps he thought it might serve as a distraction to help me cope with the fear that was causing my obvious distress.

Another important incident occurred in that chapter that illustrates the kinds of dreams that haunted me through the lengthy guilt process. The dream I had as I wrote the conclusion to the book included Charlie's actual presence for the first time. In the dream I am consoling him and reassuring him. In retrospect I think that it was at this point my healing actually began.

I want now to show that my extreme responses to his going to another war and his death were not atypical. By the late 1990s a number of academic studies began to appear about the effects of war. In particular I refer to a study by Joy Damousi on the responses of women widowed by war. The themes of the widows' responses were that they tended to remain widows; they experienced continuing sadness about missed opportunities; they were haunted by the details of their husbands' deaths; they associated their husbands' deaths with heroism; they reported recurring, haunting dreams that one called 'evil'; and they admitted they retained a sense of loyalty to their husbands that kept them from remarrying. One of Damousi's findings applied particularly to me: women remember with images of nostalgia, lost opportunities and hopes left unrealized. They often retained a romantic memory of their deceased husbands of the perfection which could not be matched by any other.[1]

This leads me to that part of the book that chronicles the phase of the Korean War in which Charlie commanded 3 RAR.

The battalion was committed for the duration of the war but in this book, I only give an account of the period of Charlie Green's command from 28 September to 1 November 1950.

In summing up the situation that Charlie faced when he took command, what is most significant is that all eyes would have been on him, especially those of the commanders in Korea (and his superiors at Army Headquarters in Australia).

As an ex-AIF officer he was not the expected choice and was confronted with an enormous task. One soldier described the battalion as a "bloody shambles", a comment that caused a lot of unhappy responses when it was published. It was a digger's way of describing the conglomerate state of 3 RAR which had been hastily formed and reinforced with intakes from two other RAR battalions and 'K Force' men. The latter were volunteers who signed up for the Korean War, were for the most part World War II veterans and they made up over half of 3 RAR's complement. How could the battalion operate as a unit without some serious training? It was a big ask. For Charlie Green it meant that if the battalion was not prepared for action there could be disastrous results. Charlie's concern would have been, primarily, for the welfare of his men.

Major General David Butler summed up the nature of Charlie Green's task in Korea, "His period of command was without parallel in the history of the Australian Army. No one has been invited to put together a unit in such short time and take it into action so quickly".[2]

In 1950, 3 RAR was the only Australian battalion in Korea and was attached to 27 British Commonwealth Brigade, commanded by Brigadier Aubrey Coad and it, in turn, was attached to the American 1 Cavalry Division commanded by Major General Hobart Gay.

The UN forces comprised sixteen nations commanded by the famous American general, Douglas MacArthur.

In the interval between the outbreak of the Korea War on 25 June 1950 and 3 RAR's first battle on 22 October, the North Korean army had overrun almost all resistance. Finally the UN forces were able to make a stand and form a defensive area around Pusan in the south-east corner of the Korean peninsula.

At that perilous stage of the war, General MacArthur executed the daringly successful Inchon landing, seizing the chance to encircle and rout the North Korean army. He soon had the UN forces advancing north. With Washington's permission but in defiance of Mao Tse-tung's warning, MacArthur put the UN forces across the 38th Parallel on 30 September with the intention of advancing to the Yalu River and ending the war.

During the advance General MacArthur conceived another daring plan to hasten the UN army to victory. He ordered a parachute drop of a large fighting force at Yongju, located between the United Nations forces and the main North Korean enemy. It is reported that MacArthur flew from Japan to observe thousands of his soldiers and tons of equipment being dropped from 111 planes with the intention of cutting off retreating North Koreans.

However his 187 Airborne Regiment (*Rakassans*) was surrounded and threatened with entrapment and, on 22 October, 3 RAR was sent to their aid. As soon as contact was made with the enemy, the Australians jumped off their tanks and immediately advanced with fixed bayonets, attacking

Men of 3 RAR on an American tank,
at the Battle of the Apple Orchard.

Troops using makeshift ladders to cross the Broken Bridge.

through an apple orchard.

It seems that the combination of daring, surprise, skill, experience and courage gave the 3 RAR diggers an impetus before which the enemy collapsed. The battalion had its initiation in battle – called "blooding" – an important marker in a battalion's history. In a few hours it achieved an immediate identity and provided an example of fighting prowess that has been a source of pride and inspiration ever since.

Though ten diggers were wounded in that defining battle, no one was killed. North Korean casualties amounted to 150 killed, 239 wounded and 200 prisoners captured.

During that "mobile phase" stage of the war, the action was described as "fighting off the march". The advancing force moves quickly towards the estimated position of the enemy and when contact is made, the enemy is immediately attacked without preparation or pre-planning. It does not require much imagination to grasp how difficult that mode of fighting is for the commander and the troops.

It was only three days after the Battle of the Apple Orchard that 3 RAR was engaged in the fierce Battle of Broken Bridge at Pakchon on 25 October. The casualties reflect the increasing resistance with eight Australians killed and fifteen wounded. Four days later, after marching 31 miles north in twelve hours, the battalion faced their fiercest battle at Chongju where nine more were killed and 34 wounded.

On 1 November 1950, the day Charlie died, the Chinese entered the Korean War and the United Nations forces were again sent into hasty retreat. China's entry into the war was climactic and it was doomed to end in a stalemate.

On 27 October Charlie Green wrote his last letter to me from somewhere between Pakchon and Chongju. It was not until I re-read it, that I detected a note of foreboding that all those years ago had escaped me. I had earlier dwelt on his missing me but today I am chilled by his words, "...until we are together again there is no answer to this cold and lonely feeling".

With his instinct for the currents of battle, he had reason to be anxious, as he would have noticed the increasing enemy resistance, such as at the Battle of Broken Bridge. He would have been aware that in the advance the lines of communication had been severely stretched and he could have had in mind the Intelligence on the North Korean battle plans that had been found on the body of one of their officers.

I find it eerie that I foresaw his death, and furthermore, I believe that some of his last words were out of fear that the battalion was under attack. He is heard to have muttered, "Are the boys all right?"

In that same letter there were words of his that gave me some solace. He wrote, "The battalion is in excellent shape and is really a pleasure to command". There was evidence that he had received affirmation, from Brigadier Coad and Major General Gay, for the way he led the battalion. It was General Gay who upon Charlie's death is reported to have said, "Colonel Green was the finest battalion commander I ever saw".[3] Charlie was not to know that under his command his battalion had already won three Battle Honours.

This book ends with Charlie's death but the story of 3 RAR had only just begun. At its blooding in the apple orchard, 3 RAR placed a footprint in history and set a standard from which it has never departed. In the months and years that followed, soldiers were to consider it an honour to serve in 3 RAR, to be identified with the battalion that became known as 'Old Faithful'.

General Butler acknowledged 3 RAR's achievement in the Green period, "He left a battalion that absolutely refused to be deterred by any setback. Its real trials were to come. Through the long retreat in the cruel winter, they fought with stoicism seldom matched. They had the courage to stop a rampaging Chinese division in its tracks at Kapyong in April 1951. In some measure, that has to be Charles Green's testament".

The Battle of Kapyong to which Butler refers, is recognized as a major turning point in the war. In April 1951, the Chinese launched their massive Spring Offensive that proved to be the last attempt to conclude the Korean War. On 23 April, at Kapyong – the section of the front that 3 RAR was defending – the battalion made a defensive stand that allowed allied troops to make a successful withdrawal. The Americans recognized the heroic feat by awarding the US Presidential Unit Citation. The battle casualty figures for the Battle of Kapyong reveal that 26 of the 33 killed in this battle were K Force volunteers.

Annual Kapyong Day parade, Holsworthy, 1950s.
Olwyn shares a joke with Lieutenant-Colonel Bruce Ferguson (ex 2/2 Battalion) who commanded 3 RAR following Charlie's death. He led the battalion at the Battle of Kapyong in 1951.

Though armistice negotiations had begun in July 1951, 3 RAR gained further recognition at the Battle of Maryang San. In that battle they attacked up hill in what was described as an exemplary manoeuvre. The Battle Honour for that action was not awarded until 1994.

There is not the scope here to detail 3 RAR's performance in the static part of the war that dragged on from July 1951 until the armistice of 26 July 1953 but the battalion was consistently outstanding.

In this book a resounding theme emerges: the Battalion. For a soldier his battalion is family, home, identity and source of pride. In the inspiring presence of courage and mateship, men enjoy a transcendence of the human spirit. At the 2008 Charlie Green Commemoration Dinner, the speaker, Major Kyle Tyrell, had pertinent things to say about what makes a battalion. He quoted Jo Gullett:[4]

> An effective battalion in being ready to fight, implies a state of mind – I am not sure it is not a state of grace. It implies giving and taking, a sharing of almost everything ... the deferment of other bonds and interests; the acceptance that life and home are now with the battalion. In the end it is possible to say 'the battalion thinks' or 'the battalion feels' and this is not an exaggeration.

Major Tyrell went on to explain that in order to arrive at 'the state of grace' a battalion needs 'exceptional leadership' and that Charlie Green 'provided the model'.

Over the years, Charlie Green's story has been emerging through a range of observations by historians, fellow officers and at least one digger.

In 1999 the British historian Michael Hickey[5] wrote, "Charlie Green's death ... cast a shadow over the brigade where he was admired especially by [Brigadier] Coad who kept a photograph of the young Australian on his desk".

In 2001, Associate Professor Jeffrey Grey, summed up the significance of Charlie Green's appointment to command 3 RAR in the Korean War:

> ...Lieutenant-Colonel C.H. Green [who] had wider experience of command in combat. Green, who was killed by enemy shelling in November 1950, has the unusual distinctions of being the only commanding officer of an Australian regular

battalion to have been killed in action, and of being the only man to command a battalion of the AIF (2/11th ) the CMF (41st) and the Australian Regular Army (3 RAR).[6]

In 2008 the digger who came forward to reflect on his "boss" was Ian 'Robbie' Robertson who was a sniper with the role of protecting the commander, upon whom the whole battalion depended.

Robbie, always close to his CO, had a view of him that few others would have had. Robbie earnestly described him:

> He would look and listen; he could get the feel of the battle and would shift the pieces, like chess pieces; he was a soldier's idea of a soldier; he was his own man; had natural ability; was firm, fair, and helpful; he instilled confidence ... he always displayed unswerving courage and confidence.

In March 2008, Nigel Steel, senior historian from the British Imperial War Museum who was visiting at the Australian War Memorial, wrote an article entitled *The Quiet Commander*. It was published in the *Canberra Times* on 21 March 2008 at the time of the opening of the post-1945 galleries at the War Memorial, Canberra. Steel referred to the Charlie Green exhibits in the new Korean War Gallery where his slouch hat is exhibited close to a small screen continuously showing a film about him. In the article, Steel wrote:

> Charlie Green is the kind of man people remember…he was an impressive, dynamic leader … he led with great style a series of battles and his death was a devastating loss … his slouch hat reflects the man himself and offers a quiet but powerful tribute to one of Australia's great commanders.

There remains to be told, the answer to my personal quest to discover if I had idealised Charlie. I turn to Ida Proctor whose words in the poem 'The One' express what is for me inexpressible:

> *We cannot weep*
> *At tragedy for millions*
> *But for one.*
> *In the mind*
> *For the mind's life*
> *The one lives on.*

Olwyn Green. 2009.

## Endnotes:

1. *Living with the Aftermath: Trauma, Nostalgia and Grief in Post-war Australia*, J. Damousi. Cambridge University Press, Melbourne, 2001.
2. *The Fight Leaders*, D. Butler, A. Argent and J. Shelton,. Australian Military History Productions, 2002. (Butler was a lieutenant under Charlie's command in 1950).
3. *The Last Call of the Bugle*, Jack Gallaway. University of Queensland Press, 1994, p. 99.
4. *Not as Duty Only*, H. *'Jo'* Gullett. Melbourne University Press, 1976.
5. *The Korean War : The West Confronts Communism*, Michael Hickey, John Murray. London, 1999.
6. *The Australian Army, The Australian Centenary History of Defence*, Volume 1, Jeffrey Grey. Oxford, 2001, p 178.

# Appendix 1

## 3 RAR ORGANISATION CHART
## SEPTEMBER–OCTOBER 1950
* Indicates officers who had served with 3 RAR in Japan

**Battalion HQ**
| | |
|---|---|
| Lt Col C. H. Green | Commanding Officer |
| Maj. I. B. Ferguson * | 2ic |
| Capt J. W. Callander * | Adj |
| Lt C. M. Townsend * | Ass Adj |
| (Later, Lt Roy Milton) | |
| Lt A. Argent * | Intelligence Officer |
| Capt B. H. Gandevia * | RMO |

**HQ Company**
| | |
|---|---|
| Capt B. S. O'Dowd * | OC |
| Capt R.G. Morahan * | QM |
| Lt. A. McCann* | TO |

**Support Company**
| | |
|---|---|
| Maj A. F. Lukyn * | LOB in Japan |
| Capt. C. C. Hall | OC (acting) |

**MMG Platoon**
| | |
|---|---|
| Capt C. C. Hall | OC |
| Lt K. W. Kennedy | 2ic (later OC) |

**Signals Platoon**
| | |
|---|---|
| Capt L. Watts OC | |
| Lt. C. MacKenzie | 2ic |

**Mortar Platoon**
| | |
|---|---|
| Capt. A Power | OC |
| Lt. P. H. Bennett * | 2ic |

**Anti Tank Platoon**
| | |
|---|---|
| Lt. K. P. Outridge | OC |

**Assault Pioneer Platoon**
| | |
|---|---|
| Lt S. W. Ness | OC |

**A Company**
| | |
|---|---|
| Maj R. A. Gordon | OC |
| Capt. W. J. Chitts * | 2ic |

| | |
|---|---|
| Lt. J. F. Wathen | OC 1 Platoon (KIA 25.10.50) |
| Lt N. R. Charlesworth * | OC 2 Platoon |
| Lt L. G. Clark | OC 3 Platoon |

**B Company**

| | |
|---|---|
| Maj G. M. Thirlwell | OC |
| Capt. D. P. Laughlin * | 2ic |
| | |
| Lt. A. L. Morrison | OC 4 Platoon |
| Lt. G. Hollings * | OC 5 Platoon |
| Lt E. O. Larson * | OC 6 Platoon (KIA 5.11.50) |

**C Company**

| | |
|---|---|
| Capt A. P. A. Denness | OC |
| Capt K. J. Hummerston + | 2ic (KIA 3.10.50) |
| | |
| Lt R. F. Morison* | OC 7 Platoon |
| Lt L.A. Eyles * | OC 8 Platoon |
| Lt. D. M. Butler * | OC 9 Platoon |

**D Company**

| | |
|---|---|
| Maj W. F. Brown | OC |
| Lt R.I. McDermott | 2ic (Hon Captain) |
| Lt D. J. Mannett * | OC 10 Platoon |
| Lt P.T. Johnston | OC 11 Platoon |
| Lt C. S. Walsh * | OC 12 Platoon |

Notes:
+ When Hummerston was killed, Eyles became 2ic of C Coy and A/Adj Townsend took over 8 Platoon.

SOURCE: Information supplied by Captain Gus Breen of 1 and 2 RAR and Lt N. R. Charlesworth. Confirmed by Alf Argent who was IO of 3 RAR at the time.

# Contributors

Oral or written contributions were supplied by those listed below.

## 2/2 Australian Infantry Battalion, AIF

|  | Rank | Awards |
|---|---|---|
| Armati, L.V. | Capt (RAAMC) | MID (3 times) |
| Austin, Vic | Sgt | MID |
| Bell, Harry |  |  |
| Blanchard, G.L. | Cpl |  |
| Boorer, Jack |  |  |
| Brock, Bruce (Effendi) | Capt |  |
| Buckley, Adrian | Lt Col |  |
| Chilton, F.O., | Brig | CBE, DSO & bar, MID |
| Dougherty, Ivan | Maj Gen | CBE, DSO, ED |
| Dunlop, J.W. | Maj | MID twice |
| Fairbrother, Don | Maj | MC |
| Goslett, Duncan | Col | OBE, MC, ED |
| Harvey, Tom |  | MM |
| Hynes, Fred |  |  |
| Mawhinney, Tom | WO1 |  |
| Osbourne, Ernie |  |  |
| Read, (Padre) | Capt |  |
| Scott, Steve |  |  |
| Smith, Dick | Lt |  |
| Toohill, W.B. | Capt |  |
| Torrington, Ray |  |  |
| Waters, Roy (Woop) | Lance Cpl |  |

## 2/11 Australian Infantry Battalion, AIF

| | Rank | Awards |
|---|---|---|
| Byers, E.J. | Capt | |
| Casper, A.L. | Lt | |
| Honner, Ralph | Lt/Col | DSO MC |
| Jackson, D.A.C. (Archie) | Lt/Col | OBE, MC |
| Matheson, A.J. | Lt | |
| O'Dowd, B.S. (Bernie) | Lt/Col | |
| Royce, G.E. | Maj | MC |
| Ryan, D.A. | Lt | |
| Waters, R. (Woop) | discharged from 2/2 Bn | |
| Wilkinson, N.A. | Capt | |
| Williams, L.J. (Bill) | Sgt | |

## 3 Battalion, Royal Australian Regiment

| | Rank | Awards |
|---|---|---|
| Argent, Alf | Capt later Lt/Col | MBE |
| Boshammer, Claude | Pte later Cpl | |
| Butler, David | Capt later Maj/Gen | US Leg. |
| Callander, J.W. | Capt | MBE |
| Denness, Archer | Maj | MC |
| Ferguson, I.B. (Bruce) | Maj later Lt. Col | MC DSO MID |
| Gandevia, B. | Capt (RAAMC) | |
| Goldsmith, John | | |
| Laing, Alan | Chaplain | |
| Mannett, David | Capt | MC |
| Morison, Robin | Capt | |
| O'Dowd, Bernard | Capt later Lt/Col | MBE |
| Opie, Len | WO2 | DCM |
| Shelton, J.J. | Capt later Brig. | MC MID DSO |
| Stanley, Arthur | WO2 | MM MBE |

Adoptee, an unofficial member of 3 RAR:
Choi, Yung Kil (Order of Australia) arrived Australia 1968, naturalised 1970

# Copyright acknowledgments

Page

"Pastorale" by Hart Crane, *Complete Poems and Selected Letters and Prose of Hart Crane* (London: Oxford University Press, 1968)

1    "Presences" by Zoe Karelli, trans. from Greek by Kimon Friar, Ohio State University, *The Penguin Book of Women Poets* (Middlesex: Penguin Books, 1979)

7    "Fern Hill" by Dylan Thomas, *The Poems 1934-1952* (London: J.M. Dent & Sons, 1952)

19    "On Receiving News of the War" by Isaac Rosenberg, *The War Poets* (London: Bloomsbury Publishing Co., 1988)

37    "Suicide in the Trenches" by Siegfried Sassoon, *Men Who March Away* (London: Heinemann Educational Books, 1965)

39    "The Soldiers" by Alexander Turner, *Poets at War* (Melbourne: Georgian House, 1944)

45    "An Infantryman in Palestine" by Val Anderson, *Poets at War* (Melbourne: Georgian House, 1944)

56    "Air-Mail — Palestine" by David McNicoll, *Poets at War* (Melbourne: Georgian House, 1944)

60    "Absolution" by Siegfried Sassoon, *Men Who March Away* (London: Heinemann Educational Books, 1965)

# Copyright acknowledgments

| Page | |
|---|---|
| 102 | "Isle of Doom" Anon, *Purple Over Green* (Sydney, 2/2 Aust. Inf. Bn. Assoc., 1977) |
| 105 | "Sacrament" by Margaret Sackville, *Scars Upon My Heart* (London: Virago Press, 1981) |
| 130 | "Soldiers Look Homeward" by Peter Middleton, *Poets at War* (Melbourne: Georgian House, 1944) |
| 133 | "Bobby Tobruk" by "Watty" Barrett, *Nulli Secundus Log* (Sydney: 2/2 Australian Infantry Battalion, AIF, 1946) |
| 138 | "Song out of Syria" by R.S. Byrnes, *Poets at War* (Melbourne: Georgian House, 1944) |
| 152 | "The Spring" by Kathleen Raine, *Contemporary Verse* (Middlesex: Penguin Books, 1950) |
| 160 | "Vision" by Frank Sidgwick, *Men Who March Away* (London: Heinemann Educational Books, 1965) |
| 162 | "The Truly Great" by Stephen Spender, *Collected Poems: 1928-1985* (Middlesex: Penguin Books, 1956) |
| 226 | "Counting the Beats" by Robert Graves, *Collected Poems 1975*. Permission granted by A.P. Watt Ltd on behalf of The Trustees of the Robert Graves Trust. |
| 236 | "Goodbye" by Alun Lewis, *Selected Poems of Alun Lewis* (London: Unwin Paperbacks, 1981) |
| 237 | "Despair" by Olive E. Lindsay, *Scars upon My Heart* (London: Virago Press, 1981) |
| 240 | "Postscript: for Gweno" by Alun Lewis, *Selected Poems of Alun Lewis* (London: Unwin Paperbacks, 1981) |

Page

256  Sonnet 2 by Charles Sorley, *Men Who March Away* (London: Heinemann Educational Books, 1965)

# Reference works consulted

| | |
|---|---|
| Alexander, Bevin | *Korea — The Lost War* (London: Arrow Books Ltd, 1989) |
| Bartlett, Norman | *With the Australians in Korea* (Canberra: Australian War Memorial, 1954) |
| Baynes, John | *Morale — A Study of Men and Courage* (London: Cassell, 1967) |
| Buckley, Christopher | *Greece and Crete* (London: Her Majesty's Stationery Office, 1952) |
| Carew, Jim | *The Korean War* (London: Pan Books, 1970) |
| Charlton, Peter | *The Thirty Niners* (Melbourne: MacMillan Co. of Australia, 1981) |
| " " | *The Unnecessary War* (Melbourne: MacMillan Co. of Australia, 1983) |
| Dexter, David | *The New Guinea Offensives* (Australian Official Publication) |
| Dupuy, T.N. | *Military History of World War II — European Land Battles 1939-1943* (London: Edmund Ward Ltd) |
| " " | *Chronological Military History of World War II* (New York: Franklin Watts, 1965) |
| Ellis, John | *The Sharp End of War* (London: David and Charles, 1980) |
| Fearnside, G.H. | *Half to Remember* (Sydney: Haldane, 1975) |
| Fewster, Kevin | *Gallipoli Correspondent* (Sydney: Allen and Unwin, 1983) |
| Firkins, Peter | *The Australians in Nine Wars* (Sydney: Pan Books, 1971) |
| Forrest, David | *The Last Blue Sea* (Melbourne: Heinemann, 1959) |
| Fussell, Paul | *The Great War and Modern Memory* (London: Oxford University Press, 1975) |

| | |
|---|---|
| Gray, J. Glenn | *The Warriors* (New York: Harper and Row, 1970) |
| Gullett, H. (Jo) | *Not as Duty Only* (Melbourne: Melbourne University Press, 1976) |
| Horner, David | *Duty First* (Sydney: Allen & Unwin, 1990) |
| Keegan, John | *The Face of Battle* (London: Jonathan Cape, 1978) |
| Keegan and Darracott | *The Nature of War* (New York: Holt, Rinehart & Winston, 1981) |
| Laffin, John | *Links of Leadership* (New York: Abelard-Schuman, 1970) |
| Lambert, Eric | *Twenty Thousand Thieves* (London: Frederick Muller, 1952) |
| Lee, Hyong Suk | *History of the United Nations in the Korean War* (Korea: Military National Defence, 1972) |
| Leed, Eric | *No Man's Land* (Cambridge: Cambridge University Press, 1979) |
| Long, Gavin | *To Benghazi* (Canberra: Australian War Memorial, 1952) |
| "    " | *Greece, Crete and Syria* (Canberra: Australian War Memorial, 1953) |
| "    " | *The Final Campaigns* (Canberra: Australian War Memorial, 1963) |
| Mackenzie, Compton | *Wind of Freedom* (London: Chatto & Windus, 1943) |
| Manchester, William | *Goodbye Darkness* (London: Granada, 1982) |
| Manning, Olivia | *The Levant Trilogy* (Middlesex: Penguin, 1982) |
| Marshall, A.J. | *Nulli Secundus Log* (Sydney: 2/2 Australian Infantry Battalion, 1940) |
| Marshall, S.L.A. | *The Military History of the Korean War* (New York: Franklin Watts Inc.) |
| "    " | *Men Against Fire* (New York: Morrow and Co., 1947) |
| McKernan, Michael | *All In* (Melbourne: Thomas Nelson 1983) |
| O'Neill, Robert | *Australia in the Korean War 1950-1953 — Volume II: Combat Operations* (Canberra: Australian War Memorial, 1985) |

| | |
|---|---|
| Robertson, John | *Australia at War — 1939-1945* (Melbourne: Heinemann, 1981) |
| Scott, Geoffrey | *Knights of Kokoda* (Sydney: Horwitz, 1963) |
| Smith, Neil C. | *Home by Christmas* (Melbourne: Mostly Unsung, 1990) |
| Snyder, Louis L. | *The War: A Concise History* (London: Robert Hale Ltd, 1962) |
| Watson, Peter | *War on the Mind* (London: Hutchinson, 1978) |
| Wellborn, Suzanne | *Lords of Death* (Fremantle, Fremantle Arts Press, 1982) |
| Wick, Stan | *Purple Over Green* (Sydney: 2/2 Australian Infantry Battalion Association, 1977) |

Unpublished

| | |
|---|---|
| Barter, Margaret | Doctoral Thesis: *The 2/2 Australian Infantry Battalion: The History of a Group Experience* To be published as *Far Above Battle* 1993. |

# Index
## General

1 Argyle & Southern Highlands Bn (UK): 254, 261
1 Cavalry Regt (US): 259
1 Middlesex Bn (UK): 254, 269
2/2 Battalion: 20-9, 35-7, 43, 51, 54, 57, 59, 62, 71, 75-8, 83, 86, 96, 99-100, 124-146, 150-1, 161-3, 167-9, 187, 203, 219, 244
2/4 Battalion: 168, 198
2/8 Battalion: 198
2/11 Battalion: 24, 26, 169-212, 240, 243
3 RAR: 24, 170-4, 240, 242-91
5 Army (US): 249
6 Division: 35-6, 43, 61, 70-1,78, 85, 141, 153, 163-5, 185, 197, 200, 211
21 Battalion (NZ): 87, 5, 99-100
24 Inf Div (US): 266
27 Brit Comm Bde: 254-5, 291
38th Parallel: 241, 257, 260, 262
41 Battalion: 1, 6, 22, 24, 44, 171
67 Bn: 244
187 Airborne Regt (US): 265
8063 Mobile Army Surg Hosp: 286

Aidhipsos: 123
*Aiken Victory* (ship): 253, 288
Aitape: 167
Alexandretta: 128
Alexandria: 64, 88
Aliakmon River/Line: 85, 93-4
Almiro: 116
Amiriya: 66
Anju: 269, 284
Antipsara: 126
Apple Orchard: see Battles
Askalon: 56
Athens: 90
Atherton: 167
Attica: 101

Bagush: 66
Bardia/battle: 49, 54, 66, 68-77, 92
Battle of Chongju: 280-2
Battle of Apple Orchard: 277
Battle of Broken Bridge: 273, 277
Beenleigh: 167, 230
Beit Jirja: 145
Benghazi: 78
Bentola River: 146
'Bobby Tobruk' (dog): 51, 79-80, 93-4, 133
Boiken: 187
But: 185

Capw Wom: 187
Ceylon/Colombo: 41, 145-7
Crete: 101-2
*City of Canterbury* (ship): 148
Chongju: 267, 278, 279 Battle of: 280-2
Chongchon river: 265, 268, 271

Danmap Rver: 167
Damascus: 142
Daphni: 89-90

Education of troops: 205-7
El Arish: 134-5, 141
El Kantara: 42, 60, 145
Elasson: 94
Euboea/Euvoia: 118, 121-2

Fort Kapuzzo: 67, 77
Features: see Hills

Gonnas: 96
Goulburn Valley: 230
Grafton: 154-5, 159, 217-8, 2325-6, 250, 279, 285, 287
Greece/Greek Campaign: 83-129
Greek escapees: 107-29

Halfaya pass (hellfire): 67, 77
Hebron Hills: 55
Helwan: 63
Hill/Feature attacks:
  Hill 282 (Korea): 254
  Hill 620 (NG): 192
  Hill 710 (NG): 174-5, 195-9, 201
  Hill 771 (NG): 192
  Hill 770 (NG): 192, 197
Hiro: 244, 249
Horana: 145
Housing (post-war): 215
Hwangju: 263

Inchon: 249

Jaffa: 54
Jane Adams (ship): 167
Julis/Camp: 45, 54-5, 58, 130, 133

K-Force: 242
Kabrit: 145
Kalutra: 146
Kalyria/Kalyvia: 113-4
Kanalia: 114-5
Kantara see El
Kapyong: 246, 273
KATKOMS: 271

Kermenie: 113
Kimpo: 255, 258-9, 262, 265
Klewalin: 191
Kokoda/Track: 151, 161
Kokorava: 113
Korea: 234, 240-291
Korean War starts: 241
Kujin: 273
Kumchon: 261
Kumusi river; 150

Lamia: 113, 117-8, 120
Larissa: 87, 90-1, 94-5, 100

Mersa Matruh: 81-2
'Metaxas Line': 85
Mt Hermon: 144
Mt Olympus: 85-6, 91-2, 94, 102
Monastir: 87
Mordhan: 127
Mudgee: 220

New Guinea: 149, 156, 161, 183
Nile delta: 60

*Orontes* (ship): 145
*Otranto* (ship): 37, 39
Owen Stanley Range: 150, 157-8
Owers Corner: 150

Pakchon: 269, 273, 275, 277-80, 286
Pachis: 120
Palestine: 43, 45-9, 61, 89,134, 145
'Panic Mountain': see Mt Olympus
Pili: 123-5
Pelopennesos: 101
Pinios Gorge: 64-6, 98
Port Melbourne: 149
Pus: 187
Pusan: 253-4, 259, 291
Pyongyang: 263, 265

Queenscliff: 232-5

Republic of Korea (ROK): 249
ROK troops: 257

Salonika: 87, 94
Salum: 67
Sariwon: 261
Seoul: 249, 259, 263, 270
Sepik river; 200, 205
Servia: 87, 93-4
Seymour: 226-7
Sidi Barrani: 42
Sinanju: 266-8
Skandura: 125
Skopelos: 125
Skyros: 125
Staff College: 232

Smyrna: 125, 128
Southport: 159-62, 230
Spelia: 111-2
Suez Canal: 42
Sukchon: 265
Sunchon: 265
Swan Creek/ Mem Gates: 7-16, 39, 216, 235, 288, 291
Syria: 138-44

Taegu: 254-5
Taeryong river: 271, 273
Talchon river: 282-3
Tel Aviv: 145
Tempe; 87, 94-6, 100, 109
Thermoplae: 87, 94, 101,109,117
Tobruk: 54, 78-82
Torricelli mountains: 194
Turks/Turkey: 118-9, 125-8

Ulmarra: 17-20, 33, 105, 152,155, 164, 208, 212, 215-8, 229

Verria: 87, 91-2
Volos: 115, 124

Wewak: 187-9
Wirui Mission: 188, 191, 197, 205
Woodlands: 230-1
Wom: see Cape
WW2 ends: 200

Yamba: 165, 223
Yongju: 259, 262, 265-6
Yalu river: 264-5, 268, 272, 277-80

# Index

## People

Ranks are the highest mentioned for the period of the book.
Bold indicates picture captions.
Does not include pages 295-302

ABBOTT Lt Bill: 197
ADACHI Gen: 21-1
ALLEN Maj-Gen Arthur 'Tubby': 43, 87
ALMOND Cpl 'Peanut': 99
ANDERSON Lt: 192, 197
ARGENT Lt Alfred 'Alf': 245, **245**, 247
ARMATI RMO/Capt L: **50**
ARMSTRONG WO R: xi
AUCHINLECK Gen Sir Claude: 134, 140-2
AYRTON Capt E: **244**

BAIRD Lt A: **50**
BANCROFT Harry & 'Tot': 216, 218, 286-8
BARRATT 'Watty': 133
BARTER Margaret: xii
BAYLIS Maj Clive 'Colin or Hotspur': 195, 198
BEAM Sam: 288
BELL Cpl G: 198
BELL Harry: 18, 56
BERGONZOLI Lt-Gen 'Electric Beard': 73, 75
BERTRAM Capt G: **50**
BINGHAM Pte H: 198
BIRMINGAM Pte F: 198
BLACK Capt B: **50**
BLAMEY Gen Sir Thomas: 43, 85, 101, 139, 141
BLAMEY Capt John: 98
'BOBBY TOBRUK' (dog) see general index
BOORER 'Jack': 31-2, 39, 40, 46, 55, 59, 65, 68, 72, 90, 92-3, 107, 113, 133, 148
BOSGARD Lt Athol: 110, 117-8, 121, 151
BOSHAMMER Dvr Claude: xi, 288-90
BOUCHIER AVM Sir Cecil: **255**
BROCK Lt Bruce 'Effendi': xi, 21, 22, **50**, 54, 93, **91**, 92-2, 107, 110-29, 132, 179
BROOKS Colonel Peter: xi, 3, 44
BROWN Pte 'Tuffy': 124
BROWN Maj W: 289
Pte 'Tuffy': 124

BUCKLEY Capt Adrian 'Buck': 31, 48, **50,** 52, 69, 80-1, 89, **90,** 96, 109, 110, 115, 121-2
BUCKLEY Barbara: 161
BURLEY Frank: 163
BUTLER Lt David: 203, 248, 254, 267
BYERS Ted: 174, 179, 187, 192-3, 196, 200, 209-10

CALDWELL Capt W: 50.2
CALDWELL Capt B: **50**
CALLANDER Capt John 'Cal': 246 249, 254, 257, **267**, 283, 290
CALWELL 'Black Prince': 31
CAMPBELL Chris: xii
CASPER Lt A 'Tropical Frog': 176
CHARLESWORTH Brig N: 2
CHAMBERLAIN WO R: xi
CHAMPION Lt A: **50**
CHIDGZEY Lt Vern: 174, 192, 197
CHILTON Lt-Col Sir Frederick: 21, 27, 31, 40, 46-7, **50**, 65, 69, 71-2, **80,** 88, 96, 107, 109, **121,** 124-8, 132, 144, 163, 166
CHITTS Capt W: 281
CHOI Yung Kil: 269-71, 284
CHURCH Maj-Gen John: 266
COAD Brig Aubrey: 254, 256, **256,** 266, 266-8, **267, 280, 284**
COHEN Capt P: **50**
COYLE Sgt G. 'Punchy': 98
COX Lt G: **50**
CROSBY Lt W: **50**
CUTLER Lt Roden: 140

DALE Pte H: 195
DARGIE William: 96
DAVIES J: 151
DAVIS Vic: 20, **19**
de VILLE Harry: 11
DENNESS Maj Archer 'Arch': 249, 267, 275, 280, 283
DIMITRION 'Hopalong': 116
DOUGHERTY Lt-Col Sir Ivan: 22, 31, 43, **50,** 59, **80,** 182
DUNLOP Sir John: 40, 54, 211
DUNLOP Lt J: **50, 211**

321

EDAN Sir Anthony: 42
EDGAR Colonel Cedric 'Boss': 27, **50**, **80, 109**, 144, 163
ELLIS Colin: 244
ELLIS Desmond: 244
FAIRBROTHER Lt Don: **50**, 76, 138-9, 140-1
FARROW Capt 'Sparrow': 206
FERGUSON Lt-Col Bruce: 170, 174, 193, 246-7, 251, 255, 261, 267
FINLAYSON George: 20, **19**
FINLAYSON Max: 20, **19**
FRASER Senator: 185-6
FULLER Pte: 126
GALLAWAY 'Jack': xii
GANDEVIA Capt Bryan: 258-9, 270, 283
GAY Maj-Gen Hobart: 259-60
GIDNEY Elsie: 230.-2
GODBOLD Capt G: **50**
GORDON Maj R. 'Speed': 274
GORDON Pte J: 140
GOSLETT Lt Duncan 'Pansy': 29, 31, **50**
GOSLETT Tammy: 29
GRANT A. 'Bill': 20, **19**
**GREEN Lt-Col Charles** (chronologically):
  Childhood: 7
  Education: 12
  Horse accident: 13
  Militia enlistment: 14
  Joins AIF: 20
  Departs for Middle East: 39
  In Palestine: 45
  Promoted captain: 82
  In Greece: 88
  Escape from Greece: 110-129
  First letter to Olwyn: 137
  Contracts typhoid: 149
  Proposes marriage: 156
  Foot infection at Bardia: 157
  Teaches at Tactical School: 157
  Marries Olwyn: 158
  Commands 2/2 Bn (acting): 167:
  Senior Tactical School: 167
  Commands 2/11 Bn: 171
  Nicknamed 'Chuckles': 172
  Receives Kato's sword: 210
  Returns after war: 213
  Starts civilian employment: 216
  Studies accountancy: 222
  Commands 41 Bn: 224
  Rejoins Regular Army: 226
  Attends Staff college: 232
  Posted to Japan: 234
  Commands 3RAR: 244-5
  Posted to Korea: 253
  Jeep accident: 261-2
  Killed in Korea: 283-7
  Funeral and memorials: xi
GREEN Alvin (brother): 7, 155
GREEN Anthea (daughter): **218, 219**, **222, 226**, 279,
GREEN Bertha (mother): 7, 8, 9, 10, 155, 220, 224
GREEN Doris 'Dot' (sister): 7, 155
GREEN H. 'John or Herc' (father): 7, 9, 21, 155-6, 204, 220, 224
**GREEN Olwyn** (chronologically):
  Meets Charlie: 36
  Charlie proposes: 156
  Marries Charlie: 158, **158, 159**
  Charlie returns; **218**
  Becomes pregnant: 220
  Gives birth to Anthea: 222
GREENWAY Capt G: 192

HAAGENSEN Alan: xii
HALE George & Mary: 233
HAMILTON Bill: 269
HARDING Lt-Gen Sir John: **255**
HARDIMAN Lt L: 194
HARRIS Ardyce: xii
HARVEY Tom: 103
HATZIS Dr: 125
'HAZARUS Herb': 51
HENDRY Lt J: **50**
HIDDINS Cpl H: 124
HICKS Sgt F: 198
HONEYWELL Capt Harry: 51, 110, 121, 151

INGRAHAM Lt Arthur 'Butch': 194
INGRAM Beth: xii

JACKSON 'Archie': 172, 179, 182
JACKSON David: 182
JAMES William: 103
JONES Lt R. 'Spud': 77

KING Lt E: **50**

LACY Cpl Allan: 98
LAING Padre Alan: **266**, 277, 286-7
LAKELAND Mrs: 232
LAVARACK Gen Sir John: 139
LEE Albert: 135
LENTON Stan: 173
LLOYD Brig John: 150
LOFTUS Lt K: **50**
'LORD HAW HAW': 48, 113, 142
LOVETT Harry: 67

MacARTHUR Gen Douglas: 131, 150, 260-5, 277, 280-2
MacKAY General: 75
MACKAY Maj-Gen Iven: 43, 71, 75

MacKENZIE Ken: 251
MAITLAND Pte: 192
MAITLAND WILSONN L-Gen Henry 'Jumbo': 139-40
MANNETT Lt David: 280-2
MATHESON Alec: 171, 173, 198
MAWHINNEY RSM 'Tom': 14, **19**, 20, 33, 60,203
McARTNEY Lester: **19**, 20
McCARREN Pte: 192
McLELLAN Lt Archie: **50**, 67
McQUEEN Pte Angus: 98
MICHELSON Capt D: **50**
MITCHELL RSM: 173
MORISON Lt Robin: 267, 274
MOURTZAKIS John: 125
MOURTZAKIS Mrs: 125
MURRAY Sgt T: 276-7
MURRELL Noel: 165

NEWMAN 'Jim': 20

'O'BLOWFLY' Sgt 'Porky': 258-9
O'DOWD Bernard 'Bernie': 175, 177, 180, 198, **201**, 208, 240, 246, 267, 282, 283
O'NEILL R: xi, 265, 267
OPIE Len: 276
OSBOURNE Ernie: 37, 62, 79,80

PAIK Gen Sun Yup: 263
PATTEMORE Errol: **19**, 20
PATTEMORE Ron: **19**, 20, 105, 132
PENGLASE Pte R: 197
PIERCE Sgt: 126
PRESTON RSM Harry: 22
PRICE Maj: 170

READ Padre: 29, **50**
REDMONDS Bill: 243, 288-9
REEDY 'Jack': 79-80, 94, 133
RISHWORTH Capt J: **50**
ROBERTS George: **19**, 20
ROBERTSON Gen Horace 'Red Robbie': 210, 249, 253, 264
ROMMEL Gen Erwin: 78, 82, 140, 146
ROYCE Capt G: 176, 192
RYAN Joe: 187
RYAN 'Tommy': 10
RYAN Lt: 176, 198

SAAGHY Dorothea: 170
SANDERS Pte: 110, 121
SANDERSON RSM D: 30
SCHOFIELD Pte: 110, 121
SCOTT Steve: 83, 104, 147
SERVOS Michael 'Mick': xii
SHANAHAN Cpl: 110, 121
SHELTON Lt James 'Jim': 247
SMITH Sgt Dick: 124, 143-4, 148

SMITH Family: 219, **219**, 221, 223, 226, 238-9, 252, 262-3, 278
SPEARS Maj-Gen: 140
STAFFORD 'Lofty': 51-3, 65, 73, 74, 80-1, 89, 97-9,132
STAFFORD Pte J: 282
STEEP Sgt 'Jack': 91
STEVENS Maj-Gen J.: 178, 198
STONE Pte Ernest: 257-8
STONEHAM Capt: 193
STUCKEY Capt: 206
SULLIVAN 'Bill': 20, **19**, 34-5, 105, 132, 136
SULLIVAN Mabel 'Sully': 105
SUMMER Sgt W: 198
SWINTON Lt C: **50**
SYMES Dvr Charles: 269

TAYLOR Harry: 244
TAYLOR Lt E: **50**
THIRWELL Maj Max: 261, 274
THOMSON Wilma and Lindsay: 223-4
TOOHILL Capt Bill: 28
TORRINGTON Ray 'Curly': 142-3
TOWNSEND Lt Colin: 267
TRAVERS B: **50**, **51**
TURNER Bill: 12
TURNER Shirley: 12
TURNER Val: 8

ULRICK 'Bill': 18.2, **19**, 20
ULRICK 'Jack': **19**, 20, 34-5, 41, 105, 132, 136

Von List F/M: 84-5, 87

WAITE Alan: **282**
WANT Mrs: 8
WARD Lt W: 99, 145
WATERS L/Cpl 'Woop': 55-8, 62, 64, 72-3, 77, 87-95, 99, **120**, 132-3, 147-8, 167, 169, 172-3, 181, 187, 189, 199, 210, 256
WATTS Capt L: 251, **244**
WATTS Padre: 206
WAVELL Gen A: 49, 53, 61, 70, 140
WHITTON Pte: 110, 121
WILKINSON Neil: 174, 189-90, 206
WILLIAMS Sgt L: 185, 187, 190, 192-4,196-7, 201
WILSON Lt A: **50**
WILSON Pte Rex: 257-8
WILSON Maj-Gen Maitland: 49, 85, 139, 140
WOOTTEN Lt-Col George: 23, 27, 28, 31, 43, 50, **50**, 52, 55, 65-6, **80**, 143, 163
WRIGHT 'Bill': **19**, 20, 105, 132

YUNG CHOI: 269-71, 284